EXTINCTION OR SURVIVAL?

The Remarkable Story of the Tigua,
an Urban American Indian Tribe

S. K. ADAM

Paradigm Publishers
Boulder • London

Copyright © 2009 Paradigm Publishers

Published in the United States by Paradigm Publishers,
3360 Mitchell Lane Suite E, Boulder, CO 80301 USA.

Paradigm Publishers is the trade name of Birkenkamp & Company, LLC,
Dean Birkenkamp, President and Publisher.

Library of Congress Cataloging-in-Publication Data

Adam, SK.
    Extinction or survival? : the remarkable story of an American urban tribe /
SK Adam.
        p. cm.
    Includes bibliographical references and index.
    ISBN 978-1-59451-594-1 (hardcover : alk. paper)
    1. Tigua (Tiwa) Indians—Texas—El Paso—Ethnic identity.   2. Tigua
(Tiwa) Indians—Texas—El Paso—Government relations.   3. Tigua (Tiwa)
Indians—Cultural assimilation—Texas—El Paso.   4. Federally recognized
Indian tribes—Texas—El Paso.   5. Gambling on Indian reservations—
Texas—El Paso.   6. Ysleta del Sur Pueblo (El Paso, Tex.)—History.
    7. Ysleta del Sur Pueblo (El Paso, Tex.)—Social life and customs.   I. Title.
E99.T52A33 2009
305.89974960764'96—dc22

                                                                2008039243

Printed and bound in the United States of America on acid-free paper that meets the standards of the American National Standard for Permanence of Paper for Printed Library Materials.

Design and composition by Cindy Young.

13 12 11 10 09   1 2 3 4 5

Contents

Introduction

I N THE EARLY 1960S, a small American Indian community situated on the outskirts of El Paso, Texas, was in trouble. It was not the first time this particular community had run into problems; indeed, during their three-hundred-year tenure in West Texas, trouble was the rule rather than the exception. The problem this time, however, would require the community to do something that it had never done before: ask for help from outsiders. The Tigua of Ysleta del Sur Pueblo had survived throughout much transition and turmoil over the years. The majority of their land had been stolen from them, and their rights to hunt, fish, and collect wild foods and plants had been abrogated. They had survived religious persecution, racial persecution, and extreme poverty. In fact, there was precious little left to take from this community, save a few acres of land and the run-down, dirt-floor shacks that the surviving members called home. The local government, however, had recently passed new provisions that would make the Tigua responsible for tax payments on their property, fees that the poverty-stricken tribe could never begin to pay. Now, on the verge of losing their homes, the Tigua turned reluctantly to El Paso attorney Tom Diamond, hoping that he could somehow help them.

Trouble, problems, and assorted difficulties had become the common companions of the Tigua Indian tribe.[1] In fact, it has been the case since shortly before members of the Isleta del Norte Pueblo had been forcibly relocated in 1680 to an area that would eventually be called El Paso, Texas. This resettlement, after hundreds of years of residence in the nearby future state of New Mexico, was the consequence of the Pueblo Revolt, a successful Native uprising that had somehow gone wrong for the small Tigua community. Forced to start over in a new location, the Tigua overcame the initial hardships and flourished in their new home, at least for a while. Their prosperity, however, was relatively short-lived, as raids by hostile Indian groups, recurrent flooding, colonial oppression, and the population encroachment of the outside world slowly took their toll. Cut off from their Pueblo brethren by the colonial establishment of state borders, the Tigua Pueblo was left out when President Abraham Lincoln, during the Civil War, formally recognized and granted land patents to the New Mexico Pueblos.[2] Additionally, the Tigua's willingness to help the various colonial governments fight hostile Indian groups meant that there was never a need for them to sign a treaty with the colonial government. That became important when the United States unilaterally "recognized" Indian tribes possessing signed treaties, a figurative stab in the back to peaceful or helpful groups like the Tigua. By the early 1900s, the situation had become bleak in the old pueblo (El Barrio de los Indios), and bad luck seemed to follow their every move. By that point in history, most of the Tigua landholdings had been stolen; high unemployment and poverty forced many community members to relocate; racism and anti-Indian sentiments meant danger for those who openly embraced their Indian heritage; both the state and federal governments had forgotten the Tigua existed; and anthropologists and other researchers were describing Tigua culture as "moribund," if not already "extinct."

The view from within the pueblo, however, was somewhat more optimistic. The community, constantly adjusting to their ever-changing circumstances (wrought by colonial subjugation), continued to follow the traditional rituals and sacred practices that had sustained them since "time out of mind." Of course, small changes had to be introduced to account for the needs of their new reality. For example, certain rituals had to be adjusted to account for their new geographic location; they modified some practices based on their relationship with the various colonial powers; and the loss of their land forced them to change aspects of their traditional hunting and gathering practices. Change was nothing new to this culture, however, and the bearers of that culture had faith that they would survive through this period of difficulty, as they always had before. While the population numbers continued to drop in the old pueblo, the remaining tribal members continued to follow their "traditional" form of leadership, they maintained their sacred religious beliefs, and they continued to assist each other and outsiders alike. The core of their worldview as Pueblo Indians remained unchanged; indeed, tribal members expressed surprise when they learned in the early 1960s that that were, and had been, "extinct."

Their luck appeared to be changing by the mid-1960s, as the "discovery" of this "lost" tribe reverberated throughout Indian Country and beyond. By 1968, the tribe had secured state recognition (and, ostensibly, federal recognition), along with the "benefits" that status implies. Money was granted for the development of a tourist complex, and a new housing reservation was built up the street from their old neighborhood. Although their financial position had improved, it was still difficult to survive on the meager amounts available through state funding, even when coupled with profits from tourism. To make matters worse, the state was dictating the terms of their continued support, and the Tigua were beginning to openly express the feeling that they had been better off before the state decided to offer its "help." In fact, by the mid-1980s, the state was actively looking for a way to get out of the "Indian business," so the decision by the tribe to seek federal recognition was largely supported in the Texas Statehouse.

Unfortunately, the process of moving from state to federal oversight, which should have transpired with relative ease, turned problematic from the start. In the first place, federal acknowledgment was a new concept, and the Interior Department, through the Bureau of Indian Affairs (BIA), was attempting to fine-tune the myriad details of the process. The Tigua, having already received state recognition and at least implicit federal recognition in 1968, opted to sidestep the BIA and go directly to Congress with hopes of passing a "restoration" bill. This path would greatly expedite the process, but the BIA protested against what it claimed was a blatant attempt by the Tigua to bypass the new process. Meanwhile, Texas, though happy to turn its financial obligations for the tribe over to the federal government, nonetheless loathed the idea that a sovereign, federally recognized Indian tribe might be turned loose within its borders. The state was against the idea of federal recognition, primarily because many feared that the tribe would enter into gaming, the hot-button political issue of the day. The Tigua, of course, were very unhappy with the state's position and felt that Texas was simply attempting to abrogate their rights as a Native American Indian community. On the verge of losing their meager state funding, however, the tribe reluctantly agreed to sign a deal that would force them to abide by the gaming laws of the state of Texas, until amended. Additionally, they were forced to agree to a tribal membership criteria that set their minimum blood quantum level at one-eighth, as well as agree to allow the laws of the state to be enforced on their reservation.[3] Although tribal members were unhappy with the agreement, they felt that they had no choice but to go along with the offer. The recognition bill passed both houses of Congress in 1987, and the Tigua proudly took their place among the five-hundred-plus Indian tribes formally recognized by the United States.

In 1991, despite its antigaming rhetoric, the state of Texas passed laws that would allow a statewide lottery. The Tigua, seizing on the amendment to state law, decided to open a casino in order to improve their still meager economic condition. The state initially agreed to allow the gaming operation to proceed, but before a compact could be signed, the state backed out. The tribe, following the terms of its recognition agreement and federal gaming laws, opened up Speaking Rock Casino in 1991 without state approval. After nearly a decade of the casino's staggering success, Texas governor George W. Bush decided to run for the U.S. presidency and determined that shutting down the Tigua operation would appeal to his conservative constituents.[4] Bush provided funding to the state attorney general to set up a task force with the unstated mission of closing the Tigua casino. After several years of legal battles, the state forced the tribe to close its profitable enterprise in 2002. The pre-casino problems of poverty, drug and alcohol abuse, poor educational attainment, poor health care, and high unemployment returned to the Tigua reservation with alarming rapidity. As of this writing (December 2006) the casino remains closed, and the Tigua community is struggling to pay its bills. Of perhaps greater concern has been the tribe's inability to change the membership criteria that set their minimum blood quantum level at one-eighth. With only 1,500 enrolled members, the tribe is facing the reality that it will be legally extinct within a few generations. The future is once again bleak, as tribal leadership must figure out a way to survive in a state and country that appear determined to finish them off once and for all.

Cultural Extinction?

The story of this small Native American Indian community is an interesting one in its own right, but it needs to be told for more important reasons. The Tigua, unlike the American Indian communities who signed treaties or the New Mexico Pueblos who have land patents, are one of a small number of Native American groups that have secured federal recognition since the termination era. The questions raised by the survival of this community have had a significant impact on how the U.S. legal system, scholars, and, more importantly, other "lost" Native American Indian tribes conceptualize the concepts of "identity," "community," "authenticity," "indigeneity," and "cultural persistence." They were written off as extinct in the early 1900s, discovered in the 1960s, and when they were subsequently recognized by the U.S. government, it signaled, according to prominent American Indian author Vine Deloria Jr., the beginning of "the modern era of Indian emergence" (1969: 243). The discovery of the Tigua, Deloria states,

> rocked Indian people in several respects. Indians had been brainwashed into accepting the demise of their tribe as God's natural plan for Indians. Yet the Tiguas plainly demonstrated that Indian tribal society had the strength and internal unity to maintain itself indefinitely within an alien culture. (1969: 245)

For over one hundred years, various anthropologists, as well as the state and federal governments, considered the Tigua tribe to be culturally extinct.[5] But how could that be? There were clearly individuals who claimed to be Tigua, so on what were these proclamations based? Why, and how, did this controversy erupt? The "discovery" of the Tigua brings to the surface a number of issues that call into question how culture and identity are defined by the U.S. government. For example, how was it possible that an Indian tribe had existed, unknown to anyone but themselves, after spending over three hundred years in the El Paso region? Or had the Tigua, as claimed by some, simply "invented" their culture and tradition in order to secure government assistance? If the Tigua were indeed a community of Native American Indians, how could they have possibly come to be lost, and later discovered? If the Tigua were still a "traditional" and "distinct" culture, how could it be proven? Moreover, why should they be forced to prove their authenticity after residing in the same location, and practicing the same traditions, for over three hundred years?

In order to respond to these questions, it is necessary to explore a number of underlying issues as well. For example, what qualifies as Indian culture, what is a tribe, and at what point does a culture or tribe cease being? In short, is culture a bounded, measurable entity? If so, what are the bounds, and how are they measured? What is traditional behavior, and how can it be tracked? What makes a particular culture an authentic culture, or a particular individual a real Native? In other words, what, specifically, is a "real" Indian, and if such a category exists, how can it be defined? More importantly, who defines it (and by what authority), what attributes is it based on, and by what mechanisms is it conceptualized and acted upon?

Of course, this series of questions fairly teems with ambiguity containing concepts and terms that, at least on the surface, defy explication.

Indeed, several of the issues raised by these questions, such as the notion that cultures can somehow go extinct, seem preposterous. Cultures change, no question about that, but "death" implies a tangible, definable quality that abstract concepts (to the best of my knowledge) fail to possess. By reifying culture, however, the government and others can discuss and describe "extinct" cultures as though culture was in some way an organism that was no longer capable of replicating itself. In fact, if one conceptualizes the term in this way, the notion may be defensible. Genocide, for example, when conducted in the traditional physical manner, achieves the goal of preventing members of a particular culture from replicating. The ultimate outcome of genocide is, indeed, cultural extinction. But, short of that, can a culture truly go extinct? Are terms like "ethnocide" and "cultural assimilation" really meaningful?[6]

These issues certainly are debatable; indeed, the debates rage on without any end in sight. Meanwhile, we know that many "Native communities" exist as living, breathing groups of people who have, nonetheless been labeled "extinct" by the U.S. government. Therefore, the question of cultural extinction, for affected groups, is more than some abstract, academic debate; their very identities and livelihoods are profoundly affected by the ways in which these terms are defined. The question for these groups is not, "Can the government reify an abstract concept such as culture?" (as clearly it can and does); the question is, "What methods does the government use to render a culture extinct, and can anything be done to prevent or overcome such extinction?" Presently, in the case of American Indians, the government no longer utilizes the traditional, violent, "kill 'em all" variety of genocide, so it is obvious that some other method has been put into place. We know it must be the case because some groups (the Tigua are only one example) need to be told by outsiders that they no longer exist. The political reality for many indigenous groups is that their existence revolves around a power struggle pitting them against a dominant oppressor, and the ability of the United States to simply define a particular group or entire culture out of existence is a very real concern for many communities. Even though attempts to legalize and define specific cultural requirements (which serve to bound particular cultural behaviors within a sphere of acceptable change) are dubious at best, it is within these bounds that groups are forced to prove their cultural veracity.

The questions raised by the development of laws and policies governing Indians are many and complex. Slippery, ambiguous, abstract concepts need to be reified and measured in order to determine who is and who is not a "real" Indian, and therefore eligible to participate in government Indian programs. It is easy enough to argue that most of these concepts defy definition (let alone measurement) and that most of the issues raised by these concepts are appropriate for a philosophy class, but certainly not a body of legal requirements. Nonetheless, reality dictates that these issues (slippery or not) must be addressed and an attempt must be made to gain some level of understanding regarding how these concepts affect members of the Native American Indian community. Although it is clearly not within the scope of this book to respond in a definitive way to questions about the ultimate meaning of particular concepts, it is within its scope to explore how one American Indian community has been affected by and responded to outside appellation of American Indian identity. Specifically, the purpose of this book is to explore the question of Indian identity as it applies to the Tigua Indians of Ysleta del Sur Pueblo. My goal is to examine the concept of cultural extinction as it applies to the Tigua community and attempt to understand how and why the Tigua Pueblo went extinct, only to be later resurrected. The issues of law, community, power, sovereignty, genocide, and culture change/perseverance will all be addressed as they apply to the issues of identity and cultural extinction. Using the Tigua as a case study, I explore the dimensions of these questions and issues and attempt to better understand not only how the above concepts came to be so intertwined, but how they influence the debate surrounding American Indian authenticity. Moreover, my goal is to explore how the Tigua community perceives its own identity and transmits that identity through multiple generations. In short, what are the mechanisms of cultural persistence used by the Tigua to survive as a Native American Indian tribe within the confines of an urban setting?

This book begins (in Chapters One and Two) with a focus on Tigua oral tradition, exploring, particularly, Tigua senses of tribal history. Tigua tradition, religious beliefs, senses of place, and senses of Indianness will all be explored as part of a narrative history that seeks to explain how the Tigua have survived as a community for over three hundred years. Specific cultural mechanisms, such as shared religious beliefs, histories, and senses of community, combined with shared values, senses of family, and commitment to tradition, have provided the Tigua a cultural continuity that lasts to this day. The issues of culture change and perseverance will be highlighted as Tigua tribal members describe their own ideas about abstract notions such as Indian identity and what it takes to be a "real" Tigua.

Chapter Three then takes a brief look at the history of the relationship between the United States and its indigenous population. The focus will be on the laws and policies created by the United States to control the Native population while concurrently devising strategies to appropriate Indian land and resources. The overarching policy of termination through "definitional" genocide will be discussed as a very real threat to American Indians in general and the Tigua in particular. This overview of Indian laws and policies provides the necessary background for perceiving the root cause of the many problems experienced by the Tigua since the birth of the United States. Chapter Four provides an overview of the role colonization and early U.S. expansionist policies played in forcing the Tigua community into the status of "lost tribe." Additionally, I explore the role played by anthropologists and other outsiders in contributing to the myth of Tigua cultural extinction. This discussion will be followed by a look at how the Tigua were "found," in which I explore how and why the Tigua were forced to fight for their rights as Native American Indians. Although the Tigua did gain state and then federal recognition, the issues of tribal sovereignty and Indian self-determination are, as we will see, largely a myth as applied to the Tigua tribe. Chapter Five explores the issue of Indian gaming, focusing on the idea that gaming has become the only viable economic strategy available to many Indian communities, including the Tigua. It describes the Tigua's creation of a successful gaming business from 1993 to 2002, as well as the role of the state of Texas in ordering the Tigua to shut the doors on this profitable enterprise. I then look at the long-term impact of this blatant usurpation of tribal sovereignty.

Methodological Issues

I have always felt strongly that anthropological research conducted with indigenous peoples should benefit the community in some significant way. Indeed, the notion of giving something back is, I believe, one of the more important hallmarks of cultural anthropology. James P. Spradley (1980: 16–17) makes a strong statement about this point with the following comment:

> There was a time when "knowledge for knowledge's sake" was sufficient reason for doing social science, at least for those who believed in the inevitability of progress and the inherent goodness of science, but that time has long since passed. In many places we can no longer collect cultural information from people merely to fill the bank of scientific knowledge.

Informants are asking, even demanding, "Ethnography for what? Do you want to study our culture to build your theories of poverty? Can't you see that our children go hungry?"

This sad (but all too often true) statement is a reflection of the poor treatment of indigenous peoples at the hands of far too many anthropologists, and not just during the colonial period (see discussion on indigeneity below). The French anthropologist Maurice Godelier (in Eiss and Wolfe 1994), discussing the importance of the anthropologists' relationship with the people they work with, points out:

> Too few anthropologists do that [give back], you know. People have to recuperate what they have been doing with the anthropologists, they have to defend them, to control what is done with the products made from their culture. But we have to do this systematically. Systematically, you understand? And so the future of anthropology is there.

In a humorous, but biting commentary, Vine Deloria Jr. (1969: 78) proclaims: "Into each life, it is said, some rain must fall. Some people have bad horoscopes; others take tips on the stock market. McNamara created the TFX and the Edsel. Churches possess the real world. But Indians have been cursed above all other people in history. Indians have anthropologists." Later, and in a more serious tone, he goes on to describe the "pure research" of anthropologists as "a body of knowledge absolutely devoid of useful application and incapable of meaningful digestion" (80). He further states (94–95): "Compilation of useless knowledge 'for knowledge's sake' should be utterly rejected by the Indian people. We should not be objects of observation for those who do nothing to help us. . . . Why should we continue to be the private zoos for anthropologists?" This is followed with a statement in response to individuals who believe academic freedom would be lost if researchers "compromised the integrity" of anthropological research: "Academic freedom certainly does not imply that one group of people have to become chessmen for another group of people. Should any group have a franchise to stick its nose into someone else's business? No" (95).

Although these words were written more than thirty years ago, their meaning is relevant today (see Smith 1998). The idea that research should be useful to the people being researched only addresses one aspect of the problem, however. An equally important outgrowth of Deloria's concerns is the notion of empowerment. Research that does nothing to help a community is one thing, but research that actually causes harm is quite another. I believe that a very simple question needs to be asked before any anthropological research begins: "Who is going to be empowered by this research?" This question, of course, can be a very difficult one to answer, but it is one that must be seriously explored because the outcome of poorly thought out research can lead to devastating consequences for innocent people. The fact that a "negative" research outcome is "unintentional" is of little solace to an affected community or individual.

Obviously, it is nearly impossible (particularly at the start of a project) to predict ultimate outcomes, but this exercise in reflexivity, if thoughtfully considered throughout the process of the project, not only strengthens the veracity of the research but also provides a recurring opportunity to ensure that the research is not empowering unintended people, organizations, or, indeed, nation-states. Although Talal Asad (1973) is perhaps the most notable critic of colonial anthropology and the (often) unintentional "benefits" of research usurped by the colonial power structure, there is no shortage of contemporary examples relevant to the empowerment question (also see Ramos 1998: 13; Warren and Jackson 2002: 3). For example, arguments over who "owns" archaeological artifacts, Native peoples or the scientific community, rages on. Archaeologists and paleoanthropologists, in particular, argue about the scientific need to study artifacts and human remains, while Native peoples fight for their right to control access to archaeological sites and archaeological findings (both material culture and human remains) and to determine how research conclusions are used. The film *Bones of Contention* (1998) and the article "Battle of the Bones" (Bonnichsen and Schneider 2000) reveal the contentious nature of this debate as well as the difficulty of ascertaining who the beneficiaries of anthropological research truly are.

Another issue that I believe is of particular importance when conducting research with indigenous peoples is the (flawed) notion that these groups have somehow become the victims of colonialism and modernity. Some, perhaps particularly within the academic community, decry the plight of the poor mistreated Natives and suggest that we should all feel sorry for them and rush to their aid. I find that attitude condescending and largely ethnocentric. Indeed, every Native American Indian that I have had the opportunity to meet has conveyed to me the sense that they were perfectly capable of survival, either without the white man or in spite of him. The notion that American Indians could not have survived this long if they were weak should not be lost on those who feel sorry for them or (perhaps especially) those who seek to hasten their demise. Every aspect of an indigenous community's ethos (including its history) is owned only by the culture itself, regardless of what certain government and religious groups may choose to believe. As Marshall Sahlins (1997: 44–45) points out, indigenous peoples often appear in writings as "neo-historyless peoples whose own agency disappeared more or less with their culture, the moment Europeans erupted on the scene." He goes on to agree with Margaret Jolly, who suggests that "when Europeans change it is called 'progress,' but when 'they' (the others) change, notably when they adopt some of our progressive attributes, it is a loss of their culture, some kind of adulteration" (45). The myth shared by many is that indigenous peoples were pristine and aboriginal before Europeans stumbled out onto foreign shores; indeed, "it is as if they had no historical relations with other societies, were never forced to adapt their existence" (45).

This is not to argue that indigenous peoples have not been victimized by dominant oppressors (as clearly they have), but to suggest that their response to that oppression has been, and should be, on their terms, not those of the oppressor. The idea that culture should change in some pre-determined direction, and that if it fails to follow this preordained path it is somehow inauthentic, speaks to the Western need to control and dictate the terms a changing culture must follow. Sahlins (1997: 50) addresses this issue:

> The struggle of non-Western peoples to create their own cultural versions of modernity undermines the perceived Western dichotomy of tradition and change, custom and rationality—and most notably its twentieth century version of tradition and development. . . . Paradoxically, almost all the cultures described as "traditional" by anthropologists, were in fact neotraditional, already changed by Western expansion.

The question is not about whether culture changes, it is about exercising control over the parameters of change. Were the Tigua, for example, affected by colonial rule? Of course, but they were also influenced by droughts, wars with other Natives, and cultural diffusion, as well as innumerable other events that helped shape and modify the Tigua worldview. That Tigua culture is the result of hundreds of years devoted to appropriate cultural adaptations, many of which took place long before the first ship sailed from Europe, cannot be overlooked or trivialized as if the only important change took place after the invasion. The Tigua have continued to change over the past several hundred years and have often been forced by the colonial power structure to adapt rapidly to the genocidal policies put into place by the United States. But the response of the Tigua to each new development, as we see throughout this book, has been thoughtful, planned, debated, and deliberate. In short, they know what they are doing. For the U.S. government to believe it can set both the conditions and direction of Native cultural change is not only unreasonable but delusional. Change, as Sahlins points out, is not the opposite of tradition, and "the best modern heirs of the Enlightenment philosophers know this. I mean for example the West African intellectuals who argue . . . that 'culture is not only a heritage, it is a project'" (50).

Indigenous peoples have been forced into a long-term power struggle against dominate oppressors for hundreds of years, and the fact that many are continuing the fight into contemporary times speaks to the notion that these groups are not as powerless as some would like to believe. In short, anthropological research that is designed to be carried out *on* a community, and not *with* the community, potentially prioritizes academic empowerment over indigenous empowerment. Additionally, it disrespects indigenous knowledge as trivial in comparison with academic ways of knowing. Scholars who enter the field believing they know more than the people they are working with are bound to be disappointed. Moreover, they are bound to conduct shoddy research as their preconceived notions (more appropriate to deductive research) will color their data and, perhaps more importantly, prevent them from building true rapport with their research partners.

One other issue I believe should be openly discussed in relation to this research is the question of research agenda. Full disclosure is, and should be, the hallmark of academic research, regardless of the methods employed. Unlike some researchers who attempt to disguise their blatantly biased research agenda, I make no bones about my advocacy for the Tigua.[7] I am convinced that the Tigua possess an Indian identity—as "authentic" as any other Indian identity—that has been passed down through countless generations.[8]

Indians?

One of the more common issues surfacing in discussions about Native American Indians is the question, Is there is a proper way to refer to "Indians"? In large part this question is an outgrowth of the 1960s political correctness (PC) movement, which ostensibly promoted cultural and ethnic sensitivity with regard to the language (particular words and labels) used to refer to members of minority groups (see d'Errico 2005; Berry 2006). Leaving the overall merits of this continuing movement aside, it is notable that the debate over this question has brought to the forefront the idea that language conveys powerful symbolic meaning and that underlying the PC debate lay the larger issues of power and control. The current debate in the United States, however (thanks primarily to the highly publicized insensitive remarks made by Hollywood celebrities Mel Gibson and Michael Richards of *Seinfeld*), has somewhat ironically focused the debate not on the power or right of one group to name or label another group, but on the right of particular individuals to use particular names when referencing others. Although the controversies relate to the derogatory words used against and (equally controversially) by particularly, blacks in the United States, there is a corollary in the historical use of the word "Indian" against (and by) Native peoples.

Before we examine the circumstances behind the creation and use of the specific term "Indian," it is important to first explore the underlying issue of power as it relates to the practice of both creating and naming human categories (see Geis 1987; Thomas and Wareing 1999). The "creation" and naming of "the other" became a very popular devise utilized by Western European nation-states during the process of colonial expansion. Indeed, O'Neil (2006) states that during the colonial period, "new ethnic groups" were created by European powers "in order to facilitate ruling their new indigenous subjects." In Australia and throughout North America, small bands of independent foraging societies "were combined into larger political units by government officials in order to simplify the control of them. Indigenous leadership positions, such as chiefs, were created for peoples who previously did not have the concept of a leader." The ability of the colonizers to name groups (on both the regionwide and the individual group level) signified to the indigenous population that the white invaders wielded great power. As Peter d'Errico (2005) points out, "Names can have great power, and the power of naming is a great power. History and law, as well as literature and politics, are activities of naming." O'Neil (2006) suggests that "identifying other people's ethnicity for them has always been a powerful political tool for controlling, marginalizing, and even getting rid of them . . . the power to label others is the power to control them." This practice, according to d'Errico, would not have run counter to the colonizers' sense of the world and their place in it. Indeed, Christian colonizers were simply following their belief structure when they set about organizing and naming the inhabitants they encountered in the "New World." Their guide was the Christian bible, which "tells a story of God giving Adam the power to name the animals and other parts of creation. An important part of the Judeo-Christian creation story is a power of naming that is a power over creation" (2005).

The history behind the word "Indian" is known to every American schoolchild who has heard the name of Christopher Columbus. Most understand that this wayward explorer believed he was in India when his ship ran aground in a region of the Bahamas and that he and his men began to refer to the indigenous peoples they saw as "Indians." Though the disoriented Columbus would die believing he had found a new route to India, it was later discovered that the place he had stumbled across was not India but an uncharted continent, indeed, two uncharted continents misleadingly dubbed the *nuevomundo*, or New World.

The word "Indian" is itself not only misleading but also loaded with pejorative and stereotypical connotations (Ramos 1998: 14). Wesaw (1995: 8–9, cited in Darian-Smith 2004: 18–19) makes this point with the following statement:

> The "Indian" is a flexible notion capable of being whatever the White world wants or does not want. The Indian can be a Noble or Savage. Indians can be evil incarnate, scalping and torturing innocents, or they can be pure-hearted environmentalists saving the forests and weeping over urban pollution. "Indians" can be anything and everything White policies want them to be. At this level of imaging, the Indian becomes a stereotype.

Stereotypes, though largely figments of a collective imagination, are, nonetheless, powerful rhetorical tools when used to rationalize certain behaviors and attitudes (also see Theodossopoulos 2003).[9] Moreover, once stereotypes become ingrained within the public consciousness, it is often difficult to prevent them from reaching mythic proportions. As Bill Wright (1992: 5) points out, "Myths create and reinforce archetypes so taken for granted, so seemingly axiomatic, that they go unchallenged. Myths are so fraught with meaning that we live and die by them. They are maps by which cultures navigate through time."

The stereotypes and cultural assumptions about how American Indians should or should not behave run very deep among the population of the United States. From the "Cigar Store Indian" to John Wayne movies to the popular Iron Eyes Cody "crying Indian" television commercial,

Americans have been bombarded with stereotypical images of American Indians that have indeed reached mythic proportions. Perhaps the largest and most damaging myth (outside the Indian as "savage" myth) is the notion that Indians comprise a singular Native culture. Contrary to this popular belief, the Indian does not exist, just as the European, the Asian, or the African does not exist. As Eve Darian-Smith (2004: 18) suggests, "All these general terms mask the extraordinary complexity and diversity that exists among different peoples living across vast continents." The danger of this myth is that it allows not only citizens, but government policymakers to lump all Native peoples together and penalize communities that do not exhibit the "proper" behavior associated with their personal perceptions of "Indianness." For example, when petitioning for federal recognition, all groups are expected to fit a predetermined mold, regardless of their individual community background or cultural traditions (see Chapter Four). The new myth, that of the "rich Indian," is perpetuated by this notion that all Native people are the same, or somehow related to each other and beholden to each other (see Darian-Smith 2004). While I was searching for funds to conduct this research, it was common to hear comments such as this one: "I thought the Indians were all rich now. Why don't they fund their own research?" Or, after being informed that few Indian communities are wealthy, "Why don't all the rich Indians help the poor ones?" The homogenization of Native peoples is so engrained that many of the people I have spoken with about the issue cannot even conceptualize the notion as false. Worst, however, is the fact that the U.S. government seems incapable of grasping this important distinction and continues to define Indianness by unrealistic, homologous standards.

The question first brought up in this section ("What is the 'proper' way to refer to Native peoples?") is, frankly, a difficult question to answer. Of course, terms that are unambiguously derogatory, such as savage, barbarian, Injun, and redskin, should never be used under any condition. The term "Native American" is often frowned on, not so much because it is derogatory but because, technically, anyone born on the soil of the United States is a Native American.[10] Other common labels include First Nations, American Indian, Amerindian, Native, Native American Indian, indigenous, and aborigine. First Nations, however, is much more common when referencing the indigenous peoples of Canada, and aborigine is most commonly used in referencing Australian aborigines (see Yellow Bird 1999: 1; Brunner 2006; Donakowski and Esses 1996; Lawrence

2004; Darian-Smith 2004: 13–14). The term "Indian," either standing alone or used in conjunction with another term, such as "American," is problematic for a variety of reasons, not the least of which is the derogatory tone some Native individuals feel that it conveys. I believe the best answer I can give in response to this question is, "With respect." Although the term "Indian" is despised by some Native peoples, it is worn like a badge of honor by others. According to Christina Berry (2006), "The first reason is habit. Many Indians have been Indians all their lives. . . . Why change now? The second reason is far more political." The replacement of the Indian with the Native American "enabled America to ease its conscience. . . . Native Americans did not suffer through countless trails of tears, disease, wars, and cultural annihilation—Indians did." Americans "do not need to feel guilty for the horrors of the past . . . this is what the term Native American essentially does—it white-washes history. It cleans the slate."

Most American Indians that I have met speak of themselves and other Natives as "Indians" and under most conditions do not assume that the word, when directed toward them, has a derogatory connotation. In my experience with the Tigua, I have found that it is often the individual using the term "Indian," not the word itself, that provokes concern. In one example, a respondent revealed that he had lashed out at a Park Service employee who was discussing the "Indian bones" discovered at an archaeological dig site, and how important the "Indian artifacts" connected to the site would be to researchers. Within this context, this respondent felt that the term "Indian" was used as a way to dehumanize the remains and put separation between the aims of science and the very real pain experienced by the Tigua community members who were present at the site.

Of course, referring to Native peoples by their tribal affiliation, whenever possible, is preferable to using generic terms. I use the terms "Indian," "Native," "American Indian," and "indigenous" throughout this book as interchangeable terms, although I do attempt to use proper tribal names whenever possible. Unfortunately, the conventions of writing English make it difficult to continually use the same proper name without disturbing the flow of communication.

Indigeneity

As the above discussion points out, the power to name carries with it the power to define. The power to define carries with it the power to control. Names, labels, stereotypes, and myths are concepts incorporated within the discourse of the dominant group in order to ease the process of subjugation and oppression (see Chapter Three). Questions about whether or not a particular group is indigenous or aboriginal ties to the related concept of authenticity, whether or not a group is made up of individuals who possess "real" identities. In the case of the Tigua (and other American Indian groups), the question has become, "How do we know the difference between real identities, as opposed to fabricated or invented identities?" In order to simplify the debate, the following discussion will focus on the term "indigenous" with the understanding that this term, for the most part, refers to the same concept as the terms "aboriginal," "Native," and "First Peoples." The related notions of authenticity, real Indians, identity, ethnicity, extinction, and recognition will be taken up in later chapters.

In order to discuss the concept of indigeneity, it is necessary to first establish a working definition of the term. For the purposes of this discussion I follow the definition provided by Justin Kenrick and Jerome Lewis (2004: 5), which "emphasizes four principles to be considered in any definition of indigenous peoples":

(1) priority in time, with respect to the occupation and use of a specific territory; (2) the voluntary perpetuation of cultural distinctiveness; (3) self-identification, as well as recognition by other groups and by state authorities, as a distinct collectivity; and (4) an experience of subjugation, marginalization, dispossession, exclusion or discrimination, whether or not these conditions persist.

The need to define indigeneity (as well as other terms that appear indefinable) is the result of the policies and laws developed by nation-states to facilitate the removal of original peoples from their land and resources (see Chapter Three for a detailed discussion). The above definition, which on the surface appears straightforward, is, of course, riddled with ambiguity. That anthropological definitions contain ambiguity would hardly be problematic if the creating and defining of abstract terms took place on a purely academic level. Indeed, the debate over meaning would be largely inconsequential. The problem, however, is that this debate is not purely academic; it addresses political and legal issues.

The current argument between anthropologists over the use of the term "indigenous" stems primarily from an Adam Kuper article entitled "The Return of the Native," published in the June 2003 edition of

Current Anthropology. In this article Kuper argues that the term "indigenous" is "essentialist" and relies "on obsolete anthropological notions and on a romantic and false ethnographic vision" (2003: 395). Such a position was destined to cause controversy among anthropologists, and numerous counterpositions were immediately proposed.[11] "In other words," according to Alan Barnard (2006: 2), "'indigenous' is simply a new word for 'primitive.'" Kenrick and Lewis (2004: 4), using somewhat harsher terms than Barnard, state: "In the July 2003 issue of *Current Anthropology*, Adam Kuper vehemently attacked the indigenous peoples' movement, claiming it to be retrograde, antiprogressive and right wing." In arguing that "Kuper's polemic is misleading in a number of ways, and would perhaps be better ignored," they go on to point out that his article is "an example of the potential academic arguments can have to reinforce discourse that serves to conceal discrimination against such peoples" and that "the article must be taken seriously. Its potential for 'spin' is confirmed by the recent explicit and implicit promotion of Kuper's conclusions by organizations wishing to justify actions that may be in conflict with the rights of indigenous people" (4). Trond Thuen (2006: 24) expands on this, arguing that "the term 'indigenous' is a political construct, not an anthropological one" Barnard (2006: 8) agrees: "There is no, and can be no, theoretically-unproblematic anthropological definition of 'indigenous.' It is a legal concept" (see also Ramos 1998: 6). Barnard makes a vital distinction that calls into question the relationship between social scientists and government legislators.

The issues and concerns raised by this debate are highly salient to indigenous peoples around the world and apply directly to a number of problems faced by the Tigua today. Kenrick and Lewis (2004: 4) sum up the importance of the debate: "In contrast to our own and other anthropologists' experience and work, Kuper's polemic ignores the context of the extreme discrimination faced by indigenous peoples and their many experiences of dispossession by more powerful groups." The argument must be placed within this "history of discrimination and dispossession against indigenous peoples," the fact that these groups have been historically "denied the rights enjoyed by other groups." That this issue is not a remnant of the past is "demonstrated by continuing attempts to dispossess them of their land and resources, and by severe and widespread pressures for cultural assimilation" (2004: 4).

Kenrick (2006: 20) later adds to this point, suggesting that "transnational corporations relish such attacks on indigenous peoples' rights since such rights act as one of the few impediments to their appropriation of indigenous people's lands." Even though Kuper legitimately calls into debate the use of the term "indigenous," he (intentionally or not) clearly provides "cherry-picking" legislators (and others) ammunition to use in defense of policies and programs designed to minimize indigenous power. Indeed, the crux of Kuper's argument appears to be that indigenous peoples are somehow seeking "privileged rights" over the rights of others (2003: 390); he even goes so far as to compare the indigenous rights movement with South African apartheid. Barnard (2006: 8), in discrediting this comparison, points out: "Apartheid was an invidious system of domination and oppression, whereas indigenous people do not seek to dominate or oppress; they only seek to be regarded as different. . . ."

As far-fetched as Kuper's comparison may be, the argument that "indigenous rights" equal "privileged rights" or "special rights" echoes the argument faced by indigenous peoples who attempt to seek redress (in the name of their ancestors) for past wrongs. The numerous problems encountered by the Tigua exemplify the way in which the U.S. government approaches groups that petition for indigenous recognition. Indeed, a primary issue relevant to the Tigua case (see Chapters Four and Five) relates to the question of "entitlements," or special privileges. It is interesting to note that for hundreds of years the tribe kept to itself and practiced its traditions and ceremonies largely unnoticed. During this period it appears that the surrounding population was happy to have a quaint little Indian community in its midst (see Chapter Four). After the Tigua began to exercise their voice and demand their rights as American Indians, however, local citizens (both private and public) began to denounce the Tigua as "frauds," "charlatans," and "Mexicanized Indians" (see Chapter Five). The notion that real Indians should be poor, powerless, and preferably isolated helped feed local dissent as the Tigua began to amass wealth and power.[12] They were real Indians while their land and resources were being stripped away, real Indians when they danced during the annual Feast Days, but "Mexicans playing Indian" when they filed land claims. In truth, the Tigua were (and are) only asking for what was already rightfully theirs.

It seems, as Kenrick (2006: 20) suggests, that indigenous peoples just cannot win. Criticizing the argument put forth by Kuper, he notes: "First, they are systematically dispossessed by European empires on the basis that they are distinct from 'us' and too backward to manage themselves or their lands." Then, when the survivors "demand some recognition of their land rights and their right to self-determination, their arguments are likened to extreme right-wing parties in Europe . . . and they are told that their land claims rely on obsolete anthropological notions and on a false romantic vision." I would also add that they are forced (at least in the United States) to meet one-size-fits-all guidelines developed by government agents and then purposely denied the ability to meet those requirements. An example provided by Mark Miller (2004: 59) points to the impossible circumstances some groups face. In the case of the Burt Lake Band of Ottawa and Chippewa, the community was denied federal recognition because they had "abandoned" their village. The fact that the government had forced them to move and burned their village to the ground after a "tax sale" did not influence the formal finding, which was that the group had "voluntarily" abandoned their community. Thuen (2006: 24) echoes these concerns, stating that the overarching problem associated with the concept of indigeneity is not "so much that the definition is complex. . . . the problem relies, among other things, on the burden that to substantiate their land claims many indigenous peoples are expected to prove their 'authenticity' by demonstrating an archaic lifestyle."

Not only is indigenous culture expected by "superordinate discourse" to undergo minimal change, but also any change that takes place is constrained by the limits imposed by (largely arbitrary) "definitions and expectations of culture" that are "required by the courts" (Kenrick 2006: 20). Thuen (2006: 24–25) points out that "essentialised presentations of self tend to be a legal and political requirement within majority discourses of indigeneity, and it is a paradox that anthropological questioning may denigrate such presentations." The laws in the United States, for example, have clearly been written to reward "traditional" behavior over "progressive" behavior, a circumstance that further deteriorates the Native right to self-determination. Furthermore, these laws, many of which are based on (and justified with) anthropological arguments, convolute the ability of ethnographers to build rapport and trust with their research partners.

My point here is not to argue that anthropologists should cease conducting research; it is simply to reiterate my earlier point that it is often difficult to predict how research data may ultimately be used. Mindful of this notion (and as stated above), my goal has not been to prove that the Tigua are indigenous peoples, regardless of how the term is defined. My goal has been to explore the "changing relationship" between the Tigua community and the successive nation-states that have oppressed them (see

Thuen 2006: 25). Indeed, I argue throughout this book that contemporary Tigua culture is a product of particular cultural responses to various and changing majority rules. I agree with Evie Plaice (2003: 24), who points out that the development of indigenous culture is specific to place, time, and circumstance. For example, she says, "Labrador Metis culture was an amalgam of other cultural traits that had developed specifically in Labrador precisely because this unique blend of place, peoples and circumstance could not have occurred elsewhere." In fact, "this interpretation adds another shade to a definition of indigeneity that neatly sidesteps and even negates the essentialising tendency of other interpretations" (24).

A final point to be made about the term "indigenous" concerns the notion that indigeneity implies "firstness" in regard to place, as well as long-term residency (preferably since "time out of mind"). That is a misleading and false notion because movement, whether before or after European contact, cannot in and of itself negate cultural continuity. As Barnard (2006: 1) points out, "being indigenous to a place is not in itself what makes a people an 'indigenous people.'" Moreover, occupancy and use of place through time (the first of the above four "principles" listed by Kenrick and Lewis) are, by themselves, no safeguard against genocide. Indeed, movement (both before and after contact) is a legitimate response to various threats, be they natural or manmade. Even though occupancy and use of place through time are criteria that assist many groups in gaining indigenous status, they unfairly penalize groups and individuals that (through no fault of their own) cannot demonstrate long-term (whatever that means) residency in a particular area.

This point is particularly relevant to this book as the issue of indigeneity, when applied to the Tigua, is complicated by their unusual (and somewhat ambiguous) historical connection with the El Paso area (see Chapter One). If we state that the Tigua are not indigenous to El Paso (which they certainly are not), does that mean that their culture is not indigenous? What about the numerous American Indian communities that were forcibly moved to Oklahoma and other places west of the Mississippi? What about the countless indigenous individuals who have been forced to leave their communities in search of employment? What about nomadic groups that never lived a settled existence? Perhaps we should simply refer to them as "refugees," or some other equally ambiguous term? As Barnard (2006: 8) points out: "It is relatively easy to say who are 'indigenous peoples' in Australia or South America, but who is 'indigenous' in this sense in Africa?" Moreover, it is true that "some peoples whose representatives claim 'indigenous' status are not indigenous (in the perpetual residence sense) to the places they presently live in. This is especially true of pastoral peoples" (8).

Tigua culture (and other indigenous culture) is the result of the "structural inequities between cultures that are the fruit of history and circumstance" (see Plaice above) regardless of where they were "originally" located. I agree with Thuen (2006: 25) when he states that "an individual's claim to belong to a certain indigenous group may not be so much the way he or she embraces the essentialized and politicized aspects of 'the culture' . . . as it is his/her position within specific kinship networks and the group's positive evaluation of performances in certain types of knowledge, behavior and competences according to shared criteria."[13]

When indigenous identity is conceptualized as a product of shared criteria, rather than essentialized and politicized criteria, groups are empowered to internally define membership guidelines that make sense to them, given their particular circumstances. One size does not fit all. Or, as Michael Asch argues, "The status of indigenous peoples [needs] to be resolved in a manner consistent with the principles of social justice" (quoted in Plaice 2006: 24). Any definition of indigeneity that does not account for particular histories, particular circumstances, and the role of domination in forcing change is not "consistent with the principles of social justice" and should, therefore, be rejected as both essentializing and political.

CHAPTER ONE

Oral Tradition, Part One

Diaspora and Survival

Introduction

The question of when and under what circumstances the Tigua found themselves occupying an area near present-day El Paso, Texas, in 1680 is contentious. An evaluation of the scholarly research is inconclusive; a reading of oral tradition is helpful but also raises several intriguing questions. What is clear is that some number of Tigua and Piro (and other) Indians residing in and around the area of Isleta, New Mexico, left with retreating Spanish forces, willingly or unwillingly, during the Pueblo Revolt. Another group, almost certainly, was forcibly taken from Isleta to El Paso one year later. Whether these contingents comprised refugees who were unfamiliar with the region or Indians who already knew the area well is unclear. That they remained and continued to practice their cultural traditions are beyond dispute. The purpose of this chapter is not to (somehow) forge a definitive answer to this question of arrival; rather, I seek to gain insight on Tigua perceptions of their own history and explore the concepts of cultural change, perseverance, and identity as they apply to the Tigua community.

Because I have stated that one of my goals in writing this book was an interest in exploring cultural change and perseverance within the Tigua community, it is important to set some benchmark against which that change (or lack of change) can be measured. Although that benchmark is largely arbitrary, historical documentation and oral tradition are sufficient, I believe, to set a date of 1680 as a fair point for departure. The methods I utilized to explore these questions and issues have combined ethnohistorical and ethnographic techniques, focused on both individual and community-wide perceptions of Tigua identity.

In this chapter, I explore oral tradition as it relates to the forms and functions of historical knowledge and its links with tribal identity. Additionally, this discussion will look at the historical knowledge and consciousness the

Tigua hold in regard to their own history as Pueblo Indians exploring the process of changing identities. My goal is not to simply present the "facts" of history, but to gain a sense of how historical knowledge is ingrained within the building and maintenance of group identity. By gathering data unavailable in written records and by exploring collective memory, we can bridge the gaps found in the individual's memory and pull together a holistic sense of the community-wide understanding of particular significant events.

Using History in Anthropological Research

The use of archival data, as well as other forms of documented history, has long been a part of anthropological research methods. Indeed, anthropologists have long sought to establish a relationship, specifically, to the discipline of history. Although history itself is subjective, when used with care it can often illuminate and provide context to particular research issues. Maurice Godelier (1999: 8), for example, states, "No society, no identity can survive over time and provide a foundation for the individuals or groups that make up a society if there are no fixed points." A community's history, its heritage, its origins, its past, they are what constitute societies' "fixed points." Additionally, in speaking about the study of the "sciences of man and society," Godelier points out: "You have to put things in their historical context. . . . An anthropologist cannot stop with the present, with the present state of local communities, there has to be an historical perspective" (quoted in Eiss and Wolfe 1994). In the United States, the tradition of incorporating history into ethnographic methods can be traced at least as far back as the work of Fenton (1952), A. L. Kroeber (1966), and later Bernard Cohn (1987) and John and Jean Comaroff (1992). The argument for both Cohn and the Comaroffs was the need for anthropology to embrace history as part of the effort to rehabilitate anthropology after the anticolonial critiques the discipline sustained in the 1970s and 1980s (Kunal 2004). One of the outcomes of these critical discussions was a greater emphasis by a number of anthropologists on the use of historical ethnography in anthropological research. As Anne Sutherland (1999) points out: "Of course, there is nothing new about history or ethnography, but what scholars . . . have advocated is a genuine marriage of the two that goes beyond Evans-Pritchard's famous speech in the 1950s exhorting structural-functional anthropologists to share a bed with history."

Ethnohistorical methods are particularly useful when conducting research that is concerned with cultural change (as this project is) because they utilize historical methods that extend beyond the usual data collection techniques, such as books and periodicals, to include data more traditionally associated with ethnography. For example, "maps, music, paintings, photography, folklore, oral tradition, ecology, site exploration, museum collections, customs, language, and place names" would all be considered important sources of data (Axtell 1979: 3–4). Additionally, the ethnohistorical approach "embraces emic perspectives as tools of analysis" and is "well suited for writing histories of Indian peoples because of its holistic and inclusive framework" (Sutherland 2005). James Axtell (1979: 2) describes ethnohistory as "the use of historical and ethnological methods to gain knowledge of the nature and causes of change in a culture defined by ethnological concepts and categories," and William S. Simmons (1988: 10) argues that ethnohistory is "a form of cultural biography that draws upon as many kinds of testimony as possible over as long a time period as the sources allow." He further describes the method as based on a holistic, diachronic approach that works best when it can be "joined to the memories and voices of living people" (10). In other words, ethnohistorical methods, particularly when joined with oral tradition, substantially assist researchers in accounting for how the members of a culture construct and understand their own past.

Oral traditions (as well as the similar life history narratives, or oral histories) are "grounded in memory, and memory [like written history] is a subjective instrument for recording the past, always shaped by the present moment and the individual psyche" (Truesdell 2006).[1] This is significant because oral tradition can reveal how individual values and actions shaped the past, as well as how the past shapes present-day values and actions. Beyond the individual is the social, however, and it is important, according to Elizabeth Tonkin (1992: 97), "that oral narratives be seen as social actions, situated in particular times and places and directed by individual tellers to specific audiences." Tonkin points out that "memory and cognition are partly constituted by social relations and thus are also constitutive of society. We are all simultaneously bearers and makers of history, with discursive representations of pastness as one element in this generation and reproduction of social life" (97). For example, although various versions of the same story exist (such as narratives related to the Tigua-Kiowa battle and the 1680 diaspora), it is possible to construct a collective understanding of the events by comparing the shared perceptions of the event outside the confines of individual bias. Indeed, people do not remember "facts" correctly or incorrectly in isolation: they are integrated within a narrative, and the narrative builds the path that connects the present with the past (Green and Troup 1999: 235–236).

One issue that must be considered when using oral tradition or oral history or both is the question of accuracy. "At the very least, one must be aware of the limitations of each technique in order not to mislead oneself into believing that these approaches automatically yield accurate renditions of past events" (Moyer 1999). Because oral tradition and oral history depend upon living people as sources, they have limits (for example, firsthand accounts can only go back as far as the oldest community member), but because these methods use spoken, not written sources, the allowable evidence expands. But what of the failings of human memory in recalling memories from a long-ago event? How do we know how closely the memories of the speaker correspond with what actually happened? What of the personal motives of the storyteller? How does the power relationship between interviewer and interviewee influence what information is revealed? What of the writers' bias and inaccuracies that affect the process of transcription?

Clearly, these are legitimate concerns, but it is likewise clear that many (if not all) of the same problems arise when relying on the written record. Written sources can carry personal or social biases, occur within a social context, and can be (and have been) unmasked as forgeries (see Bloch 1954: 62). To suggest that oral tradition is any less valid than documented history is not only ethnocentric but lacks a critical understanding of the process(es) of writing history. Moreover, criticisms about the frailty and subjectiveness of human memory do not take into account the social aspect of memory production. Speaking to this point, Tonkin (1992: 104) states: "Memory, when we look at it, dissolves its boundaries and cannot be wholly distinguished from imagination or from thought itself. These in turn cannot be understood without taking memory into account . . . memory in this larger sense is also not an individual property; it comes from outside."

This aspect of memory was reiterated by one respondent many times when, after the telling of nearly every story, he would repeat the same line: "These are not my words; these are the Elders' words." This explicit statement confirmed that this individual felt no sense of ownership over his social memories, that he understood memories as communal "property," that his role as storyteller is to act as a conduit between past and present (see Carrithers 1992: 103). The dichotomy between individual memory and social memory melts away and becomes one. Lacking ownership (and often authorship), oral tradition embeds itself within the social consciences and becomes, as a whole, impervious to widespread individual manipulation. Individuals may tell the same story differently, but it is still the same story. Particular stories persist through time because they have purpose and meaning. For example, I have heard the Tigua-Kiowa battle story (see Chapter Two) told three different ways. However, the purpose of this story, the grand narrative, remains unchanged: the Tigua outsmart the Kiowa and win the day. The moral of the story is equally clear: Tigua people are courageous, clever fighters and adept problem solvers. The addition or subtraction of some particular detail does nothing to change the point of the tale. The version a teller presents is a reflection of the version they learned, and any story can be told in infinite ways. The existence of multiple variations is to be expected. Another comment often made by the aforementioned respondent before telling a story speaks to this issue: "This is the way it was told to me."

One area of criticism relevant to oral history, in my experience, applies to the process of transcribing, or writing down, what has been said. As Judith Moyer (1999) points out, "people frequently do not speak in complete sentences, they repeat themselves, leave things out, talk in circles and tell fragments of the same story out of chronological sequence, they mumble incoherently and use wrong names. When they speak, they don't use punctuation" (see also Rappaport 1990: 11). How can an interview be transcribed without loss of meaning? In addition, readers and listeners will add their own interpretations in trying to understand what the narrator said (Green and Troup 1999: 231–234). Indeed, I would argue that transcribing interview sessions is among the most difficult aspect of the ethnographic research process. However, one of the strengths of longitudinal research is that there is ample time to present interviewees with a copy of the transcript as a way to ensure accuracy. Although some problems are difficult to overcome, such as reader bias and misinterpretation, by faithfully reproducing what has been said and ensuring that it is presented within the intended context, one can gain an accurate sense of a respondent's meaning. Additionally, as a methodological balance to oral tradition, one can enlist other sources of data such as related artifacts, written documentation, and other interviews. A single, stand-alone interview can hardly be considered compelling scientific data, but an interview (or a series of interviews) placed within the context of other data can clarify details and create a sense of the whole (Green and Troup 1999: 231–234).

Diaspora

The term "diaspora," when applied to American Indians, is often used in reference to the thousands of Native peoples who were forcibly removed from their homelands and confined on reservations across the country. Unquestionably, the forced removal of a community from its traditional and sacred homeland constitutes diaspora. The use of this term to describe the Tigua is problematic, however, and requires further discussion. Unlike the many groups that were clearly uprooted, the case of the Tigua is somewhat ambiguous. Indeed, it can be argued (see the oral tradition below) that the Tigua left their New Mexico homeland voluntarily, either with the retreating Spanish forces or perhaps even before the 1680 uprising. Moreover, their connection with Isleta Pueblo was short-term; some Tigua believe their forefathers were never incorporated into the Isleta community. Finally, a Tigua connection with the area around El Paso predating 1680 is at least arguable, meaning that "their sense of rootedness in the land is," as James Clifford (1997: 254) suggests, "precisely what diasporic peoples have lost."

Having made these points, however, I argue that the Tigua should be perceived and discussed as a diasporic population. Indeed, despite the fact that the Tigua case is atypical of many displaced peoples, it still falls firmly within the "ideal" parameters of diasporic discourse. Safran lists six features of diasporic communities that include

> [expatriate minority communities] (1) that are dispersed from an original "centre" to at least two "peripheral" places; (2) that maintain a "memory, vision, or myth about their original homeland"; (3) that "believe they are not—and perhaps cannot be—fully accepted by their host country"; (4) that see the ancestral home as a place of eventual return, when the time is right; (5) that are committed to the maintenance or restoration of this homeland; and (6) whose consciousness and solidarity as a group are "importantly defined" by this continuing relationship with the homeland. (Safran 1991: 83–84, quoted in Clifford 1997: 247)

With the possible exception of features four and five, the Tigua meet each of the six "requirements." (And, according to legend, the last living Tigua member is required to return to the "homeland" to bury the tribal drum.)

Of course, diaspora is a difficult term to define. Indeed, Clifford (1997: 247) points out that although there is a need "to sort our paradigms and maintain historical specificity" in regard to diaspora discourse, the "imposition of strict meanings and authenticity tests" are problematic and unnecessary (see also Oussatcheva 2006; van Hear 1998). The question of diaspora as it applies to the Tigua is important not for the way in which it is defined, but because of what it means to the Tigua process of identity building. The Tigua are "peoples whose sense of identity is centrally defined by collective histories of displacement," as well as "the victims of ongoing, structural prejudice" (Clifford 1997: 250–251). As Clifford suggests, "the term diaspora is a signifier, not simply of transnationality and movement, but of political struggles to define the local, as distinctive community, in historical contexts of displacement" (252).

The notion of diaspora is important to understanding contemporary Tigua cultural identity for two reasons. First, their identity as American Indians and Pueblo peoples is firmly rooted in their history of displacement, and the discourse of diaspora plays a vital role in the shaping of this identity. Second, their sense of identity has been strongly affected by the process of colonialism, a process that has forced many tribal members to relocate for economic reasons.

The discourse of diaspora utilized by the Tigua is vital to their identity as Indian peoples; it is what provides context to the later narratives of struggle and survival. That the connection to New Mexico is strong is born out of the simple fact that it has persisted for over three hundred years. In order for the connection to the homeland to be maintained, the language of diaspora must be powerful, "enough to resist erasure through the normalizing processes of forgetting, assimilating, and distancing" (Clifford 1997: 255). The Tigua "resist erasure" through a powerful oral tradition that embraces their connection to the Isleta Pueblo, and that connection is always invoked by tribal members as central to Tigua identity. The nature of the Tigua migration narrative, as well as the ongoing diasporic discourse, does not (unlike those of many diasporic communities) invoke a sense of rootedness or longing for return, however. Tigua roots are firmly planted in their present landscape; the migration narrative provides historical continuity rather than a desire for eventual return. The Tigua sense of themselves as a diasporic community simply grounds their identity as, first and foremost, American Indians and Pueblo peoples. Once the emergence story reaches the point of migration, the focus of the oral narratives shifts to the hardships and obstacles encountered by the displaced community. The goal of the community from that point in history is long-term survival in place, not return to the "homeland" (see Brah 1996).

It is, I believe, the struggle against the colonial invaders that is always the implicit (and often explicit) moral of the story as passed on through Tigua oral tradition. Movement as central to a diasporic identity matters less than European domination, as experienced by countless indigenous populations in the New World. One did not need to move in order to suffer through the oppression and subjugation wrought by colonial expansion (Cohen 1997). The Tigua fight for survival was exacerbated by their relocation (and isolation), to be certain, but it was not the overarching cause of their problems. What makes the Tigua (and many other Native communities) more properly diasporic is that many community members were forced to leave their homes and families in search of employment. As Clifford (1997: 253) points out:

> Dispersed tribal peoples, those who have been dispossessed of their lands or who must leave reduced reserves to find work, may claim diasporic identities. Inasmuch as their distinctive sense of themselves is oriented towards a lost or alienated home defined as aboriginal (and thus "outside" the surrounding nation state), we can speak of a diasporic dimension of contemporary tribal life.

Indeed, the impact of diaspora on Tigua identity building has been shaped, perhaps, more by the gradual (indirectly forced) migration that took place after the Tigua arrived in El Paso than by the original migration (forced or not). Conceptualized from this standpoint, the six "features" of diaspora outlined by Safran (above) apply at least equally as much to the events that unfolded after 1680 as they apply to the original movement away from the New Mexican homeland.

Tigua History: In Their Words

The construction of the Tigua worldview is tied inextricably not only to their sense of connectedness to the natural and spiritual realms, but also to their shared identity as Native peoples forced to survive in a world dominated by white, Eurocentric cultural values and belief systems.[2] Their ability to persevere as a community and maintain their sense of identity through three hundred years of persecution, injustice, and forced change represents a feat of astonishing proportions. The Tigua, like virtually all indigenous peoples, have a history that, for over four hundred years, has been shaped by a relationship with powerful oppressors. The story of their survival has been told by others; unfortunately, what has too often been lacking in those narratives is the voice of the Tigua themselves. The story of the Tigua people's history is, after all, their story, just as the perceptions of Tigua reality are their perceptions, and the words that describe that history should be their words. With this thought in mind, the following narrative represents a largely unedited representation of early Tigua history (1680–1900) as related by members of the Tigua community. For the sake of brevity, I paraphrase and combine redundant statements when possible. For the sake of continuity, I make brief comments as appropriate. My desire, however, is to present, as much as possible, an accurate representation of the Tigua voice and Tigua perceptions of tribal history and cultural reality.[3]

There is minor disagreement among tribal members about when the Tigua originally arrived in the El Paso region. Although several respondents believe there was a Tigua presence in the area prior to 1680, each and every respondent I spoke with agreed that some number of Tigua moved with the Spanish from Isleta, New Mexico, in 1680, followed by a smaller contingent in 1681. The vast majority feel that their ancestors were brought as slaves, and the following narrative, provided by José, accurately represents the oral tradition that virtually all tribal members ascribe to:

> I was going to talk to you about how we got here, our history. There are many variations on the history of our tribe, written in books and the tradition which has been passed on by our Elders through the generations, but our beginnings go way back. When we started as a people, well, that goes back to the creation of people, creation story. When we descended from the Earth Mother, it was in some place way up north in New Mexico, the Black Lake, the place of emergence, the place where the people came up from the other world. They were underneath the earth. There were other worlds below there before we came up to this one. But I'm not too familiar with that story, or the ceremonial terms, or if I do know them I can't say them. There were two groups, the black eyes [who reside in the sunset side of the pueblo] and the red eyes [who reside in the sunrise side of the pueblo]. The black eyes were the first to come out. One version that I heard is that they found a badger digging up from the other world, digging a hole up to this world. They saw the light from this earth

and then the black eyes came up, then the red eyes, then the chief of all people, our people, cacique, which is Tigua for chief. Then, the people came up from the different corn groups, and they traveled in all the directions. Some of the people, corn groups, some went East, some went West, South; well, eventually they settled where they originally were from. Not just Isleta but all the Pueblo people in that area [*New Mexico*]. Some settled in Gran Quivira, but those villages died off; well, they got abandoned sometime during the 1600s due to raids from enemy tribes, Apaches, Comanche, Kiowa. I think also during that time there was a very bad drought, a severe drought that came upon the pueblos. They don't know what happened to the people, because they had to leave because we had a drought. The Pueblo people, the water is part of your soul; if you don't have water you [*are*] not going to have a healthy soul. That's why some of these ruins were left. . . . They had to move because of the drought. . . . Some [*experts*] say sickness or whatever. If it were to be a sickness that happened in the pueblo, you would find a lot of bodies. You don't find that many bodies. How can you have a population of five thousand or two thousand people and the Pueblos, they always buried their people. Maybe [*in*] some of the sites they find burials, but it's very limited. You don't find thousands of people. Anyway, one of these villages, which were Tiwa, some of the survivors went to the neighboring pueblos, which was Isleta. The Piro people went to, I think, Socorro Pueblo up there, Socorro. The people were also related, they were all Pueblos and our ancestors. There were refugees from the other pueblos; they sought refuge with their kinfolk in Isleta and Socorro.

Well, OK, when the Spanish went up from Mexico looking for the [*seven*] Cities of Gold, Cibola was what they called it, maybe it was the Indians from the south, Mexico, just to get rid of the Spanish, told them, "No, there is [a] city of gold up North" just to get rid of them and the silly Spanish, always greedy and eager to find gold, they just went from village to village down in Mexico, and the Indians just said "it's way up north." "There's people that have gold sidewalks and the whole villages just shine." Maybe that's just my personal opinion, but I've heard it from other people, and read it also in books. Sometime in the 1500s, though, they came up to New Mexico, and they got up to the pueblos up north, I think. Those Pueblos told them, "No, it's [*the gold*] way up to the east over there." So they were being led from pueblo to pueblo. Somehow they brought with them, the Spanish brought with them, the missionaries, because they were looking for gold, but the missionaries were also looking

for souls to save. I don't know from what because we already had our reli-
gions and beliefs. So they came for two things, looking for gold and looking for souls to save. With that, they started coming also for our land, we
mustn't forget that, for their so-called kingdom of New Spain. They
claimed all this area for Spain and they started settling the pueblos, converting the Indians, the Native peoples, and some of it was bad. They were
ruthless in their manner of converting the Natives, they were enslaved,
poor Native people, and they got tired of it. The Indians, they say, "Enough
is enough; this isn't right." So, in 1680 all the pueblos united as a united
front to get rid of the Spanish [*which led to*] the Pueblo Revolt of 1680.
They started up in Taos Pueblo and sent runners. It actually started in San
Juan Pueblo by a man called Popé. He was the instigator; well we call
him a hero. He was the one that united all the pueblos at a set date,
I think it was August 10, 1680, and they sent runners among all the tribes
and villages and attacked the missions, the Spaniards, at that date, August
10, 1680. So there's bloodshed and massacres and deaths on both sides,
but the Spanish were outnumbered, so they got rid of them village by village. They burn the missions and get rid of the settlers on their retreat
south. The surviving Spanish missionaries and peoples, they stopped at
Isleta Pueblo, our original mother pueblo, and they see people there that
didn't leave the village. They were caught by surprise, the Isleta people,
and they attacked the village and captured our grandfathers, which were
370 something, I'm not sure about the numbers, but they catch them as
prisoners of war and as a shield in case the other Pueblo people, the war-
riors, attack. They capture our people, [*and use them*] like a human
shield, and then head south. They started out with three or four hundred.
They came down to the El Paso area. On the way some of the Indians died
because they had to walk, and some died of hunger or cold or sickness.
There were about two or three hundred that reached El Paso.

The question of precisely when and how the Tigua arrived in the El
Paso region is contentious because sufficient data, either archaeologically
or historically, are lacking. Tigua oral tradition includes several migration stories, but most of these stories deal with the 1680 movement
specifically and agree with regard to the major issues. The primary question that provokes disagreement between tribal members (and others) regards a pre-1680 presence in the region, an issue that is seldom discussed
in the literature. Because empirical data (for the most part) are lacking,
it is appropriate to approach this question intuitively. Based on this

approach, a Tigua connection with the El Paso area in general and Hueco Tanks in particular prior to the 1680 migration is probable. I make this contention based on the early willingness of the Tigua to defend this territory (an issue to be discussed in greater detail below); physical evidence (for example, and pictographic creations) that, though not conclusive, is at least indicative of pre-1680 Tigua occupation; and also an oral tradition that (albeit somewhat sketchy) maintains a pre-1680 Tigua association, if not a permanent village.

The oral tradition of a number of New Mexico Puebloan groups maintains that the first Tigua joined the Spanish (without being coerced) in the retreat because they did not want to take part in the Pueblo Revolt and feared reprisal from the actively involved pueblo communities. This interpretation of events is, of course, collectively distasteful to the Tigua because it paints them as cowards and traitors. It is not a view one would expect them to promote. However, the main reason expressed in the oral histories for discounting this particular story is not that it provokes shame, but that it does not correspond with the known evidence. For example, this version of events, which, to be fair, appears to be based mostly on speculation and hearsay, was likely exacerbated by the news that the Tigua had brought sacred items with them during their retreat to El Paso. The tribal drum, canes of leadership, *abuelo* (grandfather) masks, and other important cultural items were brought with the relocated Tigua, and, as tribal Elder Jesus points out, "the Spaniards would never have allowed the Indians to get these things if they were 'slaves.'" This point, however, was made by Jesus not to question whether the Tigua came willingly (which this fact clearly suggests, at least to some), but to argue for an earlier (free) departure from Isleta. In that instance, Tigua leaders, along with those who chose to leave Isleta with them, would have made their way into Texas prior to the 1680 uprising.

In an addendum to the story related by José (above), Jesus points out that the Indians who had arrived in Isleta from the Saline Pueblos in the early 1670s were never fully integrated into the pueblos in the Isleta area: "They move after they left that [Quarai] Pueblo, or Gran Quivira, and moved to Isleta. They moved in and never were incorporated; they never were part of that pueblo."

His point is that at least some of these Tigua may have only stayed for a short time before moving on, eventually reaching El Paso. Additionally, Teyo flatly states: "Our ancestors knew about Hueco [Tanks] before we moved here. There were already pictographs that had been there for

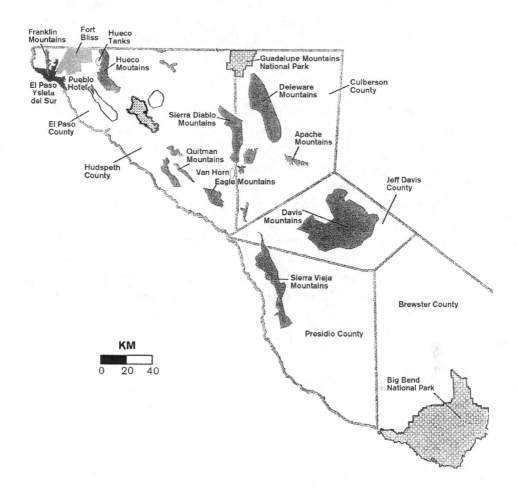

Franklin
Mountains

Fort
Bliss

Hueco
Tanks

Hueco
Moutains

Guadalupe Mountains
National Park

Pueblo
Hotel

El Paso
Ysleta
del Sur

Deleware
Mountains

Culberson
County

El Paso
County

Sierra Diablo
Mountains

Apache
Mountains

Hudspeth
County

Quitman
Mountains

Van Horn
Eagle Mountains

Jeff Davis
County

Davis
Mountains

Sierra Vieja
Mountains

Brewster County

KM

0   20   40

Big Bend
National Park

Presidio County

West Texas

years and years, and not just Hueco, further towards Van Horn there's pictographs."[4] Jesus discusses following the river from Isleta (before 1680) and of the Tigua having previous knowledge of the sacred Tigua sun symbol in Hueco. Additionally, he points to Puebloan pictographs, along with several Puebloan ruins located near Hueco Tanks, to support his interpretation. He recalls hearing a story relevant to a pre-1680 occupation but is unsure about the details. That may have been in reference to a story told to Green in the early 1970s, which describes the conditions that may have influenced Tigua movement into Texas prior to 1680.[5]

One final piece of information worth pointing out is that, even though speculation surrounds the above details, there is certainty that the date of the Pueblo Revolt was changed (moved one day from August 11 to August 10) and it is very likely that the runners who were spreading the news of this development never made it all the way down to Isleta (if the Isletans were even aware an uprising was planned). In all probability, then, the Tigua would have been surprised when the Spaniards showed up, they would have been caught with their guard down, and they would have been fairly easy to overthrow and imprison.

El Paso Settlement

In 1680 there was virtually no population in the future El Paso region, although, as discussed above, there was likely a small Indian presence in the area of the Hueco Mountains. For the most part, according to Rico, the only people were located

> across the river, [across] the Rio Grande. . . . It was Juarez, Mexico, but it was known as El Paso, because El Paso was known as the pass between two mountains, crossing the Rio Grande, passing north to New Mexico. So it was a pass between the Rocky Mountains and Sierra Mountains of Mexico and in between is El Paso. Pass of the North is what they called it.

The Spaniards wanted to settle the Tigua contingent in Juarez, but, Rico says, "the Tigua said they didn't want to settle down there, because they were farmers and wanted a place with good land. They wanted to live by what they planted, because they liked agriculture."

The Spanish told the people to find a place in the area to settle, and they found a suitable site about 14 miles from present-day El Paso. They informed the Spaniards of the location, which had good soil and was close to the river, and by 1683 they had started to build "the small mission church, which still stands today" (Rico). Then, Rico says, "our people began to plant. They had vineyards there, and they did pretty good. They had watermelons, cantaloupe, and all kinds of vegetables. For a time Ysleta produced a lot of food, a lot of vegetables, and they had a lot of wine because they had vineyards." They began to experience problems with flooding, however, and were forced to move to higher grounds.

Water from the Rio Grande was diverted into ditches that were used to water the cornfields, as well as numerous other fields of vegetables and fruits such as pumpkins, watermelons, cantaloupe, and grapes. In fact, the area, for a time, was well known for its wine and prosperous vineyards. The ability to farm, however, although vital, was not the only consideration that came into play when the Tigua were "deciding" on an area to settle.

Traditionally, the Tigua have practiced a mixed economy that included hunting, fishing, animal husbandry, and the collecting of wild foodstuffs. Although farming was important, these other concerns were of equal importance within the holistic worldview of the Tigua (Greenberg 1998). Additionally, they required various plants for ceremonial and medicinal purposes. Proximity to wild game and important botanicals, as well as (probable) existing sacred areas (such as Hueco Tanks) would have factored heavily into their ultimate decision to remain in the region. The most popular hunting grounds were over by the Hueco Mountains, but it was not unusual for the Tigua to travel hundreds of miles to hunt or gather important cultural items. José says, "I heard our people used to hunt buffalo, way back in the 1860s or 50s. We used to go over by the Pecos Valley, which is about 100 miles from here or something like that. They used to hunt buffalo over there [Pecos River Valley], but mostly it was deer and antelope and rabbit, but not mountain lion because mountain lion is sacred."

Close to the Guadalupe Mountains (in the bottom of the Guadalupe Bay), approximately 80 miles from El Paso, was a place where the Tigua, other Indians, Mexicans, and Americans went to collect salt. At the same time, while near the Guadalupe Mountains, they would gather different plants that didn't grow in their immediate region. "Some plants grow in [a] certain elevation. I know we went to find some herbs that I haven't seen in many years but we found there [Guadalupe], so that's the reason why our people went. Even today it still goes on, but it's not public and nobody talks about it" (Jesus). This information is kept quiet because of threats of physical violence from local ranchers, as well as threats of arrest made by park service personal. That the Tigua continued (and continue) to gather important items, despite the danger, speaks to the vital nature of these forays. They would also go upriver to the Indian Hot Springs region, on the way to Big Bend (now a national park), to get tobacco. While there, they collected a kind of cactus (candelabra) that grows in the area and was used to make wax. Additionally, items such as sage, mesquite beans, water crisp, nuts, and various minerals such as clay and ocher were regularly collected.

Indeed, there is documentation from botanical surveys (see Gray 1994; Greenberg 1998) that list over fifty plants traditionally (and currently) utilized by the Tigua. That, however, does not take into account the many plants that may only be used once over the course of several generations. As Jesus points out, "If you don't have any rain, nothing will grow; you need a little, just a little rain, and there are many things. If you have a good rain, you may see things that haven't been around for twenty-five or fifty years."

Why the Tigua chose to remain in the area around El Paso (as opposed to other places along the Rio Grande), or why they may have visited the area before the Pueblo Revolt likely has to do with the many similarities between the natural environments of El Paso and Isleta, New Mexico. Additionally, Pueblo ecology (unlike European political-legal conceptions of sedentary existence) conceptualizes land as sacred, and this conception is incorporated within a holistic worldview (Greenberg 1998). Native American Indians have a historical and traditional connection with the land that is deeply profound on both the individual and community level and that permeates all aspects of their ethos as Indian peoples. Senses of identity cannot be separated from senses of landscape, as each is built upon the other (see Greenberg 1998; Lawrence 2004; Clifton 1989; Bodley 1999).

The river, mountains, vegetation, weather patterns, wildlife, and mineral deposits around El Paso are strikingly similar to those found in the districts of the Isleta and Saline Pueblos. Several respondents specifically pointed to the geographic similarities between Isleta and the future El Paso as a primary reason for settling there in 1680. José discusses some of the geographic similarities between the two locations, pointing out, for example, their proximity to the Rio Grande,

> which is sacred to all the Pueblos. Plus, there's mountains all around, and there used to be a lot of cottonwood woodlands . . . where we gather our wood for fires and also a lot of vegetation that we use for our ceremonies.

. . . The willows we use for our feast days, also there's a lot of vegetation that we use for medicine. . . . There are clay deposits by the riverbanks.

This notion is reiterated by Jesus, who likewise draws a connection between traditionally utilized plants and other vegetation for food, ceremonial, and medicinal purposes, but who further suggests a relationship to water, not only from the Rio Grande, but that located in and around the Hueco Tanks area.

The similarities allowed the Tigua to make a smooth transition to their new home using the same planting, irrigating, and hunting techniques as they had at Isleta. Additionally, the Hueco Mountains (including Hueco Tanks) were within 20 miles, the Guadalupe Mountains (an important area for collecting salt and botanicals) were within 80 miles, and the Big Bend region (where wild tobacco was collected) was within 250 miles. Pueblo peoples have historically traveled great distances to collect important cultural items, and the Tigua are no exception. Jesus states:

There is a lot of stuff up there [in the area around Hueco Mountains]. My uncle used to talk about when they went, say, deer hunting or for gathering different types of food from the desert. They talk about the salt flats, close to the Guadalupe Mountains. They went there to get salt and sometimes to gather herbs that don't grow on this side. They used to talk about going up the river to around Indian Hot Springs on the way to Big Bend to get tobacco because that's where it grows. It's a ceremonial tobacco, like wild tobacco, and that's the only place it grows. So, they used to travel a lot to get a lot of different herbs.

The Tigua brought with them from New Mexico an abiding belief in the interconnectedness between the "Earth Mother" and her children. The shared understanding of this symbiotic relationship between land and people was continually referenced throughout my fieldwork. For example, José states:

The most important part of man is the Earth Mother itself. The river, there's what sustains our lives, our livelihood. From the river, it's a vein from the earth itself, the lifeblood in other words. . . . Everything is sacred to us. The mountains, every day is a ceremony to us, as a matter of fact. We are in unity with the forces of nature. You probably heard this before, you know: everything is a circle from birth to death, sunrise to sunset, the sun and moon and stars.

Luis discusses this in terms of forming and maintaining group identities when he says: "Our identity is fed by the importance . . . the value of our shared relationship with the lands of our ancestors, our *abuelos* [grandfathers]. . . . Our natural environments also feed into our belief systems and our shared rituals help bind our community together." The application of this belief system is evident in the Tigua's decision to remain in the El Paso area long after their Spanish (and Mexican and American) oppressors could have prevented a migration home (if, indeed, they ever could). Of course, the prevailing notion for the first decade or so after settlement was that there was nothing to return home to; however, after they learned that Isleta had been repopulated, it was an abiding connection to their present location that undoubtedly played a major role in their decision to remain.[6]

Survival: The "Pueblo Way"

The early period of the Tigua settlement was filled with uncertainty. The location was vulnerable to Apache attacks, the river was continually shifting and flooding, and disease and starvation were persistent problems. There were threats of revolt from the Mansos and other tribes near El Paso, and in 1692 the Piro Indians of Socorro asked the governor to order the Ysleta Indians not to encroach upon their land (Eickhoff 1996). The Spanish permitted the local Indians to continue practicing their traditional religious practices (alongside their new Catholic faith), and the Tigua remained (at least to outside appearances) friendly with the Spanish leadership.[7] In 1751 the Spanish, by royal decree, granted property to the Tigua in the amount of one league in each cardinal direction from the front door of the church (36 square miles). The shifting river caused Ysleta to become an island in the early 1830s, but by 1850 it appears that the Tigua would henceforth remain on the soil of the (future) United States (Eickhoff 1996). Mexico gained its independence from Spain in 1821, an event that was largely ignored by the local population, which by this point numbered "about 200 Indians" (Rico).

By 1900, Rico says, "times had become very hard in Ysleta and the people had to go out looking for work. It was crowded in Ysleta. . . . The reason we scattered out is because we didn't have any work. . . . Some of us went to Colorado, others to New Mexico, others California, all of us were scattered out." Those who remained in the community survived, primarily, by following traditional subsistence patterns, supplementing their cultivated foodstuffs with hunting and fishing, the collection of wild foods, and the occasional government handout. Quite a few, according to Jesus, traveled seasonally as migrant farmworkers. Additionally, an income was generated through the hunting and selling of animal pelts and meat. Food was regularly shared between tribal members, and surplus fruits and vegetables were preserved (dehydrated) for the winter months.

During these difficult times, the Tigua refused to give up on their traditions, their community, or their identity as Tigua Indians. They demonstrated a sense of innovation, self-reliance, a willingness to share with each other as well as outsiders, and a dogged determination to fight for their rights as Indian peoples. Some families moved to the village of Tortugas in Las Cruces, New Mexico, in 1881 (likely because it afforded a chance to work on the railroad) and started a daughter colony of Tigua Indians that survives to this day.

Those who remained in El Paso banded together in the fight for survival. The long-held Pueblo tradition of sharing turned out to be the key to survival as generations of Tigua passed on this vital community value. For example, Jesus states that "when they used to go hunting, whenever they kill the deer, shot the deer, [they] say, 'Here, son, go take this to the neighbor, go take this to. . . .' I mean it was no more, no less, they all got a piece of it." In a discussion about his grandmother, Luis states, "At Christmastime she would fatten up a pig for the tribe and so forth; she had a good piece of land that she had corn, squash, chili, you name it. The tribe used to come and trade for such things as chili, squash, but she never took what they were trading, she only told them to just go ahead and get what they want." He goes on to point out that "if we needed food, the other Indian families would come to us; we shared what we had." This is reiterated by Teyo, who specifically connects community values with family values. He says, "I've learned since I was little, I know my parents have always stressed helping others; this is the way I was taught by my family and I have experienced this throughout the community." The tradition of sharing continues to be an important community value, passed on through community activities such as the annual feast, as well as numerous examples (during the casino era) of sharing their (then) good fortune with others around the country. Besides sharing, the Tigua relied on traditional skills to bolster their ability to survive through the difficult economic times. For instance, Jesus discusses his ancestors' hunting skills and ability to ration in anticipation of seasonal shortages as important to their survival:

Loma means lone hill [*baldheaded*] because nothing grows on top. They used to do the rabbit hunts, using shovels or rabbit sticks right there [*Loma Paloma*]. . . . This is where they would make a living off the rabbits. They used to come and catch the rabbits and take them to the market and sell in El Paso. It was my grandfather, my uncles, that's how they used to make a living. They got 10 cents a rabbit; they take fifty to one hundred rabbits. I see them hang them up, they had skinned and opened up for days and never got smell[y]. You take a piece of greasewood, put it between a rabbit, preserves the rabbit. You do the same thing with fish. The river has a lot of fish; they used to get the fish and dry them out for the winter months. I remember growing up going out to the river to catch fish and put it up there and dry it and, you know, we had fish. We had rabbit, you know, and I know my grandmother used to make a [*de*]hydrated food, slice the food and let it dry. Preserve it for the winter, you know, the dried-up pears or tomatoes or apples. When it was getting close to winter and there was still green tomatoes on the plant, we used to dig a hole through the sand, down to the clay, and bury and just put sand all the way around. OK, so then when they needed fresh tomatoes they would dig them up and there was the tomatoes. So you see it was like a refrigerator.

The collection of salt from deposits found at the foot of Guadalupe Peak, 80 miles east of El Paso, provided the Tigua with a dependable resource that could be used not only to preserve and season their food, but also as a commodity that could be sold or traded for other merchandise. The salt flats covered several hundred acres and supplied Mexico, New Mexico, and all of western Texas (Eickhoff 1996). According to Hector: "Close to the Guadalupe (Mountains), Texas had a big fallout with the Indian people and what we call the Salt Wars. The Texans wanted to control a whole area where people used to go and get salt. . . . I remember some man would be chosen to go to the salt flats to bring salt for the tribe."

In 1877 the so-called Salt Wars of San Elizario broke out and eventually prevented the Tigua from (legally) collecting salt henceforth. A small number of Tigua (just over forty, according to Houser [2003a: 181]) earned their living working as scouts for the colonial government. Indeed, the Tigua proudly remember their scout ancestors, whose heroic deeds are venerated in oral discourse.

One other way that some tribal members were able to generate a small income was by selling various arts and crafts, but competition from nearby Juarez, Mexico, made it increasingly difficult to turn a profit. Traditional handmade crafts are very time-consuming ventures, both in the collection of the material and the actual production of the work. According to Jesus: "I guess that's why our people really did not get into the craft, because of the competition." Pottery, for example, requires the collection and processing of the clay and minerals (such as ocher), as well as plants to be processed for paint, cactus for mixing juices and making brushes, and lava rock for even heating.

Governmental Leadership

Traditional Tigua social organization was kinship-based, matrilineal, matrilocal, and matriarchal within the family group (Houser 1979; Fewkes 1902). Political structure, however, was (and is) patriarchal with regard to both religious and civil authority. Governmental leadership roles are filled by male community members and consist of two officers who serve lifetime terms (cacique, or "chief," and war captain) as well as a number of officials who are elected to one-year terms. These members make up the tribal council and are responsible for the overall well-being of the community. According to G, "Traditionally there's only five people: the chief, the war chief, the governor, and the lieutenant governor, and *alguacil* (sheriff). That's the body of the old traditional tribe, so that's five. Nobody wanted to take it." Accepting a position on the tribal council required a great deal of personal sacrifice and commitment on the part of each individual, some of whom would serve long terms because few wanted to accept the myriad responsibilities.

During a discussion about a cacique who served in the 1950s, Hector states, "That man, nobody fooled around with him, he was very strict with his belief. That's why he didn't have any young kids; they believe that [when] you take a position, it means you have to honor it and respect it." The positions of cacique and war captain are particularly stressful because they are required to be present during each ceremony and ritual, both religious and secular. Traditionally, the cacique was also responsible for providing medical treatment. Jesus describes living next to a cacique as a young child:

> You know, I remember when I was growing up, I lived next to the cacique, and he had a rooster, an old rooster, and he used to live in a little two-room house and that rooster was something special to him.[8] He was

carrying all these herbs and spices and had bags in there, a bag full of medicine and stuff. . . . That's why the old caciques, there's different bags hang down at his house with different herbs in them that he gathered [*for medicinal purposes*]. . . . I used to run errands for them [*tribal Elders*] and when I would come back and asked my grandma, I said, "Grandma, why they have all those bags of herbs?" And she said, "It's medicine that they go out to the mountains, to Hueco Tanks, and get there at certain times of the year, for purposes of healing." See, the cacique, traditionally, would be responsible to heal his people.

Traditional duties of the cacique also included presiding over funeral services, granting (or denying) permission for tribal members to marry, organizing and overseeing the New Year's Eve elections, and ensuring that all tribal officials were performing their duties (Houser 2003: 224). The traditional duties of the war captain and the subordinate captains included the following (as described in 1895):

To direct the dances in the public plaza and to preserve order during the dance; also to well regulate everything pertaining to hunts of deer, rabbits, and hares. . . . Regarding the dances, it is recognized that they are permitted on the following days only: Christmas, St Anthony's, St John's, St Peter's, St James', St Ann's, and St Andrew's (if the day does not fall at the time of the hunt). . . . It is the duty of the Capitan Major, aided by his subordinates, to remove from the Pueblo of San Antonio every kind of witchcraft and belief contrary to our . . . religion. No son of the Pueblo of San Antonio is obliged to accept . . . if so commanded, any sorcery or false belief. (Fewkes 1902. In YDSP archives, vol. 5: 125)

Many of these duties and responsibilities are still followed by contemporary officeholders, with a couple of exceptions. For example, permission from the cacique to marry is no longer necessary, and witchcraft (to my knowledge) is not an issue for this community. Reference, however, was made by H to nightly "cleansings" performed by the war captain at several New Mexican Pueblos, and Jesus discusses past and present beliefs about witchcraft in the following narrative:

My grandmother was so, she was very Indian, she believed, and in some tribes still believe, in witchcraft. People do bad things to you personally. She used to go out and sweep stuff off the porch and throw water around and the door used to face east. I would say, "Grandma, what are you doing?" "Just in case somebody comes in and tries to do bad things in the door I'm brushing it off." The sun was coming up, you know, so no evil can come in the house. That's why they sweep the dirt so, you know, and when they comb their hair, you know how when you comb your hair and you have a bunch of stuff in your brush and you grab it and throw it away? There's no way they do that. They used to comb their hair and take it off [*the brush or comb*] and put it in the walls [*secret holes in the stucco*] and close the hole. They did the same thing with toe and fingernail clippings. They did it to keep away witchcraft. Someone can do damage to you [*if they have your hair and nail clippings*]. It's really funny, I was sitting there [*at Santo Domingo Pueblo*] and she [*Santo Domingo Elder*] did the same thing my grandma did. You see the customs and you know.

Traditional Puebloan forms of governance varied somewhat between communities, but generally consisted of "a system of leaders who would be referred to as *caciques*" (Simmons 1979: 183). This style of leadership was modified (though never eliminated) by the Spanish in the 1600s with the creation of "officials" that included governor, lieutenant governor, war captains, sheriffs (*alguacil*), *mayordomos*, and church wardens. These officers were meant to deal directly with the Spanish governor in Santa Fe, and a 1620 order provided that "free elections" of these positions would be held annually on January 1. Traditionally, according to Teyo, the cacique was very powerful but neutral because he represented everybody in the tribe. The "old tribe system" of the Tigua, he states, consisted of clan leaders voicing opinions along with the consensus of the people, particularly the Elders. The cacique would then make decisions based on what he believed was "best for his people." The number of council members and the specific positions have changed in moderate ways over the years as the Tigua have adjusted to changing circumstances. For example, the position of "assistant cacique" has been eliminated, the *mayordomos* were eliminated and later reintroduced, and the number of council members and captains has varied between two and five at any given time. The current tribal government makeup is described by José:

Our tribal council is divided into two groups: the traditional council, which is headed by the chief, the war captain, and four capitanes, and the other council, which is mostly the business council, the administration council. On that council it is the governor, lieutenant governor, tribal chief, and four councilmen. They take care of the administrative and financial aspects of the pueblo. The traditional council pertains more to beliefs, that is, traditions, older traditions, ceremonials, rabbit hunts, all that pertains to the spiritual side of the village pueblo. Also, now we have three *mayordomos* [*also known as stewards or irrigation ditch bosses*], first, second, and third *mayordomos*. They oversee; make sure tradition is being followed. There is also the *alguacil* [*one of the four councilmen*], which is the tribal sheriff, sheriff of the village. He upholds the laws of the pueblo. If the laws are broken, he is the one who determines, him and the chief, what punishment is to be given to the lawbreaker. We also have some old men that are advisers to the council. They had been former members of the traditional council or the business council. So it's a lot [*of*] responsibility because the welfare of the pueblo depends on the many decisions that the council makes. The tradition is that the election [*by tribal junta, or "meeting of the people"*] is on New Year's Eve at midnight; that custom came from the Spanish. We changed that rule, though, so more people can come. It's important and we wouldn't have too many people, so we changed the time to the afternoon, 6 o'clock. Both councils are elected by only the males of the pueblo in good standing and also over eighteen years. They can vote on our tribal elections. The governor is elected for a one-year term, but he can be reelected. Also lieutenant governor; in fact, other council members are elected to one-year terms. The exception is the chief; this position is for life, so it's a lifelong position, as is the war captain. The chief has to be the most knowledgeable in the whole pueblo; he has to know all the rituals and ceremonies. We know who is up for chief, and he is selected by the men of the village. Right now we have very few Elders left, unfortunately, but it's a process that's lifelong and we know, more or less, who has maintained, who has been traditional and followed the ceremonies. Also the war captain is lifelong and he is also elected by the men of the pueblo. He is assistant to the chief in matters relating to the ceremonies and the spiritual side of the pueblo.

Survival in an Urban Setting

White encroachment and the massive land theft that accompanied it led to rapid displacement, accompanied by a direct attack on the ability of the Tigua to maintain intact the fundamental principles of their traditional practices.[9] From the earliest days of settlement, it was dangerous to be identified as an Indian in Texas.[10] The expression "There ain't no Injuns in

Texas" soon became embedded within the popular discourse of the state and was reinforced with another popular Texas saying, "The only good Injun is a dead Injun." Consequently, many Tigua would not acknowledge to outsiders their Indian heritage. As pointed out by Jesus: "They never acknowledge [admit to being Indian], our people, they always say they were farmers . . . but they weren't farmers; they were Pueblo people that farmed. Our scouts didn't say they were Indians, just farmers."

This point is echoed by Luis: "I would dare say there were a lot of people going around saying we're not Indians. It's not that we were ashamed; we weren't accepted. . . . Now, where they don't allow Mexican kids to speak Spanish, also they wouldn't allow Indians to speak Indian. You got to speak English language." In discussing the heavy loss of traditional language skills within the pueblo, Susana states that she is aware that "some of our tribal members was very particular talking about tradition, or talk[ing] about the language. . . . Something happened in the 1800s [in regard to the use of traditional language], and I heard they didn't want to talk about it, because they was being exploited, one way or another."

Another early causality of encroachment was the traditional kinship system. The matrilineal system followed by the Tigua was largely scrapped in the late 1800s. By that point, they were surrounded by U.S. and Mexican communities and had effectively become an urban tribe. Unlike their Puebloan cousins in New Mexico, who still enjoyed considerable breathing room, the rapidly shrinking Tigua population was forced to confront their ability to continue traditional marriage practices. Marriage between clan members was, of course, considered incest, and first cousin marriage had, because of outside influence, become distasteful. Marriage with outsiders was considered taboo, and the community found itself at an impasse. As explained by Pedro:

> Here it was [in Ysleta] you could not intermarriage [marry outsiders], till 1897, 1800 something, some of the people got a petition, say we don't want to marry cousins. There were first cousins marry. We were matrilineal but . . . that's why we got a lot of Mexican blood because of Mexican marriage. There's a document someplace, it was like a petition that say, "OK, we're done with this."

That the Tigua would alter their kinship rules, marry Mexicans, and (sometimes) claim Mexican heritage makes sense if one considers that the issue was confronted during an era of widespread racism, a dangerous period when claiming Indian identity could be deadly. However, it is interesting to note that, while the current kinship system follows the "Eskimo" model, the Tigua continue to perceive of themselves as matrilineal, and "we maintain our relationships and identities through our mother's side" (Wright 1993: 54).

Conclusion

The clear overriding cultural characteristic that is shared by every Tigua (young and old, male and female) is a strong sense of pride related to community survival. The fact that they are still here is a testament of epic proportions, a notion that is not lost on the Tigua. The long-term success of a cultural system, however, is predicated not on its ability to cling to usual practice under any and all circumstances, but rather on the systemic ability of the practitioners of a system to accept change and adapt in culturally appropriate ways. Although the notion of change is well understood by the Tigua, there is, as in all communities, disagreement about the specific forms and pace that change should take. For the Tigua, who consider themselves among the most traditional of Puebloan groups, change has been brought about largely through external forces, not often through conscious choice.[11]

Although individual survival understandably took precedence for many (and explains why many left), the community-wide imperative of cultural survival always occupied a preeminent place among the remaining tribal members. While maintaining a low profile (with perhaps the exception of the annual feast), the Tigua quietly persisted. Traditional rituals and ceremonies, such as dances, communal hunts, and religious practices, were followed faithfully (despite the alienation from their land); pottery making, weaving skills, and other crafts were continued; and traditional government leadership, slightly modified, continued in its role as overseer of community welfare.

The Tigua community has been forced to watch as the outside world has slowly encircled them, methodically stolen their land, marginalized them as a community of people, usurped their power, and, as a final humiliation, declared them extinct. The only problem with this notion (as a shocked academia and state power structure learned in the early 1960s) was that the Tigua were still clinging stubbornly to their identity. Far from culturally extinct, they had been quietly going about their traditional business for all these years, blissfully unaware that they were dead.[12] They were very much alive, but they were also very much changed. After three hundred years of oppression under the power of three nation-states, change was inevitable. By the early 1900s, the economic situation had become unbearable, and many Tigua were forced to leave the community to seek work. This exacerbated an already problematic situation, as population numbers were plummeting due to widespread disease, starvation, and migrations into Mexico. Some (approximately twenty-four) of the children were sent to the "Indian school" in Albuquerque, New Mexico, in 1904 for "enculturation training," traditional language skills were deteriorating, and individual and family survival began to take precedence over community survival. The "core" of the pueblo (perhaps one hundred) stuck it out, but the bulk of the tribe was forced to move away. Extreme forms of racism, dwindling population numbers, encroachment by outsiders, and severe economic despair had combined to bring the Tigua community to the brink of extinction.

But we know they have survived. Although the above narrative helps to explain Tigua survival as a physical act, it teaches us little about their cultural survival. We have seen, for example, that sharing, as a community value, was crucial, as was the importance of understanding the need to adapt traditional practices to changing circumstances. However, we have yet to fully answer the question: How has the Tigua culture survived? In Chapter Two I continue to explore Tigua perceptions of community, with a focus on Tigua senses of identity. The cultural mechanisms utilized by the Tigua to build and maintain senses of both group and individual identity are (I argue) key to understanding how their culture has persevered. In particular, I explore how religious beliefs influence the Tigua worldview and incorporate with both shared and individual senses of self. Indeed, religion, as we will see, pervades every segment of the Tigua ethos. In order to understand Tigua cultural survival, it is vital that we explore the interrelationship between religion, senses of community, and senses of self.

CHAPTER TWO

Oral Tradition, Part Two

Religion, Identity, and Cultural Perseverance

Introduction

This chapter, like the previous chapter, will explore the history of the Tigua from the perspective of tribal members. The preceding chapter focused on historical events, the surrounding environment, and economic conditions, whereas this chapter will explore how Tigua religious beliefs are tied to perceptions of landscape, ceremony, and ritual and how these perceptions have come to be inscribed with meaning and interrelated with the building and maintenance of group and individual identity. Tigua group identity (as we will see) is tied to a sense of traditionalism, a shared history, and a strong commitment by individual tribal members to maintain and pass on traditional cultural practices. Like most American Indian peoples, the Tigua conceptualize various cultural practices not as separate behaviors, but experience culture as pervasive, encircling, and all-inclusive. As Carey N. Vicenti (1995: 92) points out: "The Indian concept of the human being is one in which all aspects of the person and his or her society are integrated. Every action in daily life is read to have meaning and implication to the individual and guides how he or she interacts with tribal society or fulfills obligations imposed by society, law, and religion." Salish Indian tribal member Pat Pierre (2006) discusses "water, earth and air" as "three things that tribal peoples highly honor," but points out that these elements, in and of themselves, do not make up a system. "It takes a fourth element to understand what to do with these other three and that fourth element is spirituality. Spirituality or religion is the most important of all and cannot be separated from the other three."

The overarching key to Tigua cultural preservation has been their unwavering sense that their very existence is tied inextricably to the sacred, that their sense of identity and community is rooted in their beliefs, traditions, landscape, ceremony, and spiritual life. Maintaining, or even "bringing back," particular activities (such as the traditional, and sacred, rabbit hunt) exemplifies cultural continuity, particularly in the face of the radical social change the Tigua have endured for over three hundred years. Indeed, the ability of the Tigua to survive as a distinct culture epitomizes the embedded and enduring nature of their holistic worldview.

The following discussion explores the themes of identity and cultural change and perseverance by first looking at how personal and group identities are formed. The questions relevant to identity formation revolve around not only what identity is but how it is formed, perceived, transmitted, and bounded. How does ethnic, or community, identity affect personal identity? Is ethnic identity innate or learned? What are cultural boundaries? What is the relationship between identity formation and power struggles? What mechanisms have the Tigua, in particular, utilized in maintaining their cultural identity? After addressing these issues, I take up the role of Tigua religious beliefs in preserving traditional cultural practices that, along with identity, comprise the underlying theme of this chapter. Specifically, the discussion focuses on their ability to adapt but not abandon their religious beliefs in the face of colonial persecution. I argue that this ability, more than any other single element, is directly responsible for their long-term survival. Their belief system ties to all aspects of their worldview, permeating ceremony, landscape, cultural values, and senses of community.

The importance and perception of community events are tied to the themes of identity and religious beliefs, particularly as they relate to the pinnacle of the ceremonial cycle, the Saint Anthony's Day Feast. The relationship between the Tigua cultural landscape and their belief in the grandfathers (*abuelos*) is highlighted and connected specifically to the Hueco Mountains, the Rio Grande, and Hueco Tanks. In particular, the Tigua willingness to protect their sacred landscape is correlated with their abiding reverence for sacred geography. I discuss the issue of cultural change in relation to the Tigua response to colonial invasion and their pragmatic attitude toward bending to the forces of outside aggression while never compromising their core cultural beliefs. Lastly, cultural perseverance is explored as it relates to Tigua perceptions of survival and the keen sense the Tigua have of their own ability to continue to exist as a distinct group. Their location in an urban setting, surrounded by outsiders and threatened by modernity and government blood quantum regulations, shapes an existence that the Tigua understand is all too fragile.

Tigua Identity

Although a person's identity is shaped by numerous personal and individual factors, there can be many historical, socioeconomic, and even legal factors that can directly or indirectly influence how individual identity develops.[1] Moreover, individual and group identities are intrinsically tied together; aspects of identity formation do not take place in isolation. Rather, it is part of a collective process that is social, individual, and never-ending. Identity is connected to a sense of belonging, be it to family, community, or nation. Numerous social institutions, such as religious and governmental organizations, play a role in this process and help shape not only an individual sense of social alliance but also the nature of collective solidarity (Kriesberg 2003; Gavaki 1993: 4–5). For example, the teaching and maintenance of shared common values reinforce perceptions of collective belonging by specifying the terms of membership. The rules are internalized, and the observed actions of others help to define, and to remind us, that we belong to a collectivity (see Wade 1997: 5; Guibernau and Rex 1997: 4). Furthermore, group (or ethnic/community) identity is established through the communication of shared interests and experiences (i.e., shared history), which serve as themes of unification by forging a collective understanding, a collective worldview. As C. N. Le (2006) states:

> While there is no clear, universally accepted definition of what constitutes an ethnic group [among scholars] . . . most attempts to define ethnicity focus on one or more of the following issues: Who decides whether a group is "ethnic" or whether someone is of "ethnic origin"? Most scholars agree that ethnic identity is shaped by a process of internal definition and external labeling. That is, people who share the same ethnic origin define themselves as "us" and are categorized as "them" by people outside the group.

Group continuity, as an ongoing process, is maintained through periods of social and cultural change by reiterating and highlighting identity interests and by accentuating the group's adherence to important cultural practices and values (Kriesberg 2003; Gavaki 1993: 7). For example, religious communities stress symbolism and ritual behavior (such as the collective consumption of "flesh and blood" during communion and various rites of initiation) as concrete and unalienable foundations onto which collective identity is anchored. An important form of collective identity, ethnic identity, is a complex phenomenon, as Efrosini Gavaki (1993: 8) points out:

> It is usually associated with a way of life dictated by cultural traditions and social expectations. In a multicultural society . . . it is that cultural way of life that gives a reference point, a point of orientation for both the individuals and others. It constitutes a social, psychological and cultural reference of self, history, roots, relations, values and feelings. . . . It constitutes an anchor with our collective past and ethnic memories and provides for the blueprints of the social and cultural future.

When community members collectively rally around the protection of group identity markers, the threat of outside force aimed at destroying community institutions serves to strengthen rather than weaken group resolve, and that takes place on both the macro- and microlevels. In the United States, for example, there has developed, according to John Gledhill (1994: 163), an "interdependence" that "is deeply rooted in the historical structural processes which have constituted the 'United States.'" By constructing an "external enemy," the United States defines "the unity" of America, "as witnessed by the 'invention' of Saddam Hussein to occupy this structural position after the Soviet Union abandoned it" (163). Another macrolevel example is the use of patriotic symbolism in the United States (e.g., prominent flag waving, "Support Our Troops" yard signs, Air Force 'flyovers' during sporting events, etc.), along with the rhetoric of "protecting American values" in rallying support for the so-called war on terrorism. Microlevel examples include the Tigua response to forced religious conversion (to be discussed below), and the "blood is thicker than water" analogy for supporting family members, "right or wrong." It is likewise important to consider that, although every individual is a member of multiple groups (in the case of the Tigua, for example, Indian, Tigua, Puebloan, male, veteran, etc.), for many people ethnic identity is primary (Kriesberg 2003; Snipp 1988–1989: 6). Le (2006) suggests that ethnic identity appears to consist of two categories, each of which may play a role in ethnic identity formation:

> Scholars from many different academic disciplines have generally categorized ethnic identity formation along two main theoretical frameworks: primordial versus situational. Although these two categories ultimately represent a simplistic dichotomy to characterize processes of ethnic identity formation, they are still very useful in framing an analysis of ethnic identity.

In the first case, "the primordial (also known as 'essentialist') perspective argues that people have an innate sense of ethnic identity," which is "difficult if not impossible to change." Conversely, there is "the situational perspective (also known as the 'constructionist' or 'instrumentalist') [that] states that ethnic identities are socially defined phenomena." In this case, "the meaning and boundaries of ethnic identity are constantly being renegotiated, revised, and redefined, depending on specific situations and set of circumstances that each individual or ethnic group encounters" (Le 2006).

It is apparent from my research with the Tigua that both these categories come into play. Clearly, however, the notion that ethnic identity is "difficult if not impossible to change" is a questionable statement. Indeed, Le (2006) suggests that "most contemporary scholars are extremely skeptical of the essentialist view of ethnicity as some kind of 'natural affinity' or 'primordial attachment.' Few dispute the idea that a shared, unique origin in time and place fosters ethnic cohesion." The rejection of Tigua identity by a number of tribal members in the past, for example, was based not on a lack of innate senses of ethnic attachment, but on the circumstances of historical reality. For example, perceptions of racism and discrimination, fear of physical attacks, and embarrassment at being associated with "the poor, dirty, ignorant Indians" compelled some Tigua community members to reject their Indian identity, according to Jesus. Indeed, in the early 1960s an anthropologist conducting research for the tribe's lawyer recalled the Tigua woman who answered his knock on her door with the response: "I'm not an Indian; I'm Castilian!" She then slammed the door in his face (Houser 1979).

In fact, the Tigua community did survive through a long period of abject poverty, a painful period that individual tribal members reacted to in personal ways. For some, the reaction was to leave the community and/or deny their Indian identity. For others, embracing their identity and persevering were (and are) perceived as an act of defiance. For example, Luis states: "Many people forget, or don't have the slightest clue of what we used to go through. I went to Ysleta grade school barefoot; we all did. But we're still here! I was a proud Tigua then and I'm a proud Tigua today." This kind of response is "a product of relationships between groups—not groups in isolation. Ethnicity is essentially an aspect of a relationship between groups, not the property of a single group" (Le 2006). It is the contact between groups that gives rise to the notion that fundamental differences exist between those in the relationship and that

there is a broader power structure tied to that relationship. "Ethnic sentiment does not arise spontaneously but is related to the struggle for
power between different groups in society." It is, furthermore, "related to
the political and economic interests of those who take the lead in awakening or maintaining ethnic consciousness or by dominant groups who
wish to create and maintain inequalities and legitimize disadvantage."
For the Tigua, then, it appears that this power relationship led to an
"ethnic awakening" that was characterized by responses tied to either
identity rejection or a defiant refusal to bow to the pressures of ethnic
persecution.

One of the important notions surrounding identity issues is the idea
that identity, at least at the group level, is bounded in some way and
therefore violable. A specific cultural group, in other words, can cease to
exist as an entity based on some quantifiable criteria, typically related to
community-wide blood levels but also related to cultural behavior issues,
such as a community's adherence to traditional behavior over time (this
specific topic will be discussed in Chapter Four). The question of whether
"objectively bounded societies and cultures" exist, as Simon Harrison
(1999: 10) points out, has been largely abandoned by anthropologists as
it relates to culture. However, rejecting the notion of culture as "measurable object" does not mean that it cannot be perceived (by the members
of specific groups) as real. Groups come to define themselves within clear
boundaries that are expressed "by means of diacritical inventories . . . of
practices and symbols: modes of dress, of livelihood, language, cuisine,
music, ritual, religious belief or other symbolic content conceived as distinguishing one group from another" (10). Le (2006) quotes anthropologist Frederik Barth, who agrees that boundaries are a key component of
ethnicity and who "urges anthropologists to place less emphasis on the
substance or content of ethnicity." Rather, he suggests "that anthropologists should focus on the social processes which produce, reproduce and
organize the boundaries of identification and differentiation between ethnic groups."

Another aspect of boundary formation is the perception that they
are under threat by outside forces and therefore endangered. Harrison
suggests that there are at least two ways in which boundaries are understood to be threatened: one is through cultural "pollution," whereby "foreign cultural forms" intrude on traditional practice; and the other is
through cultural misappropriation. In other words, "one employs a rheto-

ric of cultural pollution, and the other a rhetoric of cultural appropriation, piracy or theft" (Harrison 1999: 11). By erecting boundaries, cultures are, essentially, reifying their heritage "as a form of property" that "belongs," unequivocally, to a particular group. Even though this notion is shot through with problems, it is reasonable to argue that specific cultural groups (regardless of ethnic or racial makeup) evoke the protection of identity symbols as a form of resistance (Harrison 1999: 11; see Maybury-Lewis 1997). In this way, the collective nature of the group is constructed in opposition to the threatening "other," and the group can only be protected by limiting the flow of cultural diffusion both inwardly and outwardly. Protection can be accomplished by physically keeping outsiders and outside information at bay as much as possible, as do all Puebloan groups (Whiteley 1987: 48). For most communities, however, the goal is simply to limit and control the flow. The Tigua, for example, are highly concerned with both the negative impact of outside influences and the protection of inside information. José discusses the problem of "gang" influence on the young tribal members, and Hector speaks specifically about the impact of technology on tribal members and how video games and MP3 players seem to take precedence over learning tradition. There is, of course, a high level of concern about cultural knowledge flowing out (particularly spiritual knowledge), but that appears to be linked to a concern over maintaining cultural "purity" and not over concerns that knowledge will be appropriated by "outside others" for financial gain.

For North American tribal communities, group identity extends beyond a simple connection as one of many minority groups. Senses of community and Indian identification are informed by local, regional, national, and historical connections (Kriesberg 2003). As indigenous peoples, this connection extends worldwide. Furthermore, identity is based on oral tradition, historical documentation, scientific findings (i.e., archaeological interpretation), legal definitions devised by powerful outsiders, and a host of additional factors. My goal in what follows is to briefly explore the formation and maintenance of Tigua group identity and describe how the threat, and actualization, of forced cultural change has bound the community together. Their shared struggle stands as a benchmark case study in understanding the dynamics of cultural persistence, as their story has already become a source of inspiration to other Native communities.

Adapting to Religious Persecution: Secrecy and Compartmentalization

A direct attack on the religious beliefs of the indigenous peoples of the American Southwest was, perhaps, the dominant ploy utilized by the Spanish colonizers in their attempt to break down the collective resolve of the oppressed. Attacks against the pueblo, for example, centered on destroying not only the belief itself but also the material symbols related to the belief. In the former case, the Spanish simply outlawed traditional displays of religion and severally punished transgressors. In the later case, it was the kiva, the primary religious symbol, that was destroyed. An example of attempting to destroy the belief system is pointed out by Luis: "If the Spanish caught any tribal member practicing the old religion or the traditional religion, they used to cut off one finger or an ear or some other part of their body to make the Indian understand: you do not practice that kind of religion." The widespread destruction of kivas by the proselytizing Spanish was aimed at all Pueblo peoples and largely consisted of obliterating and filling in these mostly underground religious chambers. The kiva is the traditional ritual center of pueblo communities and serves as a meeting place, primarily for religious and sacred ceremonies. Most are round, windowless, and underground, although some (the Hopi kivas, for example) are built in the form of a square (Secakuku 2005). Many Pueblo legends relate to the construction of the kiva to resemble the *sipapu*, the place of emergence into this world (Whiteley 1987: 56). Most pueblos will contain a number of kivas, each of which serves a specific function and is usually clan related (Secakuku 2006; Whiteley 1987: 59–60). Initially, there were three kivas located within the Tigua community, "one on this side of the canal, and the other was on the other side of the canal, and there was another one next to the mission" (Jesus). How long the Tigua were able to use their kivas before they were destroyed is unknown, but after their disappearance, the Tigua, determined to continue their sacred rituals, began holding their meetings at the cacique's house. The *tuh-lah*, which is similar to the kiva (the *tuh-lah* is more of a meeting hall as opposed to a praying hall), was brought into use by the Tigua in the 1900s. It represented a compromise, of sorts, serving the dual purpose of religious chamber and community meeting place.

Tigua (indeed, all Pueblo peoples') beliefs and practices are composed of highly guarded secret rituals. Discussions about traditional religion (even among and between various individual pueblos) require great sensitivity, and there is a taboo (death is a common punishment) associated with revealing sensitive religious tenets to outsiders (Whiteley 1987: 48). Indeed, some information is considered too sacred to share even with insiders. An example was given to me during a visit to a Hopi village, and several examples were provided by Tigua respondents.[2] For example, Jesus explains:

> The older persons, they kind of kept it [traditional knowledge] in their selves, I mean, because the fear [of revealing sensitive information] is there already, and that's a fear I'm facing today. . . . I mean . . . I've seen those kids and when they get drunk and start, I think that's one of my worst fears . . . that I see that kids get drunk and start doing stupid things with tradition and it's no wonder our older people didn't want to teach our kids.

The tradition of secrecy became embedded within Puebloan religious practice from the earliest days of Spanish persecution. While ostensibly practicing Catholicism, the Tigua developed a religious system that combines Native and Western religious thought, operates smoothly, and appears (at least to outside observation) to be consistent. Syncretism, however, is less evident than compartmentalization: clearly Catholic rites, such as rituals held inside the Catholic Church, are cleanly separated from indigenous rituals, such as traditional dancing that takes place on the plaza outside the church (see also Greenberg 2000: 34). This is a common similarity between Puebloan communities, particularly among the Rio Grande Pueblos, each of which celebrates saints' day celebrations (Whiteley 1987: 56). Luis points out, "It's just like burial ceremonies that we have. We don't do them inside the church; we do them outside the church. . . . We feel very strong about that . . . the ceremony, outside the church."

This separation is perhaps most evident during the Saint Anthony's Day Feast celebration on June 13, when the Tigua perform dances and religious ceremonies throughout the day, first at the traditional *tuh-lah* and then at the Catholic mission church a mile away. The dancers and other participants move back and forth between the two settings several times during the day and conduct religious ceremonies and rituals specific to each place. The "commingling of traditional belief systems with Catholicism goes back to where the Spanish tried to convert the Indian people," according to Teyo. As explained to Bill Wright (1993: 142–143):

> We fooled the Spanish when we accepted Christianity by having our own
> way of practicing in front of the churches. They thought we were practic-
> ing their religion, and at the same time we were having our own religion
> going on without them knowing it. We did it because they wouldn't let us
> do it openly, so we found our own way of doing it. They were happy and
> we were happy at the same time.

There is great sensitivity regarding discussions about traditional religion, and discussions about religious issues with outsiders are discour-
aged. As Peter M. Whiteley (1987: 48) points out, "Questions about
religion" are anathema to all Pueblo peoples and "are met with evasion or
a purposive silence." On several occasions I was with a respondent (who
operates a small craft store) when outsiders would come in and ask questions about Native religion. His response to these inquiries, although always polite, left no question that he would not, and could not, discuss
religious issues and that he felt uncomfortable being asked. Another respondent, when explaining to me his spiritual beliefs, always made clear
that he was speaking only for himself and that to say too much would
cause problems with the *abuelos* (grandfathers), whom he feared. Information that is not sensitive, however, can be discussed to the extent that
even an outsider can clearly comprehend (without the requirement of
specific detail) how profoundly Tigua religious beliefs mesh with the
overall worldview of the community.

The following synopsis regarding religion is a compilation of statements made by Jesus, Luis, and José:

> Religious tradition is based on the individual, but for us it is tied to the
> community. There are some people, just like in any other community,
> that don't want to learn and it is not for us to force it. We understand
> what religious force is about. All we've ever asked for is a place to live
> and a place to worship in our own way. Since it was taken many years
> ago, we had to find other means to do it. One of the reasons for the
> Pueblo Revolt was the Spanish attempt to enforce Christian beliefs on In-
> dian people. We went into the practice of Christianity, but we did it in
> our own way. We tricked the Spanish into thinking that we had accepted
> Christianity, by practicing in front of the churches, while at the same time
> having our own religion going on without them knowing it. Back then we
> started the whole way of worshiping their saints, who are our saints now,
> and it was done so that they didn't know. It is our way of getting around
> the Catholic system when we conduct our fiestas. We actually are doing

prayer, not only to the corn, to the earth, but to other issues. We are actually praying to our gods, to our grandfathers, because it all goes back to being thankful that we are here. Also, we are giving thanks for the things that we have received and are going to receive. We have ceremonies throughout the year that are giving thanks to different things, and we honor the *abuelos* [*grandfathers*] with our dancing, our drumming, and our chanting. We are not really practicing our real religion, because of what happened to us. But we know, regardless of the religion, we have the same God; whatever name they gave him, it was the same one. We call our God in Spanish *abuelo*, which is really "the grandfather." We believe in him and we pray to him. We pray in church, in our sacred mountain, in our house; we pray everywhere. The traditional people that are here, we always think about the grandfathers because the grandfathers, the Elders, are the ones that taught us everything we know. They are the ones that are going to be waiting for us when we go to the great beyond, showing us the way to get there. He [*one of the grandfathers*] is the father of all good Indians. He comes when the Indians do not live according to the rules or if they don't obey the cacique. No one sees him, but you can hear him cry out and yell, but he never lets himself be seen. He yells on purpose so that the people will hear him. We say that the grandfather lives on the mountains, but not just one particular place, He's all over. He can become anything. That's why our respect is for any kind of animal. I mean it might be a bird that's around and we know who it is. We look at him and he lets us know that he's around. If we do something that we shouldn't be doing, he'll punish us one way or another. (*see also Wright 1993*)

Feast Days

The Tigua ceremonial cycle begins in May and ends on January 6, which marks the start of the New Year on the Tigua calendar. The Saint Anthony's Day is, technically, the Tigua "Corn Dance" (the day corn is planted) and represents the beginning of the growing season and the opening of the irrigation ditches in all four directions. "St. Anthony was adopted by us because our traditional dance was interpreted by the Spanish as a celebration of St. Anthony's Day, which happened to fall on the same day," Luis says. If the priests wanted to believe the Tigua were praying to the Catholic God (rather than to the grandfathers), the Indians were not about to inform them otherwise. The dances celebrate and give thanks to the Earth Mother for providing corn and other forms of nourishment, as well as the rain, sun, earth, and wind. Circle dances and crossing dances symbolically represent the forces of nature and the four directions. Collective thanks for the harvest and collective prayers for community well-being are extended by the community as a whole. The dancing, drumming, and chanting are spiritual and sacred. Most Tigua ceremonies include dancing and community feasting, shared activities that bind the community together as one. Although events take place throughout the year, the June 13 festivities are recognized as the pinnacle of the community calendar. Indeed, many tribal members schedule their annual work vacation time to correspond with the many activities leading up to the June 13 feast day.

After the Tigua left New Mexico in 1680, the traditional ceremonial cycle was adapted to the similar physical environment of El Paso, and the Saint Anthony's Day Feast continued to be held on June 13. Not unlike similar indigenous ceremonies found around the world, the traditional fiestas, or feast days, were developed by the New Mexico Pueblos as a form of redistribution, a device for overcoming regional food shortages, according to Hector. The fiestas serve the additional function of promoting friendly relations with the members of nearby communities. The Tigua, who had been illegally stripped of all but a remnant of their landholdings by 1871, continued, nonetheless, to provide the free community-wide meal annually. On June 4, the preparation for the feast day begins. According to Diego and Susana:

> Every June the fourth, members of our pueblo go off in the four directions from a street corner in Ysleta, which was the corner from which our people always went off at the beginning of the season. We used to go to bless all the fields . . . go open the irrigating ditches that used to irrigate the whole pueblo. That was the center of it. And also we used to gather donations from the surrounding neighbors so we could have food and something to dress up the church with. . . . The gathering of the food for the fiesta is, it was all donations from all the people that went around. . . . You see there's four Saint Anthonys that go with each group and the people wait for the saint to come to their house so they can pray to St. Anthony. Most of the neighbors were Spanish and Mexican people and they used to receive the saint from the Indian people, and then they would make gifts, money, food, and little things, because we didn't have much in those days.

The feast represents an amazing community-wide effort that not only promotes good relations with the surrounding population but is taken by the Tigua as a time to come together as an Indian community. Personal conflicts are put aside, and the focus is placed on the maintenance of collective identity. Several ongoing personal conflicts that I was aware of were put aside during the feasts and feast preparations that I attended. Indeed, it appeared that the feuding community members went out of their way to act friendly with their "adversary." This is explained by Luis as part of the vital nature of community perseverance: "This fiesta that we are preparing for now has been going for something like 314 years. . . . It is not about the individual; it is about our survival as a community." He goes on to point out: "I can remember when I was very young, stories my father told me that when he was young the fiesta had always been the same."

Even through times of debilitating economic hardship, the importance of conducting the annual feast was never far from the thoughts of the community. Elders typically held back small amounts of surplus items throughout the year in anticipation of the annual event. As Jesus pointed out, "They were fully responsible for [the feast]. . . . It was never far from their mind. . . . My Grandmother always said we had to save for the feast." Throughout their long history in El Paso, the Saint Anthony's Day Feast has been a constant within an existence punctuated by change. Ironically, a new element was introduced as part of the festivities in the 1800s, when a minority of local people began to harass and threaten the celebrating Indians on their parade route. Some of the very people the generous Tigua were attempting to feed and befriend reciprocated by instigating violence. Nonplussed but determined to continue their tradition, tribal members enlisted "protectors" to guard the participants. A tribal member expressed the following to Wright:

> The gun carriers, the *pistoleros*, are usually chosen by the stewards for the feast day. The reason the pistoleros shoot their guns as they walk along is for the protection of the dancers. In other words, protection of the tribe. At one time, even in the early 1900s, there were people who did not believe in this tribe. There were people, that if we walked on the streets, they would try to run over the dancers. So the purpose of the gun was for protection. It was our law. We could do anything we want. Today, of course, we have the security guards. The tribal [*police*] officer is much more beneficial to us. We don't have to worry. We carry blanks in the shotguns. (*1993: 116*)

Discussing an event that occurred in the 1950s, Jesus stresses how serious this threat of violence was perceived to be by the Tigua, as well as their willingness to react to dangerous situations:

> I remember this well, these black people came in these cars [*during the fiesta*] and we wanted to stop them but they didn't want to stop, these black guys got afraid that they would be bugged by the Indians or something. They saw these people dressed up, these Indians, and they just kept on going and I remember someone grab the shotgun and shot at the car, scattered the windshield. That's how strict they were.

Hueco

Tigua religious beliefs are highly integrated with all aspects of traditional cultural behavior. Patterns of meaning, associated with not only practices but places, are derived from the spiritual connection they feel to their ancestors who occupy the traditional landscape. This is, perhaps, most evident when they speak of the sacred area known as Hueco Tanks. The Tigua have been visiting the Hueco Mountains in general and Hueco Tanks in particular since their arrival in 1680, and perhaps longer. The cultural importance of Hueco derives both from what the area offers in regard to resources (animal, plant, and mineral) and from what it offers spiritually. Indeed, many tribal members have historically visited Hueco Tanks for purely spiritual purposes, and although collecting may or may not take place during visits, praying and communing with the grandfathers always take place. Offerings of tobacco, cornmeal, or other sacred items are always made (outside public view) in honor of the grandfathers, as part of an ancient and sacred ritual. It is taboo for tribal members to point in the direction of this sacred area because that action is viewed as disrespectful. Instead, when discussing sacred regions, individuals will nod their head toward the specific area being discussed.

Tribal members initially made the 20-mile pilgrimage on foot, stopping for a brief sojourn at an abandoned pueblo 5 miles from the Tanks (discussed below). Later, horses, carriages, and automobiles would transport tribal members to Hueco, typically including a stopover at the aforementioned ruin. That Hueco Tanks has been significant to the Tigua on a continuing basis is evident by the numerous physical markers left behind (some of which are dated by the creators), which tell a story, in linear progression, about the enduring significance of the Tanks.

Regardless of their time of arrival in the El Paso region, there can be no question that the Tigua have an extremely long and abiding relationship with the area surrounding the Hueco Mountains and, particularly, with Hueco Tanks.

An area midway between Ysleta and the Tanks (around one of the pueblo ruins) was used as a stopping-off point during travel between the Tanks and the El Paso region. In fact, it has been designated the "Pueblo hotel" by the Tigua. That this site has been visited by many tribal members over the years is attested to by the sheer magnitude of pottery shards. Many thousands of pot shards litter the ground, and pottery experts have designated this style of pottery "Ysleta Brown ware" (see Brown et al. 2004). If Texas Parks and Wildlife (TPWD) would allow pottery experts to date the shards they hold in their collection, it would result in near-certain proof that the Tigua have been affiliated with the Hueco site since (in this case) at least the late 1600s.[3] Moreover, this specific area is ascribed with meaning based on its powerful identification with Tigua ancestors.

> Our ancestors, our *abuelos*, came over here to do their ceremonials before they went up to the Hueco Tanks. First, they spent . . . a few nights here to catch the sunrise coming from the east. You can see the sun anytime. They always believe doing their prayer and ceremonies here. There's abundance of food here, plenty of pecans, berries, plenty of wild food. They brought some of the seeds, like the sage, for the ceremonials, they throw off the seeds and [they] plant themselves. . . . So there are a lot of ties, is why they came to this area different times is, at the same time, they would do their offers [*ceremonial offerings*]. (*Jesus*)

Hueco Tanks is described by several respondents as a tribal "retreat." They would stay onsite for several weeks straight, during which time they would hunt and gather food, ceremonial herbs, and medicinal plants.

Primarily, Hueco is considered a "sacred place" and is "where we do our praying to the Indian religion" (Teyo, Jesus); "our grandfathers went there to 'clean themselves out' and to pray for all the people of the pueblo" (Jesus, José, Teyo). It is also described by numerous respondents as "our church." Hueco Tanks is a place that the Tigua identify with on both an individual and collective level; it is identified as an "inheritance" from the grandfathers, who continue to occupy the entire region. A particular story told by Jesus speaks to this:

And, uh, we, that reminds me of work at Hueco Tanks and this time that we have a small crew to work part-time to clean out the park. So at night, at that time, there was some old barracks over there, so we were sitting, you know, that night, you know, and just talking about different things. At that time there was a scandal between the cacique and the war captain, because the cacique was speaking too much and the war captain was saying how he doesn't pay attention to ceremonies. So, anyway, we were sitting around, and I remember looking out the window, and I was talking with a couple of the Elders about these things, and we're just talking, and we look out the window and then, you know, I looked around where everybody was sitting and you can see the expressions on everybody's face. So we were all just very silent and then we said, you know, nobody wanted to say, "Did you see that old man peering at the window?" So the next morning when we get up we said let's go find this *wayas*, which means go find a track right, but we say find a *wayas* to this man. Sure enough, outside the window, we saw deer tracks. But he can become a deer; he can become a person, different types of shapes. We really respect that; it is very powerful. I mean, you know, there are things that we wouldn't even talk about doing because when you believe in that it can happen. You know, my emotions get very strong and I believe it. At the same time, they have done stuff for me too, you know, there's some things they have guided me. So, you see, it is one of these, to me, it's very personal and very strong. I'm not talking for the others, I'm talking for myself. That's why when we go up there we [are] always supposed to leave some *macuchi* [*cigarettes*] for the *abuelos*.[4]

One Tigua respondent stated to Truhill (1992: 11–12, quoted in Greenberg 1998: 95): "Our grandfathers fought for this. Until now, we're still doing it. We're still fighting for it." The shared and individual connection with Hueco Tanks is preeminent in Tigua discourse. The enduring historical ties between the Tigua and Hueco are traced from "time immemorial" to the present day. The numerous pictographs (often incorrectly referred to by non-Natives as "rock art") are embedded with a shared meaning. To the Tigua, they are "like a bible telling a story" (Teyo, Jesus), and like a legend, the symbols serve as a cultural map, literally, spiritually, and cognitively. Cultural persistence is written in stone, as the painted and etched depictions provide the reader with direction, guidance, connectedness, and continuity. Images depict cultural information relative to wildlife, hunting tools and techniques, plants (particularly corn), birds and fish, and directions to water sources. Tribal names dating from the 1800s and spelled using Castilian Spanish establish concrete evidence of Tigua occupation, as do pictographs of *abuelo* masks (perceived as symbolic offerings indicative of their persisting presence), the sacred Tigua sun symbol, and numerous figures depicted in period (1800s) dress. The thirty-two-symbol Tigua-Kiowa battle story mural not only tells the story of the Tigua-Kiowa battle (recently corroborated by the Kiowa tribe) but is also a symbolic map that signifies caution. The weapons, snake, and headless people depicted in the mural convey an unambiguous message.

Defending the Sacred

As mentioned before, the likelihood that the Tigua have had a connection with the Hueco Tanks region since before their 1680 movement is strengthened by evidence showing that the Tigua were prepared to defend this territory from their earliest days (evidenced by the fact that they worked as scouts for the Spanish). Pueblo peoples are known, historically, for their peaceful, hospitable ways. Traditionally, violence is seen as an affront to the natural order and is to be avoided at nearly any cost (see Greenberg 1998). That the Tigua fought battles over their territory, even working as scouts for the Spanish, Mexican, and U.S. governments, indicates the strong, early ties they had to their land. Because a peaceful, hospitable nature is an integral part of Tigua identity, killing, even for food, is frowned on by some Pueblo people. Thomas Green (1974: 141) tells about a Tigua chief who would not even kill the cockroaches that overran his home. Another respondent expresses to Green his displeasure over the killing of a spider. Tribal attorney Tom Diamond tells of the time several Tigua leaders were in his car when it struck a bird that became lodged in the front bumper. After arriving at their destination, the group of Tigua removed the bird and made certain that it received a proper burial. Jesus impresses on me the importance of proper hunting skills, which extend well beyond simple technique, and include when and what to hunt as well as knowing how to utilize every part of the animal. In addition, appropriate respect and prayers of thanks are to be extended to the animal.

> The rules that were given to you was, OK, you don't just go kill a deer, or any wildlife, just because you want to kill. They're going to go and kill that animal because it's going to give you things like energy, life, shelter. You take that animal, and you make the best [*use*] of everything it gives you.

I was taught that either you going to do it right or don't do it at all because you are doing a damage to Mother Nature and they [*the grandfathers are*] always watching you.

Unnecessary killing is in opposition to Tigua beliefs. Fighting and taking the life of a fellow human being is not an act to be taken lightly. Several tribal members stressed to me the important symbolism exposed by the Tigua willingness to fight over land, drawing a direct correlation between battle and sacred landscape. "We would not have defended these lands if they weren't sacred," Teyo says. This point is expanded on by Jesus: "We were never bad guys, Pueblo people have always been very peaceful, very caring for their people. They were never fighting, but when they fought they fought. You find this style in all the other pueblos" (also see Sando 1998).

The Tigua's most popular battle story describes a fight between them and the Kiowa. Several closely related versions of this tale are told; the following represents a compilation:

The Kiowa, they were called snake people, they are still called the snake people. The story is that they had a big battle here [*at Hueco in 1837*]. The Kiowa were going out to the pueblo and try to get some of the women from the pueblo. At one time, this was the way it was explained to me, this was explained to me by two persons, it was, talk about these people going out there and picking up the ceremonies through the windows, or they try to steal the women. One time, all the men in the pueblo said, "OK, we've had enough of this," and they got a whole bunch of people together and trailed them to here [*Hueco Tanks*]. They talk about, they say they got them in there [*inside one of the caves*] and smoke them out. They use greasewood and red peppers, said put them through the top to smoke them. But, they got two prisoners and take them back to the pueblo and, matter of fact, they said they had them there and they said one was shot trying to get away. But the legend said that one of them die and the other one too because, I don't know if our tribe did something to them, that wasn't discussed with me, but that was the story that they brought them up to Ysleta. One died right there by on the corner of Socorro and Old Pueblo right there. There used to be a house there, said they died there and they got some of the artifacts. I confirmed them because a man took them out of there, something happened to him after he dug them out. He was told not to take them out of there, after he was warned "No, no" by the people, you know. I think it was part of evil stuff, but he took them out and after a week he died. Anyway, the story says that they got one still. When I talk about Loma Paloma, where we were, that's where they buried one of them, the last one, on Loma Paloma. But the Kiowas was very, that's why they're called the snake people, they come in like a snake. You can see the pictures [*pictograph panel at Hueco Tanks*]; you can see we're still dressed as in the 1800s. See they had, you can see them doing the ghost dance to scare them and whatever. But, our people have never been scared of the ghost dance. You go back, another deal, where one of our Indian scouts was killed, we're never afraid of those guys, those Apaches doing their dance, ghost dance, our people used to laugh at them, "We'll get you." But, that's [*the*] legend that has been passed that I heard. These is not my words, these are the words of our elders. That's why you see pictures in this area that shows this is a victory, or whenever it was called. About twenty years ago we had a delegation from the Kiowa and they verify, matter of fact, in this battle, I think the buffalo skin [*is*] over there on their reservation and keep on talking about you guys [*Tigua*].

Cultural Change

The rate of culture change and the direction it takes are often out of a community's control. For example, the massive land theft in the late 1800s left the Tigua poverty-stricken and unable to afford basic necessities, such as proper clothing and adequate family housing. The children were forced to wear ragged hand-me-downs to school (often without shoes) and were ridiculed and ostracized. A story related by Diego epitomizes the no-win situation many Tigua found themselves in. As a child, Diego was teased for having long hair and being too poor to afford a haircut (despite the fact that he was proud of his long hair). Nevertheless, after an extended period of ridicule, he begged his father to cut his hair. His father reluctantly agreed, but afterward Diego was mocked and derided "for being a fake" because, after cutting his hair, he no longer "looked like an Indian." Furthermore, the poor housing conditions meant most Tigua children did not have access to a quiet, well-lighted study area. As Jesus states: "We had very few who made it past the third or fourth grade, you know, most of us lived twelve or fifteen in a one-room shack. How you going to study, all them people, no electricity?"

The cycle of poverty within this community, whose members were largely unable to read or write, became self-perpetuating. Desperate living conditions were compounded by a lack of employment for those who embraced their Indian identity because "more jobs," according to Hector, "were available to non-Indians." As job opportunities diminished, more and more tribal members began to reject their Indian identity, with many moving away from the community. As José points out: "There were many other people that was Indian and never associated with us, for reasons personal or financial. . . . I don't blame them because times were rough, in the first place, and many people went out of town to seek better employment, better ways of living." The Tigua who remained, however, apparently embraced their ethnic identity openly. Furthermore, these community members instilled that sense of pride in their descendants (see "Cultural Preservation" below).

The change in economic fortunes (from bad to worse) appears to have led to a split of sorts within the community, between those who chose to disengage from their identity and those who chose to fight to the bitter end. Tales that relate to Tigua "heroes" who fought for Indian rights have, today, reached near mythic proportions. One story, which describes how a former chief once battled the local court system for his people's right to hunt and gather, is often told in epic fashion (see Adam 2007, Appendix D, Story B). Another tale, which took place in the early 1960s, describes the Tigua Elder who threatened to chop down the telephone poles on his property if the city forced him to secure a building permit for work on his house (see Adam 2007, Appendix D, Story A). The rallying cry consistently found among these stories is, "I am an Indian, this is our land, and you cannot tell us what to do here" (see, for example, the *pistolero* tale above). The sense of pride and nonconformity is palpable throughout the various "defiance" tales, and the overriding message is equally clear: "The Tigua are fiercely proud people and nobody better mess with us." The instilling and re-instilling of pride and identity throughout the course of history have created a community that today unabashedly embraces its indigenous identity. Although the number of Tigua residing in the old pueblo (El Barrio de los Indios) fell to under two hundred persons by the early 1960s, they were all that remained of the various Indian tribes and the thousands of Indian individuals that at one time inhabited the El Paso region. These survivors would prove that although change is impossible to stop, it can be understood and "managed." Moreover, the Tigua have proven that they can adapt without sacrificing their sacred traditional practices.

The introduction of the *tuh-lah*, the change in kinship rules, and the adjustment in governmental structure are but a few of the many examples of cultural change that were managed by the Tigua. Another large issue that the Tigua confront today relates to access to sacred pieces of land, as many traditional cultural properties are controlled by the government and private landowners (some of which contain sacred sites), and the Tigua have been forced to devise plans to address this problem. The casino and blood quantum issues (to be discussed in Chapter Five) are among the most contentious issues facing the Tigua today. Other changes include the following example, which was pointed out by José:

> Now, in El Paso, the bushes have been chopped down and there's nothing there but empty riverbanks. Even the river itself has been diverted; it's been diverted to the farmers into canals. That's why we have a difficult time during the ceremonies, because we go there to the river to do the ceremonies. Way back the grandfathers used to swim there for the ceremonies that we have in the wintertime.

The sacred *abuelo* dance was discontinued by the Tigua after 1936 because of the low water levels and pollution in the river. That has been difficult for the Tigua community because of their belief that the *varas* (willow branches used by council members throughout the ceremonial cycle that cleanse the community of evil), which are placed in the river during the final annual ceremony, "take away" the evil spirits from the pueblo (see also Greenberg 1998). Because flowing water is needed to accomplish the ritual, the Tigua have been forced to modify it. The *abuelo* dancers, according to several respondents, may be reintroduced at some point, but it should be noted that because the *abuelos* are perceived as the physical embodiment of the grandfathers (not just symbolic actors), they are very sacred, and the Tigua should not be expected to share concrete information about their presence.

Prior to the mid-1960s, tribal dancing, singing, and chanting were closely regulated by the tribal council, including during special occasions, such as when tribal members traveled to Austin or Dallas. "In those days," Luis says, "the dances were only for the fiesta, selected by the tribal council. . . . The younger dancers [contemporary dancers who dance for tourists] actually came about when we built the arts and crafts center that was torn down." The attire worn by the dancers has also changed over time. For most of their history, the Tigua, like the New Mexico Puebloan peoples, did not wear a "uniform" for public displays (Rico). Several tribal members, such as Diego, remember that the dress consisted of "plain old Levi's, but they weren't Levi's but something like that with a white shirt." The attire worn today is very colorful, and though every participant does not dress identically, the overall look is consistent. This style, according to Rico, "was introduced back before 1936, back in that era when the tribe was taken to Dallas to meet the president." Although it is a non-issue for the majority of tribal members, one expresses mild displeasure at this development: "That's not really the traditional dress for fiestas. . . . I don't, I never did see, that I remember from way back, all this jewelry and all this other stuff that you see now at the fiestas, but like I said, I guess it makes us look good now in the eyes of the public that comes to see us" (Hector).

Traditional dances included the Rattle Dance, the Mask Dance, the Red Pigment Dance, the Scalp Dance, and the House Dance. Contemporary dances include the Pueblo Two-Step, the Butterfly, the Basket, the Fancy Shawl, the Social Round ("given" by the Kiowa to the Tigua), and the Eagle Dance. Most of them are social dances, but some (such as the Eagle Dance) are sacred dances that have been modified for public viewing. The drumming and chanting that accompany the dancing are also important and must be executed in specific ways. In a discussion with Luis about the chanting that goes with the drumbeat, he states: "The chanting was mostly, and originally, only spiritual and that's why you would never hear words. The chanting, what it would be, everybody when they're chanting, it's a spiritual prayer, they're praying for happiness, the well-being of the tribe, giving thanks also." After the tribe received state recognition in 1968, they became eligible to receive funding for cultural resource development, which enabled them to build a cultural center and to promote tourist activities, including arts, crafts, and social dancing. The issues of dancing, drumming, and singing, as well as the modification of the rules that apply to these activities, are discussed by José:

> On the Tigua calendar our new year started yesterday, on the sixth of January; that's when our newly elected tribal council, their office goes into effect. Yesterday also marks the end of our dancing for the year. That's the day He [*the sacred tribal drum Juanchiro*] is put to rest until May when we start practicing [*for the start of the ceremonial cycle*]. The drum is covered under a blanket and put to sleep. You cannot play Him anymore. Even the songs that was used for the dancing, the ceremonial dancing, [*to play those songs*] is taboo, it is bad. It's very sacred, the Old People used

to tell us it was bad luck, taboo, to sing them. The *abuelos* will get angry and, well, misfortune will befall you if you are using those songs or play the drum. The drum is put to sleep until the last two weekends in May when we start practicing our songs and dance for our feast day, which is June 13. So now it's at rest. . . . These dances [*traditional dances*] we only dance for our feasts or for ceremonial observations; those are more of a ritual. Well, they are sacred; we can't dance them for the public viewing, only some parts of them. Like our feast day, we let people see some of our dances. Also, the old people used to say not to play any drums from now until the last parts of May, not to play the drums, but I guess it was in the 1970s when we started having our museum built here down the road, the cultural center, they gave us permission, the tribal council and the chief and war captain. We can play other drums, nonsacred drums that have not been blessed. A drum that hasn't been blessed and doesn't have a name we can use it for social dances, dances that we can dance for the tourists. Plus the songs that we sing for the social dances are not from here, from our people, from our pueblo; they are songs that we have borrowed from other pueblos, also with their permission. We could borrow their songs and dances. The difference between ceremonial songs and those for the tourists, social dances, there's a whole world of difference between the two. Right now I can play these drums [*points to a drum in the room*] because they don't have what the ceremonial drums have. They [*ceremonial drums*] have a little hole right here in the side; that's where you breathe life into it and feed it cornmeal.

Ceremonial and ritual dancing have been important to the Tigua throughout their tenure in El Paso. The dances, according to several respondents, "are tied with Mother Earth" and "represent the planting and the rain and the harvests."

A constant primary concern of the Tigua has been their ability to grow corn. The overriding order of business after their 1680 arrival was the building of a system of canals to water their fields. The importance of water can never be underestimated in this arid region, and although corn is considered sacred, so is the river, as well as the individual canals that feed the fields. The sacred nature of water and corn is pointed out by José:

It's through the river that we get the water to grow our corn, especially corn, since being the mother of all Indians, corn is very important. Not only does it sustain us, still does, but we also use corn for ceremonies throughout the whole year. We use it for all ceremonies. When a baby is born, all throughout life, until we bury the person, we sprinkle cornmeal on the person from birth till death. It has a lot of ceremonial uses, but only the chief and war captain can bless the cornmeal. You can have any kind of cornmeal, but it has to be blessed. . . . Corn is very important to us. There is a belief that corn was the first mother of the people so it's very sacred.

Although change is accepted as "a necessary evil" (Jesus), the Tigua have demonstrated great resilience in the face of both forced and incidental change. Above all, they have steadfastly refused to turn away from their core beliefs and are ever mindful of the role religion and identity play in their long-term success. Change will continue to come and forever challenge the Tigua community's ability to persevere, but their ability to see beyond the immediate and to adjust to change in appropriate ways bodes well for their community's future.

Cultural Preservation

Throughout their history, the Tigua have maintained a high level of discipline and have been extremely diligent about following traditional practice. Numerous tribal members relayed to me the importance of carefully observing traditional practice and maintaining a solemn attitude in regard to the learning and performance of tribal ritual and ceremony. The Tigua are keenly aware of their vulnerability to attack by powerful outside forces (i.e., the local, state, and federal governments), as well as with regard to conflicts over land use, and the casino and blood quantum issues, and others. Teyo points to the "priceless" nature of Tigua tradition and voices his concern that Tigua culture will end up in "old museums" if respect for and care of tradition are not maintained. He regards the passing of traditional knowledge as sacred and poignantly says: "When somebody gives you something, it's part of their heart they're giving." The importance of Tigua identity is summed up well by Jesus when he states:

I'm old-fashioned and traditional. Unfortunately most of our people are not following that role in life, but I strive and I'll do my best to teach the younger generations of kids, our grandchildren, to uphold our traditions and ceremonies. But, because there is very few of us left in this world, and if we keep up this pace, our people are probably becoming extinct. Hopefully that won't happen, and it won't happen in my lifetime. Our tribe, our people, our identity, to continue indefinitely, I tell them, our younger people, the extreme importance of following traditions. It's important to set your spirit, your heart and soul, [to understand] what it is to be a Tigua, an Indian, [to understand] we have so much rich history behind us and to look forward into the future. And, also, to look through the good and the bad. I keep telling them, be proud of what you are, always be proud of where you came from and where you're going. You are a Native American. I hope they can relate to this. Like I said, without your tradition and culture, you can be just anybody else, but we have an identity, we are a people. I just tell [them], "Don't forget what you are and be proud. You're Tigua and that's the best thing you can be. Forget those gangs, being Indian is the best."

A shared sense of group identity has fed Tigua notions of personal identity in profound ways. Every respondent I spoke with indicated that his or her individual identity (while strongly connected to a sense of "pan-Indianness" and "Pueblo-Indianness") was directly related to a sense of identification as, specifically, a Tigua Indian.

DIEGO: "Be in your own heart a Tigua, get out there and praise one another, love one another. . . . We are all brothers";
JOSÉ: "I just tell [the young tribal members] 'Don't forget what you are and be proud. You're Tigua and that's the best thing you can be,'";
LUIS: "I want every Tigua to be proud. . . . We go in a circle and we're all brothers. . . . I can tell you who he is related to. . . . I don't care which entrance [of the Tigua housing development] you go in, the first house is related to the next one, in a roundabout way. . . . The whole housing, that's a circle of society";
HECTOR: "Don't lose your heritage and be what you are; you are a Tigua so be a proud Tigua."

The importance of being identified as, specifically, a Tigua (at both the individual and group level) was reiterated and strongly stressed repeatedly. This aspect of identity correlation informs the overall argument that Tigua cultural persistence is directly related to their ability to maintain their sense of group identity throughout their long and perilous history. Furthermore, identity is tied to sacred religious beliefs that are highly integrated into all aspects of traditional cultural behavior. Every aspect of life is ascribed with meaning. Patterns of meaning, associated with not only practices but places (and senses of place), derive from the spiritual connection the Tigua ascribe not only to the interconnectedness between their ancestors and their traditional landscape, but also the spiritual awareness linked to items such as the tribal drum, canes of leadership, feathers, corn, statues of their patron saint, and other physical objects. Cortez states: "Water, corn, canals, planting, harvesting, dancing, chanting, hunting, healing, spirituality. . . . These are the things of life. Each is important, each is interconnected, and the relationship is cyclical and never-ending."

Conclusion

Tigua senses of cultural identity are closely interrelated with their perceptions of religion, and each is tied inextricably to their awareness of the cultural meanings that have been ascribed to individual and community senses of landscape, ceremony, and ritual. Additionally, the Tigua understand cultural change as an ongoing process, and they have consciously implemented modifications in order to adapt to changing circumstances. Their ability to adapt in appropriate ways is demonstrated (if by no other marker) by the indisputable fact that they are still around. However, although the focus of discussion has centered on the Tigua and their adaptability as an indigenous community, the power of the nation-state in forming and controlling the process of change has yet to be discussed.

Identity formation for both groups and individuals is based on (and conditioned by) many factors, such as individual and group economic factors, shared and personal history, spiritual beliefs, ethnic standing and discrimination, traditional beliefs and practices, and senses of historical events. Cultural change is affected by, and affects, senses of identity (both individual and group) as the cyclical process of change, self-evaluation, reevaluation, and cultural adaptation takes place. However, although some control over cultural change and identity formation is possible (as the above narrative points out), for indigenous communities, such change is nearly always reactive rather than proactive.

Although change can come in reaction to incidental events (such as technological advancements), the cause of forced change is often insidious. The ability of nation-states to purposely inflict forced change and then control the parameters of discourse and legalities relative to that change places indigenous communities in a perilous situation. The mechanism through which the nation-state exerts primary control is through a legal system that was devised by and for the majority members of the state. The use of this force relegates indigenous peoples to a minor role in shaping the relationship between oppressed and oppressor. With regard to the issue of identity, the United States has put into motion a plan for cultural genocide through legislative fiat that affects not only the long-term ability of the U.S. indigenous population to survive, but also shapes the construction of individual and group identity by usurping the rights of sovereign communities to define their own rules and ideals relative to membership criteria.

The issues of law and power and their relationship to American Indian identity will be the topic of the next chapter. Although the discussion so far describes the success of the Tigua in overcoming the many problems related to colonization, the story is far from complete. The questions of how and why the Tigua have been able to survive for so long have been addressed. But has this survival been in vain? Have the Tigua lasted this long only to be eventually snuffed out by a nation bent on genocide? Why, and how, the United States crafted its Indian laws and policies is, in reality, a story of genocide. Indeed, it is a story of genocide that makes the Holocaust pale in comparison. It is a story that most American Indians know all too well, but few other Americans do.

CHAPTER THREE

Legislating Identity

Law, Discourse, and Perceptions of Indianness

Introduction

The previous chapters have focused on the history of the Tigua Pueblo, exploring, particularly, the concepts of cultural change and perseverance as they relate directly to the Tigua tribe. I have explored the issue of identity at both the group and individual levels and related that issue to the process of change, exploring each within the context of historical events. At this point it is necessary to take a momentary detour from my specific discussion about the Tigua and take up a conversation that is more pan-Indian in nature. It is important that the historical relationship between the United States and its indigenous population be framed within the proper context. The issues of Tigua tribal recognition and Tigua gaming (the subjects of Chapters Four and Five) must be juxtaposed against the legal framework that has been devised for the government to exercise control over its indigenous population. The closely related issues of power and law affect how all Native American Indians have been dealt with by the U.S. government and must be explored as the vital ingredients within an "Indian" program bent on annihilation. The insidious nature of legalized identity profoundly affects how Indian and non-Indian alike perceive and respond to Indian issues, and the history of its development holistically affects all aspects of postcolonial Native American Indian existence.

In this chapter I explore the legal relationship between the United States and its indigenous population during the past two-hundred-plus years. The specific focus will be on the corpus of Indian laws developed by the United States in order to justify its genocidal policies, concurrent with the wholesale theft of millions of acres of indigenous landholdings. The methods devised by the U.S. government to accomplish its overarching goal of American Indian annihilation have been ruthless, duplicitous, and surprisingly transparent. As Eve Darian-Smith (2004: 39) points out, because laws reflect the power and ideology of those in charge, "we must always ask . . . whose economic and/or political advantage is furthered when any new law is made?" The development of identity legislation, a legal means of methodically defining Indians out of existence through the invention of blood quantum standards, has been integrated within the construction of a popular discourse that proposes primordial cultural standards for contemporary peoples. The ability of the United States (as colonizer) to usurp traditional authority and to determine for itself what does (and does not) constitute real Indian identity and authenticity is perhaps the most powerful tool it uses against Indian peoples.

Like all U.S racial minority groups, Native Americans are forced to confront a multitude of issues on a daily basis that white Americans rarely (if ever) confront or even think about. In her popular article *White Privilege: Unpacking the Invisible Knapsack,* U.S. anthropologist Peggy McIntoch (1989: 213–214) lists twenty-six "daily effects of white privilege" that she, as opposed to African Americans, normally takes for granted. Although this list is designed to apply to African Americans, one can easily envision such a list for each of the many racial, and other minority groups historically invented by the white European power structure (see Canessa 2005: 1). Of all the long lists that could be created as a part of this exercise, perhaps none would be quite as long as the one developed for American Indians. One of the reasons is that Native American Indians and the United States have such a long-term, complicated relationship. After becoming the first victims of U.S. hegemony, Indians have undergone a dizzying array of programs and consistently contradictory and ever-changing laws and policies designed to legally control, confine, define, and, ultimately, kill them.

The primary problem for American Indians has always been their relationship with the land: it belonged to them. They were the only group indigenous to the country and therefore the only group that could lay claim to the land and resources coveted by the colonizers. The young republic continually invented and reinvented methods for legally separating the people from their property, partly because the United States was forced, through its own treaty provisions with Britain, to account for its treatment of the indigenous population, and outright genocide was not legally plausible (if, in fact, it was even militarily possible at the initial point of colonization). Unable to devise an open policy of genocide, the United States was compelled to devise other means for divesting Native Americans of their land and wealth. This goal, it must be said, has been largely met.

During the past five hundred years (beginning with the Spanish invasion), American Indians have been systematically stripped of their land and other resources, and their population numbers have been decimated by various genocidal acts. As a group, Native Americans were stripped of their inherent sovereignty and nationhood status, placed under the "care" of the federal government, and forced to comply with a body of laws that were (and are) applicable only to Native peoples (such as identity requirements). Additionally, their position within the U.S. legal system is such that Congress can grant, or retract, "privileges" at its whim. Indeed, the indigenous peoples of the United States are the only U.S. citizens that have a branch of the legal system dedicated specifically to them. Despite the fact that technically, and legally, American Indians exist as "independent sovereign nations," their ability to wield power, political or otherwise, is essentially nonexistent.

I do not argue that other minority groups hold a significant amount of power in relation to the white majority, only that American Indians are in the least favorable position of collective empowerment. One reason is that American Indians make up less than 2 percent of the total American population. By comparison, approximate figures indicate that whites make up 75 percent; African Americans/blacks, 13 percent; and Asians/Latinos, 12 percent. Furthermore, if one factors in that anyone, in filling out a census report, can claim American Indian ancestry, it is probable that the true number is significantly lower than this. Indeed, the number of Indians who are eligible to receive benefits through the federal government (as federally recognized Indians) is below 1 percent of the total American population. That issue is not lost on politicians when running for elected office, nor is it lost on the legislators who craft social policy and create laws. There is (cliché or not) strength in numbers. For example, issues important to African Americans, Latinos, and women garner considerable discussion as part of the political discourse in the United States, particularly during an election cycle. Meanwhile, issues important to American Indians are simply ignored. The collective Indian voice has been silenced by laws and policies that have been intentionally crafted to eliminate the American Indian, and the so-called Indian problem, once and for all.

Although it is true that Native American political issues have gained some media exposure since the civil rights movements of the 1960s, that exposure has not been converted into political capital in any significant way. And even though American Indians have been traditionally Democratic in party affiliation, most will support whichever candidate is most sensitive to their personal political issue(s). Because their population numbers are so small, Indians have learned that either political party is equally likely to screw them over. The myth of the rich Indian (Indian gaming is an issue I take up in Chapter Five) buying political access has been (predictably) exaggerated: the great majority of Indians continue to live in the most depressed regions of the country. Indians living on reservations are still at the bottom of virtually every economic category. The poverty rate for Indians is the highest of any ethnic group in the United States (over 30 percent), unemployment rates often reach 50 percent on reservations (some as high as 80 percent), and the life expectancy of the American Indian is forty-seven years, contrasted with the overall American average of seventy-eight.

Indian Identity

Serious questions surround the issue of Native American Indian identity, questions that profoundly affect how individuals come to see themselves. American Indian scholar Ward Churchill (2004: 60) states: "Among the most vexing and divisive issues afflicting Native North America at the dawn of the twenty-first century are the questions of who has a legitimate right to say he or she is American Indian, and by what criteria or whose definition this may or may not be true." The question of identity, legal and otherwise, is no minor issue. At the heart of the question is the extermination of Indian peoples on both an individual and group level. As one young female Tigua member related to Bill Wright (1993: 84):

> Someday we are going to run out of blood. My blood quantum is one-eighth. The government says that after one-eighth, you are no longer a member of the tribe. Everybody my age is one-eighth, and we are the ones next in line to run the tribal government. After us, who is going to do it? The government has made us history. We helped them slash our own throat!

It is important, when exploring the question of Indian identity, to consider pre- and postcolonial identity markers. We need to understand, as best we can, "how pre-colonial non-European agrarian civilizations actually functioned"; we need to "look at the content and cultural meaning of the relationships of power and domination on which they were based and to understand them as truly historical societies" (Gledhill 1994: 68). We cannot gain an understanding based purely on "how their organizational principles differed from those of Western societies of either the modern or pre-modern period, since one of the most important things we must try to understand is how Western domination changed them" (68). "Kin-communities," for example, "provide a model for pre-state societies based on consensual authority embodied in custom rather than power relations embodied in law" (25). For Native people, identity has traditionally been much more sociocentric, with individual identity negotiated in relation to group identity, and group identity connected to a relationship with the land.

Postcolonial discourse has pounced on traditional notions of identity and created a "primordial" classification that no individual or group could ever live up to. Indian identity (in both legal and popular discourse) was, and is, defined in terms of traditional behavior, "a state of existence in contradistinction to modernity, whereby language, ways of living, and cultural knowledge . . . [are] transmitted in relatively unbroken lines from a distant past, and generally combined with 'racial' purity" (Lawrence 2004: 1). Change is forbidden as, by definition, a "changed Indian" cannot be a "real" Indian, and only "real Indians" are formally recognized by the federal government (the issue of federal recognition will be taken up in the following chapter). Of course, this already impossible task is complicated by colonial policies and programs that were designed to purposely force Native communities into change, not the least of which involved (and involves) the physical separation of the people from their sacred land. "The implication of this rupturing of ties to community, for peoples whose identities are rooted in a connection to the land and to other people, are profound" (xvi). Additionally, "alienation" is "provoked by the culture of civilization" that attacks "the sphere of 'kinship': the world of intimate personal relations, material reciprocity and mutual aid networks, community as the enactment of shared culture" (Gledhill 1994: 25). Therefore, early American Indian policy advanced a two-pronged attack against the indigenous population by concomitantly removing them from important identity sources (their land and their kinship community) and then legalizing a definition of Indianness that disqualifies individuals and groups who cannot prove continual ties to their land and community.

It is not difficult to imagine the identity problems—private, public, and legal—that the marginal Indian, the many Native individuals who do not fit cleanly into arbitrary categories of legal authenticity, must experience. As anthropologists, we know that biological determinism is a farce and that racial classifications are spurious at best. However, the idea that cultural identification has nothing whatsoever to do with "blood ties" has not, thus far, played a role in the development of government policy. The impact of these government-sponsored laws and discourses is often devastating to the construction of individual and group Indian identity formation. Bonita Lawrence (2004: 20) suggests:

> Hegemonic images and definitions of Indianness flowing from identity affect the participants' views of themselves . . . whether one looks Indian, whether a person has . . . tribal membership and grew up on a reserve or in the city, and the images and definitions of Indianness created by the colonizer to control Native people have become . . . central to Native peoples' own self-images.

And these self-images must be continually juxtaposed against nonlegal perceptions of Indianness, the powerful imagery provoked by public discourse in the United States, which continues to narrowly define real Indians as "redskins" who live in teepees; ride horses bareback; throw tomahawks and carry bows and arrows; wear feathered headdresses, moccasins, and leather-fringed jackets; and decorate their faces with war paint. Implicit in this dominant narrative structure is the notion that Indians who do not fit this model of authenticity are acting fraudulently.

Moreover, the ability of the government to cast markers of Indianness in negative terms fed the perception that Indian identity should not be embraced on the individual level, particularly by "half" or other "partial bloods," as they were superior to the "full-bloods" and should distance themselves from that tainted image. As John Gledhill (1994: 194) points out, "Valorization of European origin perpetuates the valorization of a pale complexion," and by focusing on "social movements," we begin to see how "the politics of culture" is "a process by which groups in 'society' construct or reconstruct identities for themselves in their struggles and negotiations with both dominant groups and the state." Furthermore,

> such processes are never entirely free-floating and rarely involve a radical rejection of the semiology of domination. . . . The state and dominant groups actively strive to impose their classifications on the structure of a "civil society" which never exists independently of such hegemonic processes. Even if practices of domination can never eliminate the spaces within which counter-hegemonic discourses and practices emerge, they still influence both the forms taken by counter-hegemonic movements and their capacity to articulate together to mount a challenge to the existing hegemony. (Gledhill 1994: 194)

The United States, utilizing "the politics of culture," made relentless attacks on the indigene's "pagan" religious beliefs and helped popularize a discourse that cast Indians as backward, "red-skinned savages" who indiscriminately maimed, raped, and murdered poor, innocent "White Folk." The embedded nature of these negative portrayals not only affected how the white majority constructed images of Native peoples but also affected how Native peoples responded to these falsehoods. The "valorization of a pale complexion," combined with the "valorization of Christianity" and the spread of outlandish propaganda, led to a degree of identity confusion that fragmented what had been a powerful and shared sense of Native solidarity.

In short, "the policies and politics of the US government have" added additional layers "to historically rooted systems of social distinction" (Gledhill 1994: 194). This program of casting Indian identity in negative terms worked well throughout the country, and certainly among the Tigua, as many tribal members rejected their Indian and Tigua identities. At issue, however, is not only how Indians in general conceive of their own identity, but also how the U.S. government (through the U.S. legal system) and non-Indians conceive of Indian identity. The question is simple: What makes a particular person Indian? The answer is not simple, as identity is a complex and nuanced notion.

In order to gain a better sense of who is and who is not an Indian, it is important to consider the history of U.S. and American Indian relations. As the dominant, colonizing culture, the United States holds the power to create and define the legal structure and discourse of the U.S.–Native American relationship. Hegemonic standards set the terms used to evaluate indigenous identities, and the goals of the U.S. government's Indian policy can be, and are, shaped by the creation of enforceable laws, leaving Indians with little (or no) voice in the construction of the very guidelines that directly affect not only their daily lives but their very survival as a distinct people. As Darian-Smith (2004: 38) points out: "Many people believe law is an objective and neutral system of rules agreed upon and accepted through the processes of democracy." Although most citizens believe that laws are designed to protect and benefit the community as a whole, in fact, that is rarely the case. In truth, the law "is and has always been a tool and technology of those in power. It is used to reinforce the social values and societal behaviors that most obviously benefit those who are in elite positions of economic, religious, or social control" (38). Merry (1990: 6) (quoted in Darian-Smith 2004: 38) suggests a variety of roles fulfilled by the creation of laws:

not just by the imposition of rules and punishments but also by the ca-
pacity to construct authoritative images of social relationships and actions, images that are symbolically powerful. Law provides a set of
categories and frameworks through which the world is interpreted. Legal words and practices are cultural constructs which carry powerful
meanings not just to those trained in law . . . but to the ordinary person
as well.

The overriding goal of federal Indian policy has remained unchanged
over the past two hundred years: the total elimination of Indians, or, as it
has often been called, the Indian problem. The methods used and laws
created to reach this end are instructive in comprehending how Indians
are currently viewed by the U.S. government, by scholars, by individual
citizens, and by Indians themselves. The use of legislative means combined with popular discourse allowed (and allows) the colonizers to construct powerful and legislatively entrenched methods for eventually
separating Indians from both their resources and their identity.

Indian Law

American Indians occupy a place in the U.S. legal system that is consider-
ably more arbitrary than that occupied by other U.S. citizens. Most laws
apply to the majority of the people and are open to interpretation to such
an extent that a gray area is built into the crafting of laws and legal terms.
Although this wiggle room can be an asset, allowing laws to be applied on
an individual or case-by-case basis, it can also be problematic. For example, federal Indian law is often contradictory and has been described by
Peter d'Errico (1997) as "perhaps the most complex area of United States
law (including tax laws)."[1] The complexity stems, in part, from the fact
that the federal government itself is unable (or unwilling) to define, in
any useful or meaningful way, what precisely an Indian is (leaving aside
the fact that international law prohibits sovereign nations from defining
the membership criteria of other nations). There are, for example, scores
of definitions (perhaps as many as eighty) that describe what constitutes
an Indian under various circumstances. Legal terms such as "sovereignty"
and "nation" are equally problematic.

The primary goal of the U.S. government in defining Indianness in
racial (as opposed to cultural) terms is clearly one element within its overarching policy goal of genocide. Unlike all other racial classifications invented in this country, which invariably follow the rule of hypodescent,

legal definitions of Indian identity have been crafted to limit the number of individuals who possess enough "blood" to be eligible for tribal membership or (the real issue here) "Indian entitlements."[2] The purpose behind the implementation of these rules is patently obvious: Hypodescent limits the number of privileged whites, and definitions of Indianness limit the number of privileged Indians. Why were Indians singled out for this "special" designation? They control resources. White privilege is a commodity worthy of protection in myriad ways, whereas Indian privilege (aside from personal and cultural value) is, as a commodity, useful to Indian people only as a means of extracting entitlements that are coveted by the white power structure. By reversing the rule of hypodescent for Indians, the U.S. legal system has virtually guaranteed that at some point in the not too distant future, the so-called Indian problem will disappear through its own attrition. One can only wonder what will become of the considerable landholdings and other assets currently belonging to Indian people.[3]

The Colonists Become the Colonizers

From the very beginning (or, at least, immediately after throwing off its own colonial yoke), the United States set out its own policy of colonization. Unlike the British, who were concurrently going about the business of colonizing the indigenous peoples of Canada (as well as other indigenous peoples around the globe), the U.S. treatment of "its" indigenous population was being closely scrutinized by Europeans in general and the British in particular. By this point in history, Britain had spent considerable time as a colonial power and had put forth its own notions about governing "racially inferior" populations. Although following policies of open colonial expansionism itself, the British were eager to have the Americans follow guidelines put in place by their own joint treaty negotiations. Lawrence (2004: 29) points out:

> Britain, after over a century of warfare with East Coast Native nations and anxious not to repeat the experience, affirmed through the Royal Proclamation of 1763 that a nation-to-nation relationship must govern the process of land acquisition in British North America and insisted that the U.S. government abide by these terms as conditions of peace both after the Revolutionary War and the War of 1812. But it did so largely because the specter of unfettered territorial expansion south of the border threatened Britain's Canadian colonies to the north.

The burgeoning United States, therefore, found itself in a precarious situation. How was it to justify, at least in the legal sense, the taking of indigenous lands? Moreover, how could it get around this pesky requirement of dealing with Indian groups on a nation-to-nation basis? The first hurdle was easily surmounted by invoking the doctrine of discovery and conquest (Deloria and Lytle 1983: 2; Lawrence 2004: 28; d'Errico 1997; Churchill 1999). This was a long-used European standard that was based on papal authority and invoked "Christian superiority" as ample justification for not only stealing indigenous land, but also for the brutal treatment that was to be visited upon the former owners of that land (see d'Errico 1997). Chief Justice John Marshall, in the 1823 Supreme Court case *Johnson v. McIntosh*, affirmed this rationalization for unfettered expansion when he stated:

> On the discovery of this immense continent, the great nations of Europe were eager to appropriate to themselves so much of it as they could respectively acquire. Its vast extent offered an ample field to the ambition and enterprise of all; and the character and religion of its inhabitants afforded an apology for considering them as a people over whom the superior genius of Europe might claim an ascendancy. The potentates of the old world found no difficulty in convincing themselves that they made ample compensation to the inhabitants of the new, by bestowing on them civilization and Christianity. (quoted in d'Errico 1997)

This interpretation granted the United States all the legal justification it would ever need to take Indian land (along with the resources contained on that land) with impunity. The British, and other European powers, could hardly criticize the newly founded United States for following their lead. Although appropriating land using the doctrine of either discovery or of conquest (or both) as legal justification is dubious, at best, it was apparently the closest the United States could come to providing a palatable rationalization. As for the issue of dealing with Indian peoples on a nation-to-nation basis, within eight years Marshall would resolve that little problem as well. As spelled out by Marshall in the 1831 *Cherokee Nation v. Georgia* ruling,[4] the United States would continue to view Indian nations as "sovereigns" and conceptualize dealing between the two as "nation-to-nation," but Indian people would hold a "lesser form" of sovereignty because they were not really "nations" in the general sense of the word.[5] Rather, they were to be considered "domestic, dependent nations," which placed Native peoples in the unique position of possessing a new form of sovereignty that was, in fact and law, "non-sovereign sovereignty" (d'Errico 1997; Deloria and Lytle 1983: 4). This nonsovereign status was reaffirmed in a 1973 case (*United States v. Blackfeet Tribe*), when the U.S. attorney removed slot machines from the Blackfeet reservation. During the ensuing trial, the judge ruled that "an Indian tribe is sovereign to the extent that the United States permits it to be sovereign—neither more nor less" (364 F.Supp. at 194).[6]

The United States was not content to simply remove the powers of sovereign government from the Indian peoples, however, as this act, in and of itself, did not provide the means necessary for taking the vast wealth (in land and natural resources) controlled by the indigenous population. Moreover, a decision by the United States (itself a former colony and formed on the principle of "liberty and justice for all") to conduct an open policy of genocide would strike the rest of the world (not to mention its own citizens) as hypocritical, at best. Although numerous incidents (Wounded Knee, the multiple Trail[s] of Tears, and the fifty or so Indian wars, to name just a few of the more popular examples) prove that the United States was not opposed to the wholesale slaughter of Indian people, the notion that the United States, to quote John Adams, had established "a government of laws and not men," compelled lawmakers to construct legal justification and give at least the appearance of proceeding within the law as they set about the business of legalized genocide.[7] Indeed, the government enshrined in the U.S. Constitution was designed with the central purpose of ensuring that it would govern through the rule of law. Hardly daunted by the prospect of being constitutionally mandated to create laws that would permit the United States to eliminate the Indians and steal their resources, the government created a series of laws that would allow it to do just that.

The Treaty Years

The practice of making peace treaties with Indian nations was well established by the Spanish, British, and French long before the birth of the United States. The Natives, by the 1760s, were already accustomed to the treachery of white colonialism after almost three centuries of European contact. To make matters worse, during the lead-up to the Revolutionary War, many Indians were unsure about which side to support. A small number of Indians were already subjects of colonial governments and generally supported the rebels. Most others, however, lined up with the British or sought to remain neutral, hoping to maximize their political sovereignty and cultural integrity (Washburn 2006). After the war, the Indians found themselves politically weakened, being forced now to deal with a new colonizer whom few had supported. Many of the Indian tribes were still dangerous militarily, however, so the obvious first step for the young republic to take (in order to control the Indian population) was to continue the policy of treaty making, which it had started itself, ostensibly, in 1776.[8] Beginning with the 1778 Treaty of Fort Pitt and ending with the 1868 Treaty of Fort Laramie, the United States entered into approximately eight hundred treaties with Indian nations. However, the Senate ratified fewer than four hundred of those treaties, rendering the remainder of them void. Indeed, Richard A. Monette (1996) points out: "History illustrates that the Indian tribes believed that each treaty became effective upon the solemn exchange of rights and obligations during the negotiations with government officials rather than after the document was ratified by the U.S. Senate."

The idea of crafting treaties in a way that benefited the United States, not only in terms of land acquisition but also as a way to divide communities by racial definitions, was put into play by the late 1700s. To begin, the government put into place a program that provided financial assistance to missionaries who attempted to Christianize and educate Native Americans and convince them to adopt single-family farms. Moravian missionaries, and later their Presbyterian colleagues, served as "de facto federal emissaries to the Cherokee Nation" (Churchill 2004: 65). These Christian representatives, fully believing in the moral and intellectual superiority of "white genetics," openly favored mixed-bloods over "pure" Indians. Churchill goes on to point out:

> Predictably, this racial bias translated into a privileging of mixed-bloods in both political and material terms. . . . Such a situation was quite reasonably resented by other Cherokees, most especially those whose authority was undermined or supplanted by such external manipulation. The result, obviously intended by the United States, was the opening of deep cleavages among Cherokees that greatly weakened them in military as well as political and cultural terms, circumstances which amplified considerably the decisive advantages the United States already enjoyed in its drive to dispossess them of their property. Meanwhile, similar initiatives had been undertaken vis-à-vis the Creeks, Choctaws, Chickasaws, and others. (65)

For approximately the first thirty years of treaty making, the United States did not often include racially charged language in those documents. From 1817 on, however, there are few cases in which the treaty language did not elevate "half-" or other "mixed-blood" Indians above their "full-blooded" brethren. The United States granted large individual tracts of land to the "mixed bloods," but the "full bloods" would hold land in common. The obvious point of this policy was to highlight the intellectual superiority of individuals possessing "white blood," while demeaning full bloods as too incompetent to handle their own affairs.

The right of indigenous peoples to set their own rules and terms of tribal membership was all but abrogated by 1831, as the "notion of blood quantum" was now being openly employed as a way to determine who would (or would not) "be recognized by the United States as a 'real' Indian" (Churchill 2004: 65) In addition to the racist posturing, "the treaties often employed a virulent sexist bias, tracing descent, acknowledging authority, and bestowing land titles along decidedly patriarchal lines even (or especially) in contexts where female property ownership, political leadership, and matrilineality were the Indigenous norms" (65–66). This practice further deteriorated cultural stability by devaluing traditional practice and stripping away the ability of traditional leadership to adapt to change in a way consistent with the cultural values and beliefs of their people (66). The development of Indian treaties also served the purpose of confusing many tribal governments. Tribes, accustomed to their own "sophisticated system of checks and balances" (in effect their own legal systems), were easily tricked by the white man's new and duplicitous legalistic language (Darian-Smith 2004: 23). Additionally, while conscientiously filing away the documents "that spoke of Indian nations, Indian boundaries, and Indian political rights," the U.S. government never made any mention of the bribery, threats, and force that so often preceded treaty signings, making it a simple matter for "the President, the Congress, and the Supreme Court" to maintain the formal position that cession had been voluntary (23).

Removal, Allotment, Reorganization, and Termination

The Indian Removal Act was passed in 1830 and led to the massive forced removal of Indian tribes to the western plains. Tribes from the South, as well as the Ohio and Mississippi River valleys, lost tens of millions of acres as part of the removal (Deloria and Lytle 1983: 7). By 1870 the United States realized that most indigenous nations were no longer able to resist white aggression (as least militarily) and put an end to treaty making altogether. Henceforth, "treaties" were referred to as "agreements," as what little leverage indigenous communities had was preyed away by unilateral fiat. Not that it mattered a great deal, however, as the 1903 Supreme Court ruling in *Lone Wolf v. Hitchcock* granted Congress, using its plenary power, the right to abolish the provisions of Indian treaties altogether at its whim.

Between the years 1871 and 1928 (referred to as the allotment and assimilation period), a series of laws were developed with the overarching goal of bringing Indian peoples closer to the "white mainstream." By 1880, Indian children were being removed (often forcibly) and placed in one of over one hundred boarding or mission schools. With the stated goal of "killing the Indian" in every student, the operators of these schools set about a process of forced assimilation by not only keeping the children from their families and culture for years on end but by stripping them of their language, dress, and religious beliefs (Churchill 2004: 66; also see Canessa 2005: 134–136). Owen Lindauer (1998) points out, "Once Native Americans were confined to reservations in the 1880s, the federal government embarked on a plan to bring about their disappearance—not by military means, but by assimilating their children through education" and by attempting to "suppress their tribal traditions and identities." Burke (1996: 137) states: "This systematic removal of young people to distant boarding schools contributed to a breakdown of internal tribal relations and often destroyed the ritual succession of customs from one generation to the next." The Seven Major Crimes Act of 1885 extended U.S. criminal jurisdiction to Native territories and was quickly followed by passage of the 1887 General Allotment Act (also known as the Dawes Act). This act greatly complicated the tribes' ability to govern by carving large reservations into smaller pieces. Some areas of land were "given" to Indian families, while whites were permitted to homestead on the reminder. Initially, the act called for allotments to be held in trust by the United States for individual Indians for a period of twenty-five years. After completing the "allotment" process, the federal government would identify lands to be held in common by the affected tribe and arrange for the cession of the remaining lands as "surplus" lands. This process resulted in the loss of approximately 100 million acres of tribal land between 1887 and 1934, which represented the great bulk of the approximately 150 million acres formally controlled by the indigenous population (Darian-Smith 2004: 43; Churchill 2004: 66). In addition, a large number of Indians "sold" their land, either because of impoverishment or because it was taken away for nonpayment of taxes (a concept foreign to many indigenous peoples, as was the concept of individual land ownership). As a result, much land within reservations is not owned by Native Americans, which causes confusion today about where tribal jurisdiction ends and local authority begins.

Moreover, the General Allotment Act was "expressly intended to dissolve the collective relationship to land that was the fundament of traditional cultures by imposing the allegedly superior Anglo-Saxon system of individuated property ownership" (Churchill 2004: 66; also see Deloria and Lytle 1983: 10). This confusing act was amended in 1891 and again in 1906 (the Burke Act), with the secretary of the interior granted "almost dictatorial powers" in overseeing the allotment process (Deloria and Lytle 1983: 10). The General Allotment Act was not merely crafted as a way to alienate Indians from their land (and, more importantly, their sacred landscape) but also was the vehicle used for the introduction of identity legislation, the formal development of tribal rolls in order to determine who was and was not eligible to receive allotments. Despite the fact that Indian tribes had traditionally accepted, and incorporated within their communities, outside individuals and groups (including other Indians, as well as Europeans and Africans) without regard to racial makeup, the blatantly racial notion of blood quantum was devised, now legally conceptualized, and implemented in a way that clearly distinguished Indian from non-Indian.

In 1924 a "cleanup" bill was passed in Congress that granted citizenship to all Indians not already naturalized. The stage seemed to be set for the "final absorption of Native America" when "fate intervened" (Churchill 2004: 69). Fate, as it turned out, was the discovery that the worthless tracts of land left to the Indians during the allotment process were actually some of the most mineral-rich territory in the world. Realizing the importance of maintaining control over these lands, the government's economic planners convened a committee of business and academic experts in 1925 to determine their next move. The most profitable way to approach this issue, it was determined, was to place these lands into perpetual trust status (Churchill 2004: 69; Darian-Smith 2004: 42).

The harm done by the allotment policy and the total lack of benefits to Indian tribes and people was well understood. The policy was effectively repudiated by a 1928 study conducted by Lewis Meriam and associates. Authorized by the secretary of the interior, the Meriam Report, when combined with the aforementioned 1925 committee report, was largely responsible for the development of the Indian Reorganization Act (IRA) of 1934 (Deloria and Lytle 1983: 12–13; O'Brien 1989: 82). The IRA (also known as the Wheeler-Howard Act) authorized the secretary of the interior to restore the remaining "surplus" lands to tribal ownership, to reacquire interests in land both inside and outside reservation boundaries, and to hold that land in trust. The acquired lands would be held under federal title for the use of American Indian tribes. The stated purpose of the act was to reacquire the land sold to individuals during the allotment period and reestablish Indian people with distinct tribal communities and governments. The IRA, however, also led to the near destruction of traditional Native government because it designated "federally designed tribal councils" that were "meant to serve as the medium for long-term administration of the newly conceived internal colonial domain" (Churchill 2004: 69).

The IRA was conceived of, and sold to Indian tribes and others, as a democratic policy, but tribal votes to accept or reject IRA provisions proved problematic. For example, although nearly two-thirds (181) of recognized tribes voted in favor of the act, one-third (77) rejected the act, and some who accepted it refused to organize under its guidelines (Deloria and Lytle 1983: 14–15). Additionally, Churchill (2004: 69–70) points out that "the record reveals that Bureau of Indian Affairs (BIA) field representatives obtained favorable results by presenting skewed or patently false information to voters in a number of instances, flatly rigging the results in others."[9] And although on the surface each reservation "functioned on the basis of its own 'tribal constitution,' the reality is that these 'founding' documents were essentially boilerplate contraptions resembling corporate charters hammered out on an assembly-line basis by Bureau personnel" (69–70). Furthermore, the insertion of the secretarial approval clause "empowers the secretary of the interior to approve or veto new tribal laws, to overrule certain tribal council actions, to call elections and settle election disputes, to oversee the tribes' economic affairs, to review the taxation of nonmembers, and to approve the hiring of legal counsel" (O'Brien 1989: 83). In reality, this clause permitted the federal government, through the BIA, to dominate the newly formed tribal councils. The incorporation of membership requirements into the tribal constitutions that called for a minimum blood quantum further deteriorated tribal sovereignty. Most tribal rules required members to be one-fourth Indian, and all looked to biological determination as the prevailing trait of Indian identity.

> That there was no noteworthy resistance among Native supporters of the IRA to this conspicuous usurpation of Indigenous tradition is unsurprising, given that they were all but invariably drawn from the ranks of those indoctrinated in the boarding schools to see themselves in racial rather than national, political, or cultural terms. . . . The government could increasingly rely upon Indians themselves to enforce its race codes for it. Indeed, whenever the existence of the latter has been made a point of contention, Washington has been able to lay the onus of responsibility directly at the feet of the IRA governments it not only conceived and installed, but which remain utterly and perpetually dependent upon federal patronage for their base funding and whatever limited authority they might wield. They, in turn, defend such negation of Indigenous sovereignty in the name of maintaining it. A more perfect shell game is impossible to imagine. (Churchill 2004: 70)

The ability of the United States to regulate Native identity by policy implementation represented the crowning achievement of Indian legislation to this point in history. After dispossessing Indians of their land and with it their ability to sustain themselves, the government was now in a position to demand conformity from the indigenous leadership. Indeed, Indian leaders were henceforth compelled to negotiate the terms of their coexistence with a federal body that wanted nothing more than to starve them into submission and then force them into extinction. The "disciplinary power" wrested over American Indians by the BIA dovetails with the example of the Australian aborigines provided by John Gledhill (1994: 147). In discussing a theory proposed by Barry Morris (1989), Gledhill states:

> The basic principles which Morris derives from Foucault are that disciplinary power requires the creation of a body of knowledge about the subject group. The Aborigines were turned into an object of specialist knowledge (which has taken various forms historically). Others thereby came to become dispensers of truth about the needs and requirements of Aborigines, and the Aborigines themselves were increasingly called upon to fulfill the constructions of their identity created by those in authority over them. They thus lost control over their communal identity (or more precisely, their ability to define themselves). (1994: 147)

That is precisely the purpose for which the BIA was devised. The Native voice has been silenced, except in cases in which the BIA allows it to be heard. The Indian "experts" are not the Indians but the BIA, to whom Congress turns when Indian issues surface. The Native voice is likewise largely drowned out by the federal recognition process, which relies on cultural anthropologists, linguists, archaeologists, and other credentialed experts in determining whether or not a petitioning group is authentic or not.

By 1949, the United States had grown weary of dealing with the "Indian problem" and the Hoover Commission was recommending the "complete integration of Indians into white society" (Pevar 2002: 11). When Dwight Eisenhower took over as president in 1953, the Hoover recommendations were formally acted on, and federal Indian policy entered what would become known as the Termination Era. House Concurrent Resolution No. 108 was adopted in 1953 and called for the rapid removal of Indian benefits and services, such as health and educational services. Additionally, land ownership rights would be removed, state judicial authority would be imposed, and Indians would lose state tax exemption (Pevar 2002: 11; AILTP 1993: 13). During the next ten years, 109 tribes had their trust relationship with the United States terminated, their reservations eliminated, and full jurisdiction over the land and people was granted to the states where the former tribes were located. Public Law 83–280 (PL 280) was also approved in 1953, and although most terminated tribes were later reinstated, PL 280 continues to apply to a large number of tribes. The 1956 relocation program, aimed at further "assimilating" Indians, offered work training and "housing assistance to Indians who would leave the reservation for urban areas" (Pevar 2002: 12). Many of the individuals who participated in this program, however, returned to the reservations disillusioned about their opportunities in the unfamiliar city settings.

In summary, from the early 1800s to the early 1960s, the U.S. government crafted a series of policies designed to eliminate the Indian problem through legislative fiat. The failure of the earlier policies, some of which took the form of outright genocide, culminated in the overt attempt at removal through termination. Indeed, as we can see, Indian legislation became much more than simply a body of laws used to justify control over every aspect of Indian life. It has produced a "conceptual framework that governs ways of thinking about Native identity. . . . Its overarching nature as a discourse of classification and regulation . . . has produced the subjects it purports to control, and . . . has therefore indelibly ordered how Native people think of things 'Indian'" (Lawrence 2004: 25). I do not mean to suggest that Native peoples have "blindly internalized colonial frameworks," but that the development of identity legislation has produced a system within which Native peoples must engage the government (utilizing the terms and rules defined by the colonizer) as part of their struggle against the institution itself (Lawrence 2004: 25; see also Gledhill 1994: 20–21). In other words, "the colonial discourse embedded in identity legislation has even invaded how resistance is conceptualized" (Lawrence 2004: 25).

Self-Determination

This discussion, so far, has focused on the development of specific laws and policies designed by the United States to disenfranchise and disempower its indigenous population. The overarching policy of subjugating, if not eliminating, Indian peoples was accomplished through various means, including the wholesale theft of indigenous land, resource plundering, the marginalization of traditional forms of tribal leadership, the forced removal of Indian children from their communities, attacks on indigenous spiritual and ceremonial life, starvation tactics, and the use of violence (as well as threats to use violence) in enforcing policy. These methods were given a patina of legality throughout the process and sold to the public as just and fair. Every atrocity committed against Native peoples was promoted as "for their own good," and every policy failure was attributed to the incompetence of the Indians. Along the way, "Indians" were invented, defined, and expected to live up to the legal standards devised for them. Henceforth, Native people would need to incorporate into their personal and group identity-building process a new element: legal identity.

The construction of Indian policy and Indian law, however, took a decidedly different turn near the end of the 1960s. This tumultuous decade saw advancements in civil rights legislation applicable to minorities, women, and the socially disadvantaged in general. For their part, Native Americans drew the public's attention to Indian issues through the use of highly organized protests and demonstrations, not the least of which was the takeover of Alcatraz Island in 1969. Indeed, the takeover of Alcatraz was perhaps the most successful Indian protest action of the twentieth century, fueling the rise of modern Native American activism. The creation of the Alcatraz–Red Power Movement (ARPM) led to a decade that witnessed over seventy planned Indian occupations of federal facilities. These occupations brought Indian rights issues to the attention of the federal government, the American public, and (perhaps more importantly) Native peoples themselves, as Indians began to change the way they viewed Indian cultures and their inherent rights of self-determination. Russell Means (Oglala Lakota), an early and influential American Indian Movement (AIM) leader, states: "Before AIM, Indians were dispirited, defeated and culturally dissolving. People were ashamed to be Indian. You didn't see the young people wearing braids or chokers or ribbon shirts in those days. Hell, I didn't wear 'em. People didn't Sun Dance, they didn't sweat, they were losing their languages" (Churchill 2003).

The takeovers and protests succeeded in getting the federal government to end its policy of termination and adopt an official policy of Indian self-determination. From 1968 to 1982, the government entered what would be termed the Indian Self-Determination Era. During this time span, the government passed a number of laws aimed at improving Indian welfare. From 1970 to 1971 alone, Congress passed fifty-two legislative proposals on behalf of American Indians to support tribal self-rule. Notable acts included the passage of the Indian Civil Rights Act (1968), the Indian Finance Act (1974), and the Indian Self-Determination and Education Assistance Act (ISDEA, 1975), which began phasing out the role of the BIA in overseeing all aspects of Indian affairs. The Indian Child Welfare Act and the American Indian Religious Freedom Act both passed in 1978.

The Indian Self-Governance Era began in 1982 and continues through the present. Tribal tax status, Indian mineral development, Indian gaming, and Indian law enforcement have been addressed during this era. The 1990 Native American Graves Protection and Repatriation Act (NAGPRA) requires consultation with affiliated tribes regarding the handling and display of human remains and funerary objects, as well as the repatriation of those objects under appropriate conditions. In 1994, the ISDEA was amended to authorize a self-governance demonstration program in Indian Health Services (IHS) to enable selected tribes to explore self-determination in management of health delivery initiatives. Whether this new round of laws and policies will have a positive impact on Indian identity, or indeed Indian survival, is a question that cannot yet be answered. However, recent policies that have been purposely crafted to limit tribal sovereignty and regulate tribal membership qualifications (such as have been forced upon the Tigua and others) indicate that the "new" policy is little more than "old" policy in a slightly altered guise.

Conclusion

As discussed above, identity is a very complex and nuanced notion. Although few people give much thought to their own identity, it plays a major role in how an individual's life unfolds. Indeed, the pervasive power of identity and the various ways identity is perceived within popular discourse can assist or, conversely, socially handicap people from birth, simply because they were born rich, poor, a member of the majority race, or a member of one of the minority races. It is not simply that people have differing opportunities to "succeed" but that their sense of personal worth is achieved through their perception of their own social standing, both as an individual and as a member of a group. The invention of identity markers has allowed the United States to create and impose powerfully pervasive and stereotypical portraits that have become socially engrained within the public psyche. By attaching value to particular forms of dress, language, behavior, gender, level of education, race, religious beliefs, and so on, the government found it simple to rank certain identity markers on a sliding scale of "proper" to "improper" or, more often than not, "high class" to "low class." Although this "classificatory system" is often confusing and contradictory, the vast majority of Americans ascribe to its dictates. Indigenous peoples, occupying a position on the lower end of the power relationship, have been traditionally ranked among the lowest of the low. The prevailing dominant attitude (up to the late 1960s) encouraged all ethnic minorities (except blacks) to be "hopeful" that they would eventually be absorbed into the mainstream. In regard to Indian identity, G. P. Castile (1996: 744) states that

> the promise was one of eventual equality through assimilation. It is not surprising that in such a market many made the trade, and by the 1920s, when the value of Indian identity was at an all-time low, there were few claiming to be Indians—only 250,000 counted by the government.

The "promise" of "equality through assimilation" was of little value to most Native peoples, however, as the discourse relevant to Indian peoples had already done its damage. Furthermore, the last thing many indigenous individuals wanted was to embrace the values and beliefs of the white majority. There were those who "made the trade," but many (such as the Tigua "core") refused to consider assimilation, even though, historically, the indigenous population of the United States was ranked at or below the level of African Americans (and other blacks), Mexicans, Asians, indeed all ethnic and racial groupings. The discrimination and racism practiced against Native American Indian people were so brutal and socially accepted in some geographic areas that many Indians (including many Tigua people) were forced to purposely pass themselves off as something else, in most cases as "Mexicans." As one Tigua respondent tells me, at that time (up to the 1950s or so), "You could either be a live Mexican or a dead Indian." The sense of fear that led tribal members to deny their Indian heritage was aided by a popular discourse that degraded "dirty" Indians as uncivilized, wild, barbaric, and lacking in "culture." These derogatory stereotypes have been perpetuated by some up to recent times. Even as late as the 1960s, there were Tigua tribal members who hid from their identity: "There are still some people that are Indian people that used to deny being Indians or were ashamed to be Indians. I remember some of them, I won't mention names, but I used to go to school with them. They use to degrade us, call us derogatory names" (José). Castile points out:

> In most of American history, barring the occasional "noble savage," these reprocessed "images" were almost entirely negative. . . . To define Indians as cruel, ignorant savages without civilization served a practical purpose for the larger society. Cotton Mather was able to observe, of the destruction of the Pequots, that "these barbarians were dismissed from a world that was burdened with them." . . . Raw conquest of these people, with subsequent expulsion from their lands, might otherwise seem unjustified; it eases the collective conscience if they had it coming. (1996: 743)

The danger in the creation and perpetuation of these kinds of myths is that, eventually, they become entrenched elements within a classificatory system that produces "a way of thinking . . . a grammar . . . which embeds itself in every attempt to change it" (Lawrence 2004: 25). The creation of indigenous subjects, through legislative means and through the dissemination of popular discourse, reduces indigenous people's identities to measurable traits. Identity is measured against blood percentages, biological phenotype, and degree of "traditional" dress and behavior. Native peoples have been systematically removed from their former identities and reinvented as Indians (41). That the poor qualities popularly associated with Indianness drove a large number of individual Indians to reject their true identity should come as no real surprise. Indeed, it is perhaps more surprising that more did not follow the path of least resistance.

At issue here is not only the marginalization of identity but the confusion of identity that is forced through the creation of arbitrary legal, biological, and social identity markers. The perpetuation of this classification system is reinforced not only through a discourse that assigns value to particular traits or behaviors, or groups of traits and behaviors, but also through the use of "scientific" myth that validates these markers. Researchers invent and conduct "unbiased" tests, such as Samuel Morton's (in)famous 1820s skull measurements, or they purport to measure other "quantifiable" criteria such as "intelligence," and then popularize as "scientific fact" the notion that the racial superiority of the dominant culture has been proven. Of course, the will of God is invoked as rationalization for racial stratification, as well, for He must have created people differently (some "better" than others) for some reason. The values of the dominant culture are promoted as the proper values, and this discourse is further legitimized by the creation of laws that ensure and enforce their adherence. Moreover, the moral and ethical beliefs of the "other" are called into question and portrayed as backward or barbaric. Particular cultural practices, such as kinship rules that allow bigamy, are outlawed as immoral, and behaviors such as homosexuality are deemed sinful. In short, the power of the U.S. government to create public policy, control discourse, and make laws, allows it to not only create a public sense of what identity is but also to create, control, and shape the parameters of identity within the system of laws. This power goes beyond the ability of the government to simply legislate morality at will, particularly as it applies to American Indians. Today, American Indian peoples are forced to behave in certain ways for certain periods of time (see Chapter Four for a detailed discussion), and their authenticity is called into question (or outright rejected) if they do not meet the standards of cultural behavior put forth by the dominant society.

This discussion of law, discourse, and perceptions of Indianness helps to shape the remaining chapters of this book. Each of these issues plays an important role as I explore the process of government recognition and the power of the United States to dictate the parameters of sovereignty and self-determination to an extent that the meanings of these terms have become obsolete. As my exploration of the Tigua continues, I show that the government has not been content to simply steal from and marginalize the Ysleta del Sur Pueblo but has also used its position of power to extract a recognition deal with the tribe that postpones, but ultimately leads to legalized termination.

CHAPTER FOUR

State and Federal Recognition

Introduction

Unlike their Pueblo brethren in New Mexico and Arizona, the Tigua have spent much of the past three hundred years engulfed in a legal quagmire, both in regard to their status as Indians as well as the legal boundaries of their landholdings. Their current status as American Indians recognized by the federal government, and the unusual legal predicaments that they have long experienced, are largely the result of a nearly unfathomable series of historical occurrences, many of which transpired without their notice or care. To understand why and how the Tigua came to be who they are as a people, it is important to briefly explore the history of their geographic location in West Texas.

Their location is important not only because of the physical features found in the region, but also because of the legal features associated with the development of the United States as an expanding nation and the creation of Texas as a state. Like many indigenous groups who have maintained a traditional lifestyle while the outside world slowly surrounded them, the Tigua wanted nothing more than to simply be left alone. Like countless others before and after them, the Tigua discovered that the encroachment of the West and the laying down of borders where none existed before would force them to confront their very existence as a people. Victims of circumstance and place, the Tigua have emerged as survivors, but they are not unscathed. The tribe's situation today, as a "legally ambiguous" tribe unable to exert their sovereign rights of self-determination, is the end result of, more than anything else, simple bad luck.

The Tigua of Ysleta del Sur Pueblo were "given" their land in 1751 when Charles V, then king of Spain, granted them a section of land that was one league in each direction from the church. These grants, which were likewise made to the other pueblos in what is today the state of New Mexico, encompassed approximately 17,000 acres, or 36 square miles (Thick 2005; Eickhoff 1996: 9; Houser 1979: 340). By making land grants, Spain was attempting to place traditional land "ownership" rights within the legal framework of the dominant structure. Each pueblo was

103

to be viewed as an independent, sovereign government, and authority would rest within each individual pueblo (Schulze 2001: 18–19). Charles gave each of the pueblo governors a cane that would be an outward symbol of his authority, which was in addition to the written documents that were on file with the Spanish government (Thick 2005). These canes were modeled after the canes used by the viceroy in Mexico, the various Spanish governors, and the court officials in Spain. Forty years later, the Recopilación de las Leyes de los Reynos de las Indias was issued, stating that "the Indian grants, their rivers, and other water sources could not be sold or taken away from them" (Eickhoff 1996: 70–71). Further laws issued in 1811 prohibited the sale of Indian lands. As we will see, however, the laws and treaty promises that were made became worthless to the Tigua (see Eickhoff 1996).

Shortly after the issuance of these land grants, France "sold" the United States a vast reach of land, which extended into the northeastern corner of the future New Mexico. This sale, known as the Louisiana Purchase (1803), led to a dispute between the United States and Spain over the boundaries of the area the United States had "bought." According to the Spanish, Louisiana consisted roughly of the west bank of the Mississippi River and the city of New Orleans. The United States, however, claimed that the border of its purchase stretched all the way to the Rio Grande and the Rocky Mountains, a claim unacceptable to Spain, as it would mean the loss of Texas and half of New Mexico, both Spanish colonies. The dispute was settled in 1819 with the signing of the Adams-Onís Treaty, which renounced any claim of the United States to Texas. "It fixed the western boundary of the Louisiana Purchase as beginning at the mouth of the Sabine River and running along its south and west bank to the thirty-second parallel and then directly north to the Red River" (McKeehan 2001).

Texas Becomes a State: A Brief History

The 1810–1821 Mexican War of Independence brought Mexico its freedom and removed Spain from the picture, but the United States, Mexico, and Texas still could not agree on the boundaries of the soon-to-be state. The good news for the Tigua was that when Mexico won its independence from Spain in 1821, the new government reaffirmed the laws and the protection of Indian rights and lands "granted" by the Spanish in 1751. The bad news was that although the Constitution of 1824 gave

Mexico a republican form of government, it failed to define the rights of the states within the republic, including Texas (Barker and Pohl 2001; O'Neal 1969: 61–62). This oversight opened the door to later legal maneuverings that created problems for the Tigua. The independence of Mexico also allowed a reopening of the controversy regarding the border with Texas, as the United States claimed that the Sabine and Neches Rivers had been switched on maps, which meant a loss of land for the United States (Block 1976: 43; experts.about.com/e/a/ad/adams-on istreaty.htm, 2006).

The new Republic of Texas (1836) inflamed the controversy by claiming borders that encompassed all the present state of Texas, as well as parts of present-day New Mexico, Oklahoma, Kansas, Colorado, and Wyoming. Additionally, the Cuevas-Smith Treaty signed between Mexico and Texas in 1845 guaranteed Texan independence, but only so long as it remained a separate republic (Silverthorne 2003). Texas preferred to align with either Great Britain or the United States, but the U.S. Congress did not want to abrogate its treaty agreements with Mexico and was embroiled in debate about admission of slave states to the Union. Finally, in 1845, President John Tyler used the fear of British encroachment to swing the offer of annexation to Texas, even though it was certain to lead to a war with Mexico. Texas accepted, becoming the twenty-eighth state of the United States (Barker 1935; Crapol 1997).

The annexation of Texas, as expected, led to the Mexican-American War (1846–1848). Mexico had continued to refuse recognition of Texas as a legitimate state after the 1836 Texas Revolution, considering the state to be "a breakaway province" (Lee 2005). However, nearly a decade had passed since Texas had declared its independence from Mexico, and the expansionist United States was not about to give Texas back. Annexation was beneficial to both Texas and the United States: Texas was in a difficult position following independence, with a weak government, little industry, and minimal infrastructure (Callicott et al. 2006: 29). After Texas was admitted to the Union and the Mexican-American War ended, the Treaty of Guadalupe Hidalgo (1848) assigned the United States all territories east of the Rio Grande (today known as the American Southwest) in exchange for an end to hostilities, the removal of U.S. troops from Mexico City, $15 million cash to Mexico, plus the assumption of slightly more than $3 million in outstanding Mexican debts. The treaty also provided recognition and the promise of protection to individuals owning private property acquired under Spanish and Mexican laws, including the land grants to the Indians. The exact boundary with Texas remained uncertain, and Texas initially claimed all land north of the Rio Grande (an area that extended far westward into territory claimed by the United States) but later agreed to the present boundaries (Eickhoff 1996: 71; Pletcher 2001; Minter 1976: 3).

The annexation of Texas to the United States, along with U.S. gain of territory from the Treaty of Guadalupe Hidalgo, created more problems between North and South regarding the extension of slavery into the territories. The North wanted to stand by the proposal made in the Wilmot Proviso, which excluded slavery from all the lands acquired from Mexico (Fuller 1935: 235). Other issues, such as questions about the slave trade and the fugitive slave laws, had led many to conclude that the southern states might just withdraw from the Union altogether. When California sought admittance to the Union as a free state in 1849, the issue threatened to erupt into civil war. A series of measures designed to end the controversy (put forward as a single omnibus compromise bill) failed. The measures included the admission of California as a free state, the organization of New Mexico and Utah territories without mention of slavery, the prohibition of the slave trade in the District of Columbia, a more stringent fugitive slave law, and the settlement of Texas boundary claims by federal payment of $10 million on the debt contracted by the Republic of Texas. After long debates and failure to pass the omnibus bill, Congress passed the measures as separate bills in September, which would collectively become known as the Compromise of 1850 (Griffin 2001; Stegmaier 1996: 135).

Meanwhile, many people, North and South, hailed the 1850 compromise as a final resolution to the question of slavery in the territories. However, the issue reemerged in 1854 with the Kansas-Nebraska Act, when proslavery congressmen protested having a free territory (Kansas) west of Missouri. The Missouri Compromise of 1820, which barred slavery from both Kansas and Nebraska, had infuriated Missourians, who had believed that Kansas would be a slave state. Indeed, the Kansas-Nebraska Act flatly contradicted the provisions of the Missouri Compromise, and an amendment had to be added that specifically repealed that compromise (Hurd 2004). Congress debated this aspect of the bill for three months but in the end saw it adopted.

This series of events, no doubt unnoticed by most members of the Tigua community, would soon lead to grave consequences for the Ysleta del Sur Pueblo. In 1861 the conflict between the free states, slave states, and the federal government erupted into the Civil War. Texas seceded from the Union to join the Confederacy, along with ten southern states, and their inclusion in the Confederate States of America (under President Jefferson Davis) meant that the Tigua were no longer a part of the United States.[1] The previous events, having led to the creation of the present-day Texas boundaries, separated the Tigua from their New Mexican relatives. In 1864, while Texas was in the Confederacy, Abraham Lincoln issued the famous "Lincoln canes" to the governors of the New Mexican Pueblos. These canes acknowledged the sovereignty of the pueblos and were patterned after those provided by Charles V. Along with the canes, Lincoln extended land patents to all the pueblos, which made their inhabitants the only Indians to hold fee simple title to their own lands (Eickhoff 1996: 72; Sando 1998: 112–113; Wright 1993: 15). The Tigua, of course, were left out of this gesture.

The Civil War ended in 1865, and Texas was readmitted into the Union. Unfortunately for the Tigua, when Texas had become a state in 1845, it negotiated a deal whereby it entered the Union retaining its public lands, like the original thirteen colonies (a fact unique among western states). The lack of a federal presence meant that, although Congress had exclusive jurisdiction over Indian affairs under the Constitution, the federal government could not establish reservations for Indians in Texas as it did in other areas of the American West (Dickerson 2001). However, the 1848 Treaty of Guadalupe Hidalgo, executed between the United States and Mexico, had obligated the United States to protect and recognize the land rights of Mexican citizens in the territory ceded to the United States. Indeed, section 6 of the treaty bound the United States to recognize the full rights, property, and other interests of Mexican citizens, and the Mexican government had declared Indians to be citizens. At the time of that treaty, the 1751 grant to the Ysleta del Sur Pueblo was located in an area claimed by Texas, Mexico, and the United States. In 1850, when the United States and Texas signed the compact setting the present boundaries of Texas, the United States, though ceding the Ysleta grant portion of the state to Texas, nonetheless inventoried the Ysleta Pueblo in Texas as one of the pueblo tribes under federal control and jurisdiction (Minter 1976: 3; Houser 1979: 340; Schulze 2001: 19). However, because Texas public land was retained by the state (which felt no responsibility for the Indians who were on that land) and the federal government believed that it could not solve the Indian problem without having land to set aside for relocation and settlement purposes, the Tigua (and other Texas Indians) were left in a sort of legal limbo (Mintor 1969: 12).

In 1854 Texas did authorize the United States to set aside land for two Indian reservations, but difficulties arose between the whites and the Indians, and, as a result, most Texas Indians were transferred to federal reservations out of state (Minter 1969: 12). Unlike most other Texas tribes during the course of the nineteenth century, the Tigua managed to avoid removal by helping defend El Paso against Apache and Comanche attacks while continuing to farm their lands. Although they avoided expulsion, by the end of the century the Tigua had lost most of their land and, because they lacked federal status and protections, became an essentially landless people, working as laborers on farms they had once owned.

Not Extinct

By the early 1900s, the Tigua had been visited by a number of "salvage" ethnologists who, frankly, considered them to be near their cultural end. Researchers such as J. Bourke, Ten Kate (who stole sacred tribal property), A. F. Bandelier, James Moody, and Jesse Walter Fewkes of the Smithsonian Institution each concluded that the Tigua were all but "Mexicanized," retaining only a handful of traditional pueblo practices (Schulze 2001: 21). Fewkes (1902: 58) found the Tigua had "practically become 'Mexicanized' and survivals of their old pueblo life have . . . long since lost their meaning." Living on the border, surrounded by Mexican society, and lacking a federal reservation, the Ysleta del Sur community clearly had adopted certain cultural practices from the Hispanic population. Most spoke Spanish, dressed in Mexican-style clothing, and lived in adobe dwellings. Although Fewkes (1902: 58) found the Tigua "almost indistinguishable from the surrounding society," he also reported that they had maintained significant cultural customs. For example, the Tigua still lived in El Barrio de los Indios near the Ysleta Mission, calling their community by the Tiwa name, *Chiawipia*; they still faithfully practiced religious ceremonials containing elements of both indigenous and Catholic practices and beliefs; they continued to worship St. Anthony as their patron saint; approximately twenty-five individuals still spoke Tiwa, and he noted that many more could understand but not speak the language; group members performed ceremonial dances, or *bailes*, in front of the church on the various saints' days; the Tigua performed a mask dance referred to by the Tiwa name *newajilra*, or *baile de tortuga* (for the turtle shell rattles used), a rattle dance (*Shiafuara*), and the "red pigment dance," among others; and the Tigua still remembered the *Kufura*, or scalp dance, though after the cessation of warfare they ceased to perform the dance for obvious reasons (Fewkes 1902: 62–69).

Additionally, the Tigua "wore face paint and buffalo skin masks of red and yellow and used the ancient tribal drum and gourd rattles to maintain a beat" (Minter 1976: 5). Other similarities between the Tigua and the New Mexican Pueblos included an emergence story related to origins in a *Shipapu* (an ancestral opening into the earth in a lake) and a matrilineal descent system (Fewkes 1902: 71). Moreover, Fewkes's publication of the Tigua Compact of 1895 (see Chapter One) was vital to the Tigua's later recognition efforts. Indeed, the fact that the Spanish had attempted to alter indigenous political organization into more formalized structures and that the Tigua had maintained this (dual) structure over the centuries would (in part) provide concrete evidence that they were still a viable culture. Overall, however, this early research contributed to the misperception that the Tigua had become "extinct" after the turn of the century. Nothing could have been further from the truth.

By the beginning of the twentieth century, the Tigua settlement at Ysleta had become the "last vestige of the once thriving Indian population in El Paso" (Schulze 2001: 21). Ysleta offered the only refuge for those seeking to maintain some semblance of tribal existence. "It seemed that the various Indian groups of the area—Piros, Sumas, Mansos, and Tigua—had widely intermarried and amalgamated into the Tigua community at Ysleta. After 1910 the Mexican Revolution apparently disrupted the communities on the Mexican side to such an extent that the refugees fled to the United States," with many joining the Tigua (Minter 1969: 11). Nicholas P. Houser (1979: 337) points out: "The Piro tribe of Senecu ceased to exist as an organization around the first decade of the twentieth century," and descendants of the Piro tribes of Senecu (near Juarez) and Socorro, as well as the Manso, "can still be identified within the El Paso–Juarez area." Tigua oral history is replete with stories connecting themselves with these other tribes, and one Tigua Elder still has possession of the original Piro drum (which he calls the brother of the Tigua drum). In a discussion about the Piro, Diego states:

Now, one side of the river, on the Mexican side, there was a little tribe called the Piro, the Piro tribe, and they were not a Mexican tribe, it was an American tribe. They met the Tigua and got together with the Tigua and used to cross the river and join in when the Tigua had their feast in Ysleta. The Piros came to visit and when the Piro had a feast the Tigua would join them. Some of the people intermarried; some of the Tigua women marry Piro men and some of the Piro women married Tigua men. So, we had part of the Tigua blood in our tribe and part of the Piro. The Piro, as time went on, disappeared, and they don't exist anymore, as we know. The people live, but they don't claim as a tribe anymore.

Around the old mission complex, Tigua elders maintained traditions that enhanced Indian community and identity. The Tigua maintained their cultural distinctness by clearly delineating tribal membership, although the ethnic boundaries of the village were constantly changing. Although the aboriginal language was largely forgotten, there were still some around, even in the late 1960s, who could converse in Tiwa. As José points out, "Many of, during the early 1960s or early 1970s, we didn't speak much of the Tiwa language. Even our fathers and grandfathers, they didn't speak much of it. Only the older ones, in their sixties or seventies, they understood it and they spoke it. I remember my Father spoke a few words only." Even today, many older tribal members remember hearing the language spoken, but after three hundred years of submersion within a Spanish- and later English-speaking environment, most tribal members drifted away from their mother tongue.

The loss of language skills did not prevent the Tigua from maintaining traditional practices, however, as they adapted to changing cultural conditions. To determine membership, the Tigua recognized ancestry and blood quantum to some degree but placed more emphasis on ceremonial participation. To be Tigua, individuals had to respect the power of the ancient tribal drum and also had to show respect for St. Anthony. It was essential that Tigua participate in the St. Anthony's Day ceremonies and other saints' day celebrations. Young members learned traditional Tigua ritual chants and dances and performed them during ceremonies (Houser 1979: 337; Mintor 1969: 12; Miller 2004: 221). Additionally, their isolation from other Indian communities was embraced as a strength rather than a weakness. "One of our big advantages over the other pueblos is that we have always been surrounded by white people. We learned to take the criticism of the white people and lived through all of that. We fight back and still keep our own customs" (Hector).

By the early 1960s, there were approximately 166 people living in thirty-two households in the Tigua community. Of these, a "core" group of approximately twenty families lived near the Ysleta church and the *tuh-lah*. Overall, this core group was "less integrated into mainstream culture, was more likely to be unemployed and poor, and had chosen to emphasize a Tigua identity over others or, in the alternative, was unable to pass as Mexican in the surrounding city" (Miller 2004: 221). Except for on special occasions, however, few outside visitors could distinguish the Tigua from the surrounding Mexican Americans, whom the Tigua called *vecinos*, or neighbors. The Tigua had "no trouble distinguishing between themselves and the *vecinos*, however, and the Mexican Americans had no trouble distinguishing either" (222). In the late 1950s the town of Ysleta was annexed by the city of El Paso, and the Tigua suddenly had to pay property taxes. Too impoverished to pay these taxes, they soon faced foreclosure proceedings on their property. After surviving (in relative obscurity) for over three hundred years "with no outside aid," the tribe now had their backs to the wall and would have to obtain outside assistance to continue surviving as a community (219).

Government Acknowledgment of Indians

In the United States, the government has developed a system whereby Native culture is (in essence) "means tested" to determine whether it is "viable" or (at least as far as the government is concerned) "dead." Any group that fails to pass the test, known as the Federal Acknowledgment Process (FAP), is deemed inauthentic and is considered extinct. Although a rejected group can continue to practice its "traditional culture," a failed FAP application does convey the idea that the petitioning group is "acting fraudulently." This process raises several fundamental issues that call into question the concept of culture itself. In order to develop legal terms, the abstract (culture) must be made concrete somehow; there must be a way to quantify and measure this unmeasureable notion. The government has devised a number of strategies to help it bridge this conceptual chasm, using a combination of methodological techniques, including historical documentation, ethnohistory, prehistory (largely archaeological findings), and present-day ethnography. In essence, the government sets a "cultural baseline" and proceeds from that point in its bid to "measure" the various ways in which a particular culture has changed. Diana Loren and Emily Stovel (1997) make the following observation:

Unwittingly or not, archaeological units of study facilitate nation-states in the definition of indigenous groups as remnants of the past, imbued with characteristics that can be acted upon toward assimilation or ignored all together. The characterization of ethnic identity in the past formalizes differences, solidifies the somewhat ethereal and changing nature of self-definition outside of historical context, making identity an object that can be captured by science and changed by politics.

The flawed logic behind the development of these measures of cultural change aside, the U.S. government has, indeed, devised a system not only for measuring change but also for determining at what point change results in cultural extinction. The criteria for groups petitioning for recognition through the FAP, for example, include the following:

- The petitioning group must have been "identified as an American Indian entity on a substantially continuous basis since 1900."
- The petitioning group must "comprise a distinct community that has existed as a community from historical times until the present."
- The petitioner must show that it "has maintained political influence or authority over its members as an autonomous entity from historical times until the present."
- It must also submit its group's present governing document, including its membership criteria, and its membership must consist "of individuals who descend from a historical Indian tribe or from historical Indian tribes which combined and functioned as a single autonomous political entity."

As one can easily imagine, the process involved in proving cultural viability is a nightmare for petitioning groups. The FAP guidelines are riddled with subjective terminology such as "substantial," "distinct," "autonomous," "historical," "influence," and many more. Indeed, the former Branch of Acknowledgment and Research (BAR) chief listed "thirty-five words or phrases requiring interpretation, while Assistant Secretary Kevin Gover later admitted the entire endeavor was inherently subjective" (Miller 2004: 63). How, for example, does a tribe "prove" that they have been "identified" as a "distinct" Indian "entity" on a "substantially" continuous basis since 1900? The FAP process was initially designed in 1978 to take under three years to complete, yet today ten years is the average, and twenty years is not uncommon. The cost of the process for petitioning tribes ranges from a low of $50,000 to a high of over

$1 million, for a process that retired former branch head Bud Shapard, testifying before Congress, referred to as a "monster" of his own creation: "After 14 years of trying to make the regs which I drafted work, I must conclude that they are fatally flawed and unworkable. The convoluted administrative process cannot be revised, modified, or altered in any way that will make them work" (54).

Particularly infuriating to petitioning tribes, however, is not the capricious nature of the guidelines but the idea that they are being forced to prove aspects of cultural persistence that the U.S. government purposely and actively worked toward removing from them. A good example of this catch-22 is provided by Mark Miller (2004: 59):

> Most unacknowledged tribes have come to despise having to prove that their community has always existed. For centuries non-Indian officials did their best to destroy tribal communities, and it now seemed unjust to require groups to prove they existed every twenty years despite the government's best efforts to the contrary. As Michigan Indian leader Carl Frazier told Congress, "My tribe, the Burt Lake Band of Ottawa and Chippewa had its reservation allotted . . . [by the government] yet we maintained a strong and vibrant Indian community on these lands until the entire community including our homes were burned to the ground to force our eviction after a tax sale." Even so, because in theory a tribe faced with these forces may have "voluntarily" abandoned its community, many non-Indians continue to remain unconcerned with the causes of the tribe's demise. They simply believe the tribe in question became extinct.

It is this issue, perhaps more than any other, that raises concern that although the government has ostensibly put into place a program designed to assist Indian groups, the FAP is in reality an outgrowth of the overarching genocidal nature of federal Indian policy. Historically, governmental policy and law (as argued in Chapter Three) have been crafted with the obvious intent of eliminating the Indian problem one way or another. That the policy is ongoing is reflected in the attitudes and statements made by top government officials. As recently as 1988, for example, President Ronald Reagan was reported to have argued that it was "a mistake for the country to have 'humored' Native Americans with treaties and special status." Shortly before Reagan made this statement, his secretary of the interior commented that "Indians suffered from a wide range of social problems because they lived under 'socialistic government policies' promoted by the federal government" (Miller 2004: 73). President George W. Bush is on record as opposed to Indian sovereignty, and he played an instrumental role in denying the Tigua their rights of self-determination.[2] The recent discovery that billions of dollars of Indian trust fund money have "disappeared" is now being used by the government as a way to further punish Indian peoples. The United States, rather than admit its mistake and pay a fair settlement, has chosen to fight a lawsuit meant to hold it accountable. In an order dated February 7, 2005, District Court Judge Royce Lamberth criticized the Department of the Interior for having allowed Bureau of Indian Affairs (BIA) officials to stop payments to accountholders for a short period in September 2004.[3]

In short, the government has seized on its own ineptitude as a ploy to appropriate even more from its longtime victims. The government, in a blatant blackmail attempt, is trying to (literally) starve Native Americans into accepting a "settlement" in lieu of accounting for all of the funds lost due to its incompetence.

The most overt example of a continuing government program of genocide, however, is the fact that blood quantum standards remain as the true measuring stick used by the government as part of its recognition criteria, despite the fact that government officials know that culture is transmitted through learning and is not innate. The Tigua are an example of a federally recognized Indian community who, unless changes are made, will be legally extinct within a handful of generations. Unfortunately, they are far from alone.

Historian Patricia Limerick exposes the intention of the government, which recently attempted to craft an outright policy of genocide. Limerick (1987: 338) quotes the following from a BIA document: "Set the blood-quantum at one-quarter, hold to it as a rigid definition of Indians, let intermarriage proceed . . . and eventually Indians will be defined out of existence. When that happens, the federal government will finally be freed from its persistent Indian problem." This statement was in response to a 1986 Reagan administration initiative seeking proposals to reduce overall federal spending. Although this proposal was blocked, the very fact that it was written and not immediately rejected is very telling. Equally telling is the government's open willingness to allow poverty-stricken Indian communities to designate their reservations as dumpsites for toxic wastes. As one American Indian remarks in regard to this policy: "The Nazis used to bring the victims to the gas chambers, the new Nazis bring the gas chambers to the victims" (Craven 2006).

State Recognition

In 1961 the mayor of El Paso learned of the Tigua situation, and he responded by writing the BIA, hoping to acquire aid for the Indian group. However, many bureaucrats still believed in termination, and the BIA denied any obligation to the Tigua (Mintor 1969: 30–31; Schulze 2001: 17–18).

In 1965 El Paso attorney Tom Diamond was in the early stages of assisting the Tigua in their bid for recognition. Diamond, who was advised of the Tigua's problems by the director of a local television station, initially knew very little about Indians or Indian cultures. After conducting background research and visiting the tribe for the first time, Diamond noted several Pueblo customs:

> A small cage in the front yard of the cacique . . . contained a small white rooster which, as the cacique later informed Diamond, served as a symbol of authority for the chief. Inside the house the cacique had small paper bags hung on nails, which contained "*Yerba Buena.*" He informed Diamond that part of his job as cacique was to provide medical care for tribal members. (Schulze 2001: 22).

The Tigua present at that first meeting showed the attorney their grandfathers' discharge papers from the U.S. Calvary, "sang a few of their Indian language chants, and showed him poll tax receipts marked with the phrase 'Exempt-Indian'" (Miller 2004: 224). Although initially distrusted (as outsiders always are), Diamond earned the trust of the Tigua leaders, eventually earning the respect of even the most disillusioned tribal members. In recounting the early days of the recognition process, Jesus recalls Diamond's influence:

> I remember years ago, in 1966 we were trying to be recognized as a tribe so Tom Diamond got all the history together and presented it to Congress. . . . We proved that we were recognized way back in the 1800s, but the BIA, the federal government just forgot about us. . . . I have a lot of respect for Tom Diamond, he put his money to buy shoes for the Indian kids out of his own pocket. He's been a very good attorney for the tribe, he didn't charge us for legal fees; he just did it because he believed in our Indian people, he believed in the old people.

Diamond learned that the Tigua maintained a very specific tribal government and they also perpetuated many Pueblo-influenced customs, such as the annual Saint Anthony's Day celebration on June 13. Convinced that the case was worth pursuing further, in October 1966 Diamond took the first step in the fight for Tigua recognition by serving notice to city tax and county tax assessors and collectors that the Tigua would no longer be responsible for tax payments. "Diamond based their refusal on the fact that the title to the Ysleta Grant was recognized by the Texas Legislature in 1854 as being held by the Tiguas, thereby exempting them from any and all tax liability" (Schulze 2001: 23). The county attorney announced that individuals who qualified as tribal members would be exempt from outstanding and future property taxes. Tribal members, however, would need to prove their lineal descent to the satisfaction of the county tax collector. As for the question of how to prove lineal descent, it was determined that "birth, baptismal, death, and family records that trace descent back to 1854 would all suffice for tax purposes" (23).

At the start, Diamond uncovered evidence that the Tigua had once possessed a Spanish land grant that unscrupulous state and local politicians had gradually usurped during the nineteenth century. Diamond now realized that the Tigua had a strong land claim case that would gain the attention of policymakers. As Teyo points out:

> A long time ago there used to be like boundaries for our land. When we used to go hunting there were traditional territories because this was all ours for as far as the eyes can see. That's where we used to hunt deer, antelope, up here in the mountains. We used to hunt rabbits. There is not much left there; there is urban sprawl. But all these mountains and hills where we used to hunt rabbits have been stolen from us. I use the term stolen liberally, because I think all these individual settlers, the Anglo and Mexican, Spanish, and whatever, just took it over and stole it. They [*outsiders with government support*] took our land away from us. . . . They just came, and the Indian people, so hospitable, Pueblo people to other people. The people were coming from the east, "Oh, you can stay here, it's OK." But, finally, they took advantage, told us, say, "OK, you stay here" [*in Ysleta*].

Although the claim held financial potential, the Tigua pursued the action primarily to provide leverage to work a recognition deal with the state and federal governments. The BIA was determined to give the tribe a hard time, even after "Diamond presented evidence that the Tiguas had attended the Albuquerque Indian School, had served as Pueblo Indian scouts, and had been inventoried in 1849–50 by the U.S. Indian agent" (Miller 2004: 227). The BIA response to this was to repeat its earlier contention that it had no trust responsibilities to the tribe. The BIA informed Diamond:

> A tribe needed a treaty, an executive proclamation, or an act of Congress to qualify for BIA trusteeship. When Diamond informed the BIA that he intended to pursue formal recognition through one of these means, they replied: "The President no longer issues executive orders recognizing new tribes. Congress no longer passes laws recognizing Indian tribes. We don't make treaties with anyone unless we are at war with them." (Schulze 2001: 24)

Unhappy with this response but determined nonetheless, Diamond began working with State Representative Richard White to secure some form of justice for the Tigua. A visit to Texas attorney general Crawford Martin's office "resulted in their first clear strategy" (Schulze 2001: 24). Martin agreed that something needed to be done for the Tigua, but because the "federal constitution denied states the right to assume responsibility for Indian groups . . . taking the case to the federal level was unavoidable" (26). Knowing the BIA's position, White advised that the BIA would oppose any bill that established trust responsibility for the federal government and suggested the state could help the Tigua. Thus Diamond decided to do both: "Get a bill through the Texas Legislature recognizing the tribe and agreeing to assume trust responsibility subject to getting a federal bill through recognizing the tribe and transferring trust responsibility to the State of Texas" (quoted in Schulze 2001: 24). It would be an attractive option from the perspective of the BIA since "this was the height of termination. They wanted to get rid of Indians, not create Indians" (27). Responding to this strategy, White's office drew up legislation in 1966 to "recognize the Tiguas by designating them the Tiwa Indians of Ysleta del Sur Pueblo" (Miller 2004: 228).

In April 1967 the Tigua went to Austin to prove their identity. "Unacknowledged Indians often have to 'play Indian' to gain access to valuable state and federal resources. For unacknowledged tribes, their 'Indianness' is not a given and must be constructed to meet the expectations of the dominant culture" (Miller 2001: 224). This fact was not lost on the Tigua, who, even after winning recognition, had to continue "playing Indian" at the statehouse every year. Tribal member Jesus, in particular, loathed the experience: "Those white people in Austin [the Texas capital] only see an Indian when they are wearing feathers and acting like a savage." Conceding that "you have to play along sometimes to get what you need," Jesus, nonetheless, expresses his displeasure that the Tigua were forced to prove themselves. "Why should we have to? We've been here over three hundred years. How much more 'proof' do you need?"

In order to prove the Tigua authentic to the gathered state legislators, Diamond assembled a panel of experts, such as anthropologists Nicholas Houser and Bernard Fontana, who presented scholarly reports. Additionally, Isleta governor Andy Abieta and National Congress of American Indians (NCAI) executive Georgeann Robinson provided Indian validation as a complement to the expert testimony. Tigua leaders Jose Granillo, Miguel Pedraza, Trinidad Granillo, and others came ready to play Indian for the legislators, bringing Indian food and wearing traditional outfits, including headbands, feathers, and ocher paint. During the hearing, Tigua members chanted and preformed several dances to the beat of the Tigua drum and gourd rattles (Schulze 2001: 26; Miller 2004: 228). Miller (2004: 229) states: "The Tiguas' performance, coupled with Abieta's and the NCAI's confirmation of their Indianness, had clearly met the expectations of the Texas legislators as to the group's 'authenticity.'" In addition, the Tigua (fortunately for them) possessed stereotypically Indian phenotypic characteristics, which many whites require when determining whether someone is a real Indian. After seeing the evidence, members of the Texas state government agreed to assume responsibility for the group.

In 1967 the Texas Legislature enacted House Bill 652, extending to the Tigua the services of the state's Commission for Indian Affairs, while House Bill 888 authorized the governor to accept a transfer of responsibilities from the United States. The Tiwa Act, unfortunately, did not provide the Tigua any legal status as Indians under federal law; therefore the Tigua continued to be subject to state civil and criminal laws. On April 1, 1968, the U.S. Congress passed House Bill 10599, which recognized the Tigua of Ysleta del Sur as a community of Indians and concurrently transferred to Texas any responsibility that the United States might have for them. On April 13, 1968, President Lyndon Johnson signed Public Law 90–287, recognizing the Tigua and establishing a trust relationship with the state of Texas.

The Texas Commission for Indian Affairs Takes Over

When the Tigua came on board in 1968, the Texas Commission for Indian Affairs was composed of non-Indians who appointed a superintendent for each of the two reservations at opposite ends of the state. The governor selected the commissioners, and the Texas legislature appropriated funding to support seventeen employees at the Alabama-Coushatta Reservation and eight at the newly created Tigua Reservation.

> This all came about, and what happened was, we were recognized by the federal government and the federal government turns around and says, "We recognize you as Indian, but we will turn the tribe over to Texas." That's when they put the law in there that we have to apply to Public Law 280, and that's a sticky law. . . . and then we went on to form the Indian commission, and the Indian commission said it will fund so much of your proposals, and that's when all the mess started. (Reya)

By the late 1960s it was "in" to be Indian, and the Texas Indian Commission hoped to exploit the dominant culture's interest in Indians (Miller 2004: 232). The prevailing image of American Indians, projected in popular media up to that time, centered around the "Injun" as a cruel, scalp-taking savage, hardly human in look or manner. "Whether depicted as savage, fierce, or childlike, Indians were above all presented as objects of curiosity belonging to a very different age and society. Seeing them dressed in war paint and feathers, people found it difficult to imagine them functioning in modern urban cities, traveling unattended, and managing their own performances" (Darian-Smith 2004: 30). This image has been gradually "inverted and romanticized into that of the 'Native American.' They are now seen as having been upright, clean-living peoples whose practices were a model of environmental preservation" (Jahoda 1999: 24). This newfound but largely romanticized respect for American Indians and their "connection with the land and environment" was largely a result of the 1960s civil rights movement, an "increasing awareness of ethnic diversity and alternative lifestyles," and the popularity of the 1971 "Keep America Beautiful" advertising campaign, which called for an end to gratuitous abuse of the environment (Darian-Smith 2004: 31). This television commercial (popularly referred to as the "crying Indian" spot) "cleverly manipulated ideas deeply ingrained in the national consciousness. The central idea is that on matters involving the environment, [the Indian] is pure" (Krech 1999, in Darian-Smith 2004: 31). This belief in the "ecological and spiritual purity of Native Americans" began to permeate the mainstream media, along with the notion that Native Americans have a unique relationship with the land (31).

The popularity of the New Age movement (see Chapter Five for discussion) was fed by (and fed into) the image of a symbiotic relationship between nature and spirituality. "For the first time, many Americans were introduced to crystals and channeling. Reincarnation staged a comeback. Shamanism and Native American spirituality captured the imagination of many. People turned from traditional medicine and embraced holistic health practices" (Kyle 1995: 1).

The Texas Indian Commission, with this knowledge in mind, set out to create a program through which the Tigua could market their Indianness. The new Texas commission had realized some success with the tourism plan currently being followed by the Alabama-Coushatta and believed it could do the same with the Tigua. The commission planned to develop a tourist complex, with the Tigua living in a recreated cliff-type Indian pueblo that would display their "Indian village" lifestyle (Miller 2004: 233). Additionally, there was a plan to build a *tuh-lah* to serve as a ceremonial center (complete with bathrooms built to resemble sacred Pueblo kivas), which, as the Tigua pointed out, could not serve as a religious center as it was not only disrespectful but "was made for those souvenirs . . . for when tourists come" (234). The retired grocery store executive who was, oddly, appointed as Tigua tribal superintendent decided (without consulting the tribal council) to establish a formal tribal roll using blood quantum criteria. The Tigua tradition of basing membership more on ceremonial and community participation than blood quantum was rejected, and the tribal rolls were opened to anyone of Tigua ancestry. This greatly concerned many of the Tigua because, as Jesus points out, "this let the people who only care about money into our tribe." Several, in particular Hector and Jesus, questioned these newcomers, asking: "Where were you when we had nothing?" Others, such as José, were a bit more conciliatory:

> And, also, many other people that was Indian and never associated with us, for reasons personal or financial, started coming back, started coming back to Ysleta and applying for housing and benefits and scholarships. I don't blame them because times were rough, in the first place, and many people went out of town to seek better employment, better ways of living.

The state felt that it should control membership guidelines because it controlled the funding. Tigua leaders, as Hector puts it, "resented being pushed around" and forced into "putting our culture on public display." The notion of building a multistory pueblo (particularly with kiva-shaped bathrooms) was, Maria says, "ridiculous. . . . It showed these people knew nothing about us." Tribal leaders protested the "dictatorial" methods of commission director Walter Broemer, accusing him "of side-stepping the tribal council," creating plans and making decisions without regard for tribal input (Miller 2004: 239). Broemer defended himself against charges of paternalism, although in a strange way: "I do try to sell my program, but at any time the Tribal Council can vote it down. Yes, I push people [because] sometimes it's very difficult for an Indian to assume the responsibilities a position requires" (quoted in Miller 2004: 239). Patronizing and ethnocentric remarks like that exacerbated an already uncomfortable partnership between the state and the tribe. Realizing, however, that they needed to do something to bring in money, the Tigua reluctantly agreed to approach tourism as a way to reach self-sufficiency, which was their overarching objective all along. "We had to feed the family," Jesus recalls. "There was no other alternative."

The initial goal behind seeking recognition was to avoid losing the little land they had left to the tax collector, and they also hoped to gain a small reservation along with some educational and medical assistance. Educational assistance was viewed as vital to their future self-sufficiency. As Hector points out, "Our average education level was second grade. . . . We needed to improve that to have any hope for the future." Maria concurs: "We wanted our children to have the chance we didn't have. Most of us had to go to work in the fields to help our families; we went to school barefooted and didn't have any place to study. We were teased and made fun of every day." With the help of state and federal government grants, the Tigua were able to build an Arts and Crafts Center where Tigua artisans marketed items such as Pueblo pottery, ceramics, and jewelry. They also built *hornos* (domed adobe ovens) to demonstrate the group's bread-making skills, and they opened a restaurant that served Indian influenced Mexican dishes. However, gaining financial independence through tourism and crafts-related ventures proved difficult, largely because, as Rico points out, "we couldn't compete with the venders across the border" (in Juarez, Mexico).

By the early 1970s, the Tigua had begun to secure federal grants for the purchase of a 27-acre block of land for a residential housing reservation. The chance to move into new homes with electricity and indoor plumbing was "incredible" and, "a dream come true," according to Hector. Although some of the Elders preferred to remain in their old homes, most of the tribal members with children jumped at the opportunity to provide their children with comfortable, quiet, and lighted rooms for study.

I think in recent years, that they built the other housing, the new housing, the urban development housing. That's when many of the people started selling their houses here in the old pueblo and moving over there to the new housing. The majority moved over here . . . but it was an entirely new experience because many, like I said, didn't have running water. (*José*)

Along with the $3 million in grant funds, the Tigua were required to provide 250 hours of work to be eligible for a home, a condition most embraced as "not a problem" (Pedro). By the early 1980s, however, the Tigua were growing weary of the Texas Indian Commission and its scarcely veiled threats of termination. The state, for its part, was growing weary as well. In fact, in 1984 it decided, belatedly, that under the Equal Rights Amendment of the Texas Constitution, Indian tribes are prohibited from receiving special treatment. It was clear that they planned to seize on this constitutional interpretation to withdraw support for the two Texas tribes. The fact that Indians are political, not racial, organizations was a concept that was lost on the state, and its threat to end funding for the Texas Indian Commission was viewed by the Tigua and Alabama-Coushatta as a very real possibility. It had, apparently, been searching for an excuse to abandon its responsibility to the Indian tribes for a number of years before it stumbled onto this little gem of a law. The Tigua, for example, had been required since the beginning to "put on a dog and pony show" every couple of years in order to prove they were still real Indians, so by the time the state decided to "get out of the Indian business," the Tigua were not overly upset (Miller 2004: 211). As Reya puts it, "The state never really did anything for us anyway."

In about 1980 the state says, you know, "We can't afford you. I'm sorry we can't pass your propositions, you need to go." Then we went back to the federal government and said, you know, "The state of Texas really can't afford us." So they said, "OK, come back to being federal." The government is so full of shit. When this started they came and talked, "The state of Texas is going to do this like always." We were glad to be rid of the state but we didn't know if the feds would be any better. The government always lies; they never keep their word, all the treaties that have been broken with other tribes. How many times have we got the federal government tried to, was taking from us and putting into a white man's school, make him to learn the white man's ways? They would take him out to Oklahoma or someplace and you see some of the history, how they took Indian people and put them in schools, so the intent of the government was to get the savage out of the Indian people, not to speak their language. They wanted them to be the white man's way. (*Jesus*)

Federal Acknowledgment

Leaving the state behind and pursuing federal acknowledgment (along with the federal trust status that would go along with it) appeared to be the Tigua's best option. The decision by the Tigua to seek federal acknowledgment was a risky path to choose, however, as the federal acknowledgment process was brand-new in 1978, and many unknown issues were yet to be worked out. Nobody knew, for example, how long the process would take, or even how to define common terms such as "tribe," "political influence," or "community." Congress had only recently begun framing Indian recognition guidelines after the long Termination Era had ended, so neither tribal attorney Diamond nor the government had a precise idea of how the Tigua should proceed. Although other Indian groups were pursuing claims against the government by this point, a standardized acknowledgment process was still in its early stages, and the Tigua, unlike most petitioning groups, came to the process with state recognition already in hand. Primarily, the government wanted to create a sort of checklist for the newly established petitioning process, "thus providing unrecognized Indian groups the opportunity to pursue their claims to Indianness in a more systematic and controlled manner" (Schulze 2001: 30–31). However, because the Tigua's case was utterly lacking in precedent, Diamond was forced to prepare a series of arguments that would address the requirements of a newly petitioning group.

The alternative route was to seek out congressional support for "restoration" as a federal group. The Tigua firmly believed that their tribe had received federal recognition in 1968 when the government placed them under the care of the state of Texas. Although the tribe had not been technically "recognized," it was clear that the intent of the federal government was to ensure the Indians would be viewed, and assisted by the state, as a legitimate group. Moreover, the congressional route made sense, given that Congress had recently taken to "restoring" a number of the "terminated" tribes, which seemed to be a much quicker and more painless process than working through the BIA. Additionally, it bypassed the scrutiny of already recognized tribes who tended to dislike acknowledgment legislation much more so than restoration legislation. Because the Alabama-Coushatta were working in conjunction with the Tigua in their recognition efforts, when the recognition bill was drafted, the two groups were lumped together. It was clear, however, that Congress had passed termination legislation only for the Alabama-Coushatta and not the Tigua, creating a potential problem from the very beginning. Although that was thought of as a fine distinction that would go unnoticed, the BIA threw up immediate objections (Schulze 2001: 31; Miller 2004: 242–243).

During hearings in 1984 and 1985, the Interior Department had adamantly opposed the Tigua's position, insisting that the group go through the BIA acknowledgment process. In the first place, the BIA argued that "it had not evaluated the Alabama-Coushattas under the department's restoration criteria to determine whether the group still was maintaining 'tribal relations' since termination" (Miller 2004: 242). Additionally, it rejected the Tigua claim that the tribe had received federal recognition in 1968. Although the BIA later agreed that, in fact, the Tigua had been recognized by the federal government, it very much resented the idea that these tribes were sidestepping the BIA process. For their part, the Tigua put together an information package that met the BIA requirements and convinced the BIA that they were worthy of a special exception. The BIA reversed its position not only because of the new evidence presented, but also because of the 1968 Tiwa Act and the Tigua's relationship with the state of Texas, each of which clearly demonstrated their status as Indian peoples (Schulze 2001: 32). Most important, however, was their strong relationship with other recognized tribes, notably numerous Pueblo groups, the Kiowa tribe, the All Indian Pueblo Council, and the National Tribal Chairmen's Association (Schulze 2001: 32; Miller 2004: 245). The support, specifically, from the Isleta, New Mexico, Pueblo was vital.

Having surpassed the BIA hurdle, the groups next responded to the growing opposition to their legislation, which was linked to the gambling issue. At this point in history, Indian gaming had become a controversial and contentious issue, and the hapless Tigua found themselves embroiled in the conflict. Primarily, Texas state comptroller Bob Bullock opposed the bill because he was afraid that the tribe would engage in gaming activities and wanted the legislation to contain a clause forbidding gambling. Both U.S senators from Texas voiced their concerns about gaming, and the Tigua were forced to secure the aid of Hawaiian senator Daniel Inouye, who introduced a Senate bill on their behalf. Texas senators Phil

Gramm and Lloyd Bentsen appeared to want to wait and see how the national Indian gaming debates came out before making a commitment on the Tigua/Alabama-Coushatta bill. As Kevin Gover (2002) points out, "The State of Texas was not necessarily opposed to federal recognition of the Pueblo, but was concerned about having a sovereign Indian nation loose within its borders." In order to placate the concerned legislators, "in one of those deals-with-the-devil that unrecognized tribes are sometimes forced to make," the tribe agreed that it would not conduct gaming within its reservation, "if the state would not oppose federal recognition of the tribe."

During negotiations in the Senate Select Committee on Indian Affairs, the Tigua accepted a series of compromise measures put together by the Department of the Interior. Both the Tigua and the Alabama-Coushatta passed tribal resolutions completely banning gaming while agreeing to an unusual provision limiting membership. Tribes normally set their own membership criteria, yet to pass the bill the Tigua agreed to limit eligibility to receive federal services to individual members who could demonstrate at least one-eighth blood quantum (Schulze 2001: 32: Miller 2004: 251). The Texas comptroller proposed a provision in the legislation specifically providing for state regulation of gaming on the reservation, which the Tigua tribal council found totally unacceptable. The provision would represent a significant infringement upon the tribe's power of self-government, and would set a potentially dangerous precedent for other tribes.

> The BIA says, "OK, we recognize you but this is what you have to do." I do not know but somebody else [in the tribe] said, "OK, we recognize the federal government but we will not do this" [agree to the government deal]. They [Department of Interior] wanted too much, wanted to be able to control the tribe like the state. I'm not sure if it was the [Tigua] governor or one or two others who finally agreed, but we really had no choice. They [the federal government] got us in the late 1980s. (Jesus)

To avoid state regulation and the wrath of recognized tribes, the Tigua council decided to pass a tribal resolution banning all gaming on the reservation. The Tigua asked the U.S. House to amend its bill to prohibit all gaming as defined by Texas law and even passed their own resolution "stating that the tribe had no interest in bringing gambling to their reservation" (Schulze 2001: 34). However, because the bill prohibited gambling "where gambling is prohibited in Texas," state officials believed that

Texas bingo regulations would not apply to the Tigua reservation, as recent federal cases (see *Seminole Tribe of Florida v. Butterworth*, 1981) made it clear that state civil and regulatory laws were inapplicable to Indian reservations. "Since gambling is not expressly forbidden on any federally recognized and controlled Indian reservation, this wording left the Tigua open to reconsider their stance on gambling at any time" (Schulze 2001: 34). The Senate Select Committee on Indian Affairs redrafted the bill to include a provision prohibiting gambling, but neither Senator Gramm (who had been refusing to sign off on the bill) nor Comptroller Bullock realized that the wording of the bill had been altered. The bill that passed the U.S. House in 1986 contained a compromise stating that tribal laws on gaming were to be identical to Texas law until amended. The Tigua also accepted the blood quantum provision and agreed to state civil and criminal jurisdiction over their lands, making them, in essence, a Public Law 280 tribe. The Tigua and Alabama-Coushatta bill passed in the House in 1985 on a voice vote with no debate; it passed the Senate on August 18, 1987. Within two weeks President Reagan signed the bill, formally establishing the federal trust relationship for the 1,124 Tigua then on the tribal rolls.

Conclusion

The Tigua, it seemed, had finally received the legal rights and standing owed to them. Their years of fighting for survival, apparently, had at long last reached its end. As the Tigua took their place among the other five-hundred-plus officially recognized American Indian groups, their future looked brighter than ever before. During the next fifteen years, the Tigua would, indeed, reach the pinnacle of their success and realize their long-sought dream of self-sufficiency. The above mentioned "deal with the devil," however, would shortly come back to haunt them. The state of Texas, unhappy that the small Indian community was growing in wealth (not to mention power and prestige), determined that successful Indian communities were not welcome within its borders. The sovereign rights and self-determination of Indian peoples were not concepts the state took any positive interest in. Indeed, its interest was just the opposite. The story of the Tigua's financial rise and ultimate fall will be the topic of the following chapter.

CHAPTER FIVE

Speaking Rock Casino

The State of Texas Versus the Ysleta del Sur Pueblo

Introduction

After the Ysleta reservation received federal recognition in 1987, its economic situation remained bleak. Unemployment continued at a rate of over 50 percent, and the few tribal members who had jobs often had to commute long distances or move away altogether. Poverty, alcoholism, and drug use were prevalent on and around the new reservation, as were the crime and violence that often accompany impoverished settings. The Tigua had discovered that state and federal recognition was hardly the economic panacea many had hoped for.

Economic independence and the dream of self-sufficiency continued to remain outside the community's grasp. Government grant funds and economic development projects allowed the tribe to collectively raise its meager standard of living, but poverty continued to be the rule rather than the exception. Then, in 1991, Texas passed its State Lottery Act, and the Tigua found themselves in a unique position. The 1987 Tigua and Alabama-Coushatta bill had disallowed gaming on tribal land, stating that tribal laws on gaming were to be identical to Texas law until amended. Now that the state had clearly amended its own gaming laws, the Tigua were free to pursue gambling as a possible source of economic development. As we will see below, however, gaming was not openly embraced as an option by the entire community. The decision to reject or accept gaming on the reservation was contentiously debated, and the tribe did not reach its decision unanimously. Once the decision was made and the casino opened, however, it was immediately apparent that the tribe had created a very profitable enterprise. The state, which for the most part ignored the Tigua and their casino, initially did little to prevent the gaming activities that were taking place on the small West Texas reservation. Toward the end of the 1990s, the circumstances suddenly changed, as Indian gaming (indeed, gambling in general) emerged as a hot political issue and the state, under Governor (and soon-to-be presidential candidate) George W. Bush, decided it was time to put a stop to the tribe's profitable enterprise. After several years of legal wrangling and a series of dubious legal rulings, the state succeeded in forcing the Tigua to shut down Speaking Rock Casino on February 12, 2002.

The issues of law, power, and identity once again emerge as central to our discussion. The Indian gaming debate revolves around the surface issues of American Indian sovereignty and self-determination, but underlying these arguments are accusations that call into question the authenticity of tribes who embrace gaming as an economic option. Opponents of Indian gaming suggest that it is a nontraditional activity that goes against the nature of the spiritual, pure Indian who is connected to nature. Others believe gaming tribes are frauds who are only interested in money and are cashing in on their ancestors' identity. Conversely, gaming is seen by many indigenous groups as a possible solution to myriad economic and social ills. As pointed out in Chapter Three, American Indians as a group have the highest mortality rates, the highest unemployment and poverty rates, and the lowest life expectancy in the United States. Debilitating disease (including drug dependency and alcoholism) and high rates of illiteracy are common throughout Indian Country. Indeed, gaming has become an attractive option for a number of Indian communities, who see it as the only economic remedy currently available to them. Individual states have also entered the debate, arguing (ironically) that Indian gaming is a direct attack on *their* rights of sovereignty, actively fighting against the growth of the Indian gaming industry. The goal of this chapter is to explore how and why Indian gaming has become such a contentious issue, along with how and why the Tigua came to gain and then lose their lucrative gaming enterprise. The issues of identity (i.e., authenticity), tradition, law, and politics each play a role in explaining the dynamics of this contentious issue.

Contested Identity

Before we discuss the issue of Indian gaming in general and Tigua gaming in particular, it is important to further explore the concept of "authenticity" as it relates to Indian gaming. A small number of gaming tribes have experienced a drastic reversal of their economic position. Although the notion that gaming has transformed many poor

Indians into rich Indians is absurd, for a select few tribes this change has been very real. For those groups (the Tigua among them), perceptions of identity are affected by both internal and external issues related to "new" wealth, because the tribe's change in fortune after opening Speaking Rock Casino affected not only the way the community viewed itself but also had an impact on how the tribe was perceived by local outsiders.

Felipe recalls: "We've come a long way. I remember when we used a go to downtown El Paso they told us, 'Get out of here Indians, go back to the people.' That was sad. It's just funny, when we got Speaking Rock Casino everybody changed their tune and called us 'Mr.' and 'How are you doing?' Funny how money changes people." Others, upset because they believed that the Tigua were cashing in on their identity, expressed doubt about the tribe's legitimacy. The popularity of the New Age movement and the influx of wannabe Indians, combined with the myth that Native Americans were wiped out during colonial times, have led to the assumption by far too many people that anyone who claims an Indian identity is acting fraudulently. Randy Eickhoff (1996: 107) recalls the attitude of some El Paso residents:

> Today, some individuals charge that those claiming to be Tiguas really are not, since the Tiguas of Ysleta del Sur have disappeared and those individuals claiming to be Tiguas are in all actuality poverty-level Hispanics who are taking advantage of aboriginal laws. "You can't tell me those people are Indians," one El Paso citizen complained. "Those people down there were broke and about to lose their homes until someone decided, Hey! Let's pretend to be Indians and take advantage of the government that won't know any better!" Unfortunately, that citizen is not alone. Many people refuse to believe that the Tiguas are not extinct. They believe that the land set aside by the government as a reservation in reaffirmation of laws it once broke is the result of clever legal manipulation, not legal right.

It was not only particular citizens who felt the Tigua were "created" by El Paso attorney Tom Diamond; indeed, a number of prominent local government officials are on the record questioning their authenticity. For example, Jim Speer, attorney for El Paso County Water Improvement District Number 1, had this to say after the Tigua filed suit to seek control of a large portion of the county's water system: "There's a saying around here that God made the world, but Tom Diamond made the Tigua Indians" (quoted in Olsson 1998). And in an open letter to area residents regarding water rights, Brewster County judge Val Beard (2004) states:

> Our neighbors are gearing up for a new Indian War, but unlike the bat-
> tles of the past, this one will be fought by lobbyists, lawyers, politicians
> and citizens' groups. Yes, after over 100 years, the Indians are back, big
> time. We're talking about the Ysleta del Sur Pueblo, aka the Tigua, some-
> times spelled Tewa. The Tigua are *the brilliant legislative creation* of El
> Paso attorney Tom Diamond. The tribe *claims* to be the remnant of Na-
> tive Americans who fled from New Mexico to El Paso along with the
> Spaniards during the Pueblo Revolt of 1680. Arguments about whether
> or not the Tigua are really Indians still go on. . . . The fledgling tribe *lit-
> erally had to reinvent itself.* And attorney Diamond became one of the few
> Americans to *create* an Indian tribe, as opposed to trying to wipe them
> out. (emphasis mine)

Karen Olsson (1998), in an article about George W. Bush and his mo-
tivation for wanting the Tigua casino shut down, suggests: "Maybe El
Paso developers asked Bush to do it: the Tigua are undeniably a litigious
group, having filed various claims of titular and usage rights to large tracts
of land and to 100 miles of canals and ditches in El Paso County." More
serious for the Tigua, however, was a 2002 report commissioned through
the Texas Parks and Wildlife Department (TPWD), written by anthropologists, and concluding that the Tigua have no significant historical affiliation with Hueco Tanks State Park. This report, written by Kurt F.
Anschuetz (with a written contribution by Polly Schaafsma) for the Rio
Grande Foundation and entitled *Senses of Place and Construction of Affiliation: Hueco Tanks State Historical Park Ethnographic Study,* is riddled
with misperceptions and was written with the apparent (unstated) goal of
perpetuating stereotypes, myths, and outright falsehoods. It (thoroughly
debunked by Greenberg in 2003) brings to the surface a number of issues
relevant to the discussion of authenticity.[1]

The stated goals of the Rio Grande Foundation (RGF) report were to
identify cultural groups affiliated with Hueco Tanks and document
"land use and associations between specific cultural landscapes and cultural entities." Other purposes ascribed to the project included identifying traditional cultural properties (TCPs), identifying associated
management implications, and improving interpretative efforts (1.3).
Needless to say, these goals and purposes were driven by the TPWD
agenda and not the tribe's. The real purpose behind the study, as we will
see, was to build a case that not only denies a Tigua affiliation with

Hueco Tanks but argues that the Tigua of Ysleta del Sur Pueblo (YDSP) are, in fact, culturally extinct.

The groundwork for this argument is laid early when the authors suggest (without citation) that "communities today manipulate their relationship with the past for their present and future purposes" (1.6). Although they agree that culture is dynamic, they go on to state that tradition, although constant, is often modified by communities to help fulfill desired ends (see Garcia 2005: 158). In other words, people will make up anything to get their hands on desired resources (i.e., the Tigua have modified their traditions in order to support their claim to Hueco Tanks). The authors are apparently pouncing on ambiguities regarding the definitions of terms such as "culture" and "tradition," arguing, albeit subtly, that the Tigua are "inventing" their traditions. Anthropologists such as Jocelyn Linnekin (1983) and Roger M. Keesing (1989) have helped to popularize the notion that because the past, in Keesing's words, was "never a simple, unambiguous reality . . . ancestral cultures [have become] symbols rather than experienced realities." Traditional culture, in short, does not exist "in reality" but has been reified, "fetishized," "commoditized and packaged." The purpose behind this capitalist "commodification" of culture is primarily related to economic reality. Therefore, culture has become a product that can be "sold to tourists" for a profit (Kessing, 32–33). Even as the debate over invented traditions continues (see, for example, the pointed response to Keesing's arguments by Trask 1991), this shift in academic discourse provides further ammunition for those who would like to see the pesky, troublemaking Native peoples wiped out by simply declaring *all* culture inauthentic.

The bid by Anschuetz and Schaafsma to remove the Tigua from their sacred landscape continues (3.15), with a quote that refers to the possibility (no examples offered) that people who have been removed from their homeland reinvent it in often fantastic ways. The use of cultural tradition as a strategy to gain access to and/or protect resources of interest or value to a community is offered without one concrete ethnographically documented example of any community modifying its tradition in order to assert an affiliation to a locale or place. Yet, the authors would have us believe it is a frequent occurrence. Next (5.17), Schaafsma suggests that claims by the Tigua to the Tanks are recent, as a result of some emergent political agenda, which she refers to as a "revitalistic" movement. Thomas Green (1973) is cited extensively by the authors to support this position, but apart from the fact that Green labels Tigua political efforts using an outsider appellation with little supporting documentation, he actually calls it a nativistic movement. A revitalistic movement is an organized, conscious effort to create a more satisfying culture, whereas a nativistic movement seeks to perpetuate and protect tradition (see Linton 1942; Wallace 1956). Schaafsma's incorrect use of the term "revitalistic" betrays her specious argument that the Tigua have appropriated the tradition of others through some kind of "constructed history" in order to secure land. This argument is absurd. As we have seen, the Tigua interest in Hueco Tanks is part of their oral tradition, predating any documentation provided by outsiders who have their own interests and agendas in mind. Certainly the protection of sacred spaces would figure prominently in any political agenda for any American Indian community, and the interest in protection is nativistic and continuous, surfacing as a political discourse in the face of and to counter emergent threats to locales. Surely the authors understand the difference between periodic political agendas surfacing in communities as a result of an extralocal threat (i.e., the public use plan by TPWD for the park) to their religious shrines and traditional cultural properties, and opportunistic behavior by those seeking to appropriate another's property to which they have no connections. Had ethnographic research been completed, the author's would have realized that the Tigua did not "reconstruct" a history, but rather they constructed documentation needed for legal and political purposes.[2] Furthermore, the observation that landscapes are dynamic, and that each generation imposes its own cognitive map on an anthropogenic world, is proffered in an attempt to downplay contemporary concerns. In brief, the authors are saying that even if the Tigua once had a sacred affiliation with Hueco (which they know to be a fact), that was a long time ago and the Tigua today are not *really* interested in continuing that relationship. Significantly, the authors fail to point out that although culture is dynamic, there are continuities in tradition (especially in American Indian communities where elderhood means something), and each generation affirms the cognitive map passed down from previous ones by ceremony, pilgrimage, and so on. Importantly, each community and each generation may have to protect areas from outside interests, even if they did not have to before. Hence, the reason some areas, such as Hueco Tanks, are contested more is not a reinvention of tradition but a more focused political action. Conflict does not change the tradition; rather it changes the politics of protecting that tradition. As Michael Carrithers (1992: 10) suggests, "The sense that the younger generation makes of things, and the sense that they impress on events, must reflect their own situation and not be a mere parroting of their parents."

In short, this report portrays the Tigua community as lying and deceitful, a community that will do or say whatever is necessary in order to meet its goals. Apparently, the fact that the Tigua refuse to directly divulge sacred information to outsiders is interpreted by the authors as evidence that no sites of importance to the Tigua are to be found at Hueco Tanks:

> The challenge to the people of the Pueblos of Isleta and Ysleta del Sur in their efforts to establish claims of significant continuing affiliation with the Hueco Tanks State Historical park as part of their traditional homeland is to communicate effectively with outsiders, especially individuals who occupy or manage the land and its natural and cultural resources. (6.22).

Rather than recognizing that secrecy about religious concerns is an ingrained Puebloan trait and rather than understanding that secrecy is necessary for their protection against government and Christian-backed programs of assimilation as well as public desecration of sites (not to mention slanderous academicians), this report willingly contributes to the interpretation and reinterpretation of a people and their identity in ways that meet the needs of the authors. Indeed, the authors of this report take Tigua secrecy as proof that they are acting deceitfully.

Additionally, as though seizure of the role of dominator were not sufficient, author Anschuetz continues to dictate the standards to which the dominated must conform:

> This chapter provides background material that potential [sic] can serve as a framework for the community in articulating its continuing cultural-historical relationships with its landscape and why these interactions are important to the people of the Pueblos of Isleta and Ysleta del Sur for sustaining their respective identities. (6.22–6.23)

Although Anschuetz has no qualms about directing the "proper" response of the Tigua to the theft of its TCPs, he does struggle with the notions of culture, identity, tradition, and change. For example, he erroneously points to the loss of certain traditions as evidence of a disappearing identity. Although he points out the decrease in the use of the Tigua language and other elements of material culture and cultural traditions, he fails to point out that these kinds of changes always take place as communities change. Instead, he suggests that the adoptions of physical traits, such as Mexican clothing, are indications of assimilation, denoting the loss of identity. Likewise, his search for a sense of a cultural landscape in accordance with his personal notion of what is to be expected in a traditional Puebloan construction disregards the basic facts. A continuing community has a culture and an identity. He himself has acknowledged the fact that the Tigua are a continuing community, yet he fails to recognize that community, culture, and identity are connected, regardless of changes that may take place. Indeed, Anschuetz essentially contends that the Tigua are not Pueblo enough by standards that he himself wants to set (7.48–7.66). He takes an extremely arrogant stance, insinuating that Pueblo communities should fit the frozen image of what he expects them to be, maintaining static cultures with persisting traditions. Again, a community's culture is just that: the culture of a community. The YDSP community has persisted; the unique circumstances of the Tigua, living within a major U.S. city, are consequences of adaptive strategies responsive to their environment. His prejudicial view would have Pueblos (and other Indians) surviving as "noble savages," were they to remain at all.

"Authentic" Indians

It is important to keep in mind that although common American public and government perceptions of Indianness are stereotyped and patently false, individual Indians cannot always divorce themselves from the reality that they are expected to play the part. The Tigua learned this lesson during their tenure under the Texas Indian Commission. There is a definite "white need" that Native people are expected to fulfill, and they must "be capable of demonstrating to white people the primordial nature of their claims to Indianness" (Lawrence 2004: 5). The contested nature of identity, of course, extends into everyday behavior: "real" Indians must always look, dress, and act like "real" Indians. As Bonita Lawrence points out:

> In such contestations of identity (which are always on white terms), Native people who are revealed as transgressing the boundaries of so-called authenticity through their modernity can be dismissed as fakes, or severely restricted in their abilities to develop their communities in contemporary ways. The Western imagination continues to paint the world as populated by "endangered authenticities," always juxtaposed to modernity. (2004: 5)

The Tigua, for example, understand that when they perform "traditional" dances for the tourists, they are expected to look and act a certain way. Without the drums, ribbon shirts, moccasins, and feathers, they would simply not be seen as acting authentically, and the public would stop visiting and denounce them as "fake." The tourists seek out a commodity for consumption, and the Tigua provide it. This is not to say that the Tigua are acting fraudulently or even that they believe that they are just giving the tourists what they want. Indeed, they look and act the way they look and act because that is the way in which they happen to look and act. I am not making a circular argument here, just simply pointing out that the Tigua are who they are, and, happily, at this point in history their perceptions of self are congruent with outsiders' perceptions of Indianness. The Tigua look and behave as they do independent of outside observation, but identity, as Lawrence points out, does not exist in the abstract. It "must be recognized by other individuals before it can be lived as real" (2004: 11). Or, as Trond Thuen (2006: 26) states:

> The claim to be indigenous is not just a one-sided issue; it has to be confirmed by others, and ideally by those who constitute the family of indigenous peoples worldwide. Its similarity to the concept of ethnic identity is relevant here; it rests on self-ascription as well as a confirmation from others. (see also Guenther 2006: 17; Kenrick 2006: 19; and Kenrick and Lewis 2004: 7)

Identity is a reciprocal process, and the Tigua are aided in their own sense of Indianness by the approval of others, be they outsiders or other Indians. What is at issue here, then, is not what constitutes authentic appearance and behavior, but what constitutes perceptions of authentic appearance and behavior. As long as the Tigua (as well as other Native peoples) and the outside world continue to agree on the boundaries of Indianness, as long as change is reciprocal, authenticity is assured. Unfortunately, many authentic American Indians do not fall within the boundaries, particularly during times of work and leisure, and are consequently forced to prove themselves in order to be accepted.

The issue of authenticity does not stop at perceptions of boundaries regarding looks and behaviors, however. The ability to identify oneself as a real Indian is at least partially dependent on both public perceptions of authenticity and legal definitions of authenticity (Warren and Jackson 2002: 10). The ability to be recognized as Indian on the individual level (which is the first hurdle to overcome in the process of becoming real) is contingent on the colonial regulation of an "arbitrary cutoff point for definitions of Indianness," linked to the question of "sufficient" blood quantum (Lawrence 2004: 15–16). This process, however, almost always works in tandem with group affiliation and whether or not community connections are legitimate. A "pure blood" without ties to a federally recognized community is often simply not recognized, legally or socially, as authentic. Likewise, individuals who are on the rolls of recognized tribes will not be seen by outsiders as real Indians if they do not look or act according to expectations. The issue is further complicated by generations of intermarriage between Indians and whites, blacks, Mexicans, and others, which has led to the creation of "legal"—but white-looking or black-looking or Mexican-looking—Indians.

Moreover, by lumping together over five hundred distinct groups, mainstream culture has marginalized the unique history, culture, and tradition of each community, although a few of the better known groups have a small segment of their story incorporated into the grand discourse of Indian history.[3] Identity for most Native people and groups is multilayered, comprised of markers that include American and Indian, as well as specific affiliations such as nation, tribe, and clan. Each is important, each has meaning, and to gloss over this point is to strip individuals of their right to express their particular sense of group specific identity. This method of lumping all into one, of course, flies in the face of logic as well as traditional practice. G. P. Castile (1996: 743), for example, points out:

> Native North American peoples, like all peoples, had a myriad of ways of defining their group's membership. Like most human societies, they generally relied on kinship criteria—consanguinity and affinity—of many varied types. . . . These systems of self-definition were group specific, and there is little evidence of any shared label of common identity that was pan-Indian, one including all of the hundreds of separate linguistic and cultural entities of North America.

Recasting all indigenous peoples as just "Indian," however, simplified the process of defining and controlling the indigenous population and helped promote the simultaneous development of Indian stereotypes. Stereotypes, of course, feed popular notions about group identity, as they are "uncritical generalizations that resist authentication and change" (Bausinger 1989: 13, in Senjkovic 2002; see also Theodossopoulos 2003). The generalizations and stereotypes associated with Indian identity have, in the past, promoted negative images and behaviors tied to an overall discourse of the Native American as savage or barbarian. The "new" reality (since the 1960s), however, is tied to a discourse of romanticism and mysticism, which has firmly attached itself to perceptions of Indianness in the American public at large. That led to an influx of "buck skinners" and "wannabes," many of whom exploit their newfound identity status with financial schemes, often at the expense of the legitimate Native. "Indian" craft stores and marketplaces have been springing up around the country since the 1970s, many headed by proprietors of dubious character. The so-called New Age movement (aside from its promotion of "healing crystals" and other pseudoscientific claims) sells Indian spiritualism and "ancient Indian medicinal techniques" that are not only a blatant theft and misappropriation of indigenous intellectual property, but also help perpetuate the media myth of the "Indian in nature," the "noble savage" as the embodiment of the "real" Indian. More frightening to some is the attempted practice of traditional religious ceremonies by non-Indians: "Native religious leaders express horror at the monstrous cloning of their visions of the sacred. For them, the New Age is a kind of . . . evil imitation close enough to the real thing to upset the delicate balance of spiritual power maintained by Indian ritual specialists" (Brown 1998: 201, quoted in Harrison 1999: 11).

The era of Indian gaming has also brought out a large number of people, both individuals and groups, who are seeking to make it rich as members of a gaming tribe. These imposters help perpetuate the most recent myth about the rich Indian. Indeed, the actions of those possessing questionable ties to Indian identity would be laughable, if not for the real damage they cause as part of their moneymaking schemes. Their actions further blur the line between real and fake and force traditional Indian communities to continually tighten their membership guidelines. As we have seen, the United States has indeed put into action a no-win policy that Indian communities are forced to contend with. And, for now, the government is content to sit back and watch as Native Americans slowly regulate themselves out of existence.

The "Real" Tigua

Of course, the question of who is a real Indian extends far beyond questions related to blood quantum; however, this issue is vitally, and specifically, important for the Tigua as the U.S. government, during the federal recognition process, set their blood quantum limit at one-eighth. By creating artificial boundaries that rigidly divides Indian from non-Indian, by quantifying Indianness, the government has set the terms necessary for the legal extinction of the Tigua. The consequences of this blatant usurpation of tribal sovereignty extend beyond the reality of eventual tribal extinction, however, as the daily impact of this dictate is felt across the community. A "legal" Indian is eligible to receive government funding and participate in government programs; a "nonlegal" Indian is not. Important health and education services are denied to many nonlegal tribal members, and the tribe cannot provide housing assistance or make per capita payments to individuals not listed on the tribal rolls. Additionally, individuals who would like to be more active in tribal ceremonial and government functions (for example, participating in tribal juntas) and who would like to embrace their Tigua identity are (often) legally prohibited from taking part. Though these individuals are not shunned by official members, their marginal status clearly affects their sense of belonging and leads some to reject their own Tigua identity altogether.

Complicating this issue are the notions of cultural boundaries and legal (e.g., federal) recognition. To even further confuse an already confusing issue, consider the numerous marginal individuals who are unable to place themselves firmly into one category or another. An example of this would be a non-Indian (e.g., Chinese) child who is legally adopted by an Indian family, raised as an Indian, and instilled with a sense of Indianness but who, because of legal definitions, is not technically Indian. Moreover, few people (even outside the legalisms of the government) would consider that person, as a member of the "Chinese race," to be a real Indian, and their reaction to and treatment of him or her would convey that attitude.

The question of identity, though tied to notions of legality and popular discourse, is informed by multiple factors. As previously mentioned, blood quantum requirements generally only govern legal senses of Indianness, and although that is important for various reasons, "legal" Indian does not necessarily translate into "real" or "authentic" Indian. Besides self-identifying as Indian, one must be viewed and accepted by others before that identity can be lived and experienced as real. Acceptance or nonacceptance by outsiders affects perceptions of self, but it is the primary group or community with which an individual wishes to identify that must set the terms of its own membership. Senses of authenticity must be brokered at this level, and degree of blood may have very little to do with meeting qualifications. According to Jesus, a "real Indian immerses themselves in their culture":

> To me it's very traditional; it's the way I think. Not a lot of the elders know about these things [*traditional practices and knowledge*] because they were going away so much from the tribe early on and got more on the outside world than on the inside of the Indian world. And that's why there's a friction between the new kids and the older kids, because they came late into the tribe and they come in and try and tell you how it is done, what they saw in a book. And they're trying to mix the Plains Indians with the Pueblos. They advertise, like a billboard, "I'm an Indian." First thing they put on their license plate or bumper sticker says, "I'm an Indian." What is an Indian? Well an Indian knows and understands the traditional ways. There are [*legal*] tribal members that don't understand the traditional ways, you know.

"Authentic" Indianness, to this Tigua member, is not tied to legal descriptions or degrees of blood or to what outsiders may or may not think about Indian authenticity, but to traditional knowledge and understanding. It is also tied to a sense of desire, a positive attitude, and a willingness to listen, learn, and ask questions. The passing on of traditional knowledge to descendents (not "official" tribal members) will take place provided the individual displays the proper respect and interest. "This is not about me; this is about our people. I will help anyone [tribal or descendent], but they have to want to learn for the right reasons," Jesus says. This sentiment is closely echoed by José, as he discusses his perception of life around the pueblo during the early 1960s:

> There was more of a unity here with the Indians in the village, the ceremonies were still intact, everybody helped with the fiestas and there was more of an Indianness. Even though we were in poverty everybody knew each other, everybody helped each other because we were all pretty much related, everybody was related to the other Indian families. I remember there were, at that time, less than 200 [*Tigua*] but in the village itself there were about 150 give or take. But, the real core of the pueblo, the real Indians, came out for the ceremonies, the dancing and rituals; there was maybe 80 or something like that. That was the nucleus of the pueblo.

He makes a clear distinction between senses of Indianness, or the makeup of "the real Indians," as opposed to the other Indians who are "Indians in name only." Indeed, I found both of these respondents to be open and sharing with tribal descendents (and tribal members alike), and each expresses a willingness to assist others, provided that the knowledge is sought after for the proper reasons. The "proper" reasons relate to "a genuine, heartfelt desire to learn your culture, to learn the history of your people, to learn the right way and pass that knowledge on" (Teyo). One tribal member, Cortez, is perhaps most knowledgeable about the traditional language, but before he will agree to discuss other aspects of tradition, the requesting person must prove that she is serious by learning a set number of Tigua words. Several tribal members discussed being "tested" as youths, as the Elders, according to Jesus, "were always watching," and they would only provide one piece of the "puzzle" at a time. You had to "prove yourself, prove you were ready to learn," before they would reveal new knowledge.

The question of authenticity, therefore, clearly extends beyond the black and white of classification; there exists a gray area that defies definitive explication. As pointed out by Jesus and José, embracing and practicing traditional behavior are key to "real Indianness" for them, whereas for other tribal members it is the simple embrace of Tigua identity that is most important. Luis has this to say: "I have heard it since I was little, 'I am more Indian than you.' Who is more Indian than who? If you are a Tigua you are a Tigua. I've heard that since I was little, 'He is more Indian because you lived in the city.' No, Tigua is Tigua." Many tribal members share this notion and express the belief that if you have an ancestor of verifiable heritage, then you are Tigua. Although the learning of traditional knowledge and active participation are encouraged, neither is necessarily mandatory.

If there is one consistent sentiment regarding senses of Indianness among the Tigua, it would be that it is not something that you prove but something that you feel. In short, a "real" Indian does not need a card from the government, a particular look, the approval of outsiders, or a certain degree of blood. A "real" Indian, many Tigua say, simply knows it in their heart:

> It's wrong that they say we are not real Indians. I think, what is a real Indian in the first place? We're just trying to survive in this world; we're doing the best we can. . . . You know, it's in your heart, you do your own thing, you don't follow anybody else and I think you'll be all right. . . . Don't listen when they say you have to do things this way or this way; if you follow your heart it will take you to the right place. (*Teyo*)

Of course, *serious* arguments about the Tigua's authenticity have long since ended. The notion that they were "created" is absurd by any standard. But, preposterous or not, there will always be those who refuse to believe that the Tigua are real Indians, deserving in their rights as indigenous people. There will always be those who believe Tigua lawsuits are frivolous, those who refuse to believe that Tigua land was stolen, and those who believe the "Mexicanized Indians" fooled the government.

A Brief History of Indian Gaming

As we have seen, questions relevant to the issues of authenticity and tradition are contentious and multifaceted. Perhaps more than anything else, the era of Indian gaming has brought these questions to the forefront of public consciousness. Charges of fake Indians growing rich on the gaming gravy train have become commonplace. A book by Jeff Benedict, for example, argues that the Pequot tribe is an "inauthentic" gaming tribe only seeking to make money in gaming, and the widely popular television program *60 Minutes* aired a program on January 1, 2000, titled "Wampum Wonderland: Legitimacy of Casinos Run by Indians," which quoted Benedict and cast doubt on the "legitimacy" of Indian gaming (see Darian-Smith 2004: 100). Indeed, the issue of Indian gaming has been contentiously debated between and among Indians and the public for the past thirty years. It stirs up controversy for a variety of reasons, not the least of which is the notion that Indian gaming is somehow an assault on traditional Indian behavior. White America seems to prefer "their" Indians poor and isolated, not rich and vocal. The production of arts, crafts, jewelry, and bread are appropriate (i.e., traditional) moneymaking ventures, not gaming.[1] There is a sense among many Americans that a rich Indian cannot also be an authentic Indian. Indianness, to the general public, is associated with poverty, isolation, and ties to the earth, not money.

> The cultural myth of Indians as spiritual, pure, and connected to nature, land, and family is no longer sustainable in the face of Native Americans participating in contemporary society and behaving as savvy business people. Running lucrative casinos, bringing legal actions against government agencies . . . are not typical ways in which our dominant society imagines Native Americans acting. (Darian-Smith 2004: 34)

Furthermore, Kathryn Shanley (2000: 93) suggests, "when associated with the 'natural world,' Mother Earth, we are good Indians, but when we are involved in the business of making money from gambling, we are bad Indians." Or, as Kathryn Gabriel puts it, Indian gaming is "an economic struggle involving the redistribution of goods. Yesterday, horses, blankets, rifles; today, hard cash" (1996: 3). There is also the paternalistic notion that Indians are incapable of running sophisticated gaming operations without being swindled or taken advantage of by crooks and charlatans. Additionally, and perhaps most significantly, gaming has become a power struggle between states and Indian communities, each of which seeks to exercise its own rights of sovereignty. Sioux Harvey (2000: 25) points out:

> The Indian Gaming Regulatory Act of 1988 (IGRA) was introduced in response to the confusion about federal and state jurisdictional control over reservation casinos.[5] The goal of the IGRA was to regulate Indian gaming operations as well as to provide some federal protection for tribes from state governments, which in many cases tried to curb Indian operations.[6]

The sovereignty issue strikes at the heart of the conflict: states and tribes have each, obviously, attempted to shape the IGRA to serve their own sovereignty needs. Most Native Americans felt they were giving away far too much in allowing states to have a role in negotiating compacts and explained, correctly, that revenue sharing with states was simply a disguised form of taxation. States, however, claimed they would incur costs from the gaming activities, based on their belief that gaming leads to higher crime rates, higher levels of addiction treatment, and other assorted administrative costs (none, that I am aware of, cite the influx of tourist money as problematic). In short, tribal leaders believe that since their operations are on federal trust land, the state should have no jurisdiction. States have complained that IGRA exempts tribes from paying taxes while reducing states' regulatory control. Some, such as Eugene Christiansen (president of a gambling consultation firm), believe that Indian gaming is responsible for forcing states to change their gambling laws. He suggests: "Indian gambling is goading state legislatures to authorize casino games and other forms of gambling. If the Indians have casinos and states can't tax them, there is a natural tendency for legislators to say 'Hell, we'll have our own casinos that we can tax'" (Lawrence 1999).

This "blame the victim" attitude belies the reality of gaming. Approximately 40 percent of all gaming revenue in the United States is derived from state lotteries, 5 percent from Indian gaming, and 55 percent from commercial entities in Nevada and New Jersey. It is consistent, however, with the notion some states (e.g., Texas) hold that the lottery is not technically gambling. In large part, however, most anti–Indian gaming states attempted to sell their position against Indian gaming to the public based on issues of morality and public safety. Although most of the antigaming rhetoric revolves around morality concerns, that argument (outside the Religious Right) falls largely on deaf ears (polls indicate 70 percent of Americans approve of gaming on Indian reservations). Ironically, the vast majority of Americans now support most forms of gaming, in part because of the promotion of gaming by states and churches (Lambert 2002: 35, quoted in Darian-Smith 2004; see also Mason 2000).

Genuine independence is all many Indian communities aspire to, and it has become clear that (with the exception of tribes whose lands contain mineral or other forms of natural wealth), gaming is often their only path to self-sufficiency. Eve Darian-Smith (2004: 96) points out the cyclical nature of Indian dependence:

> Without economic independence, Native Americans are caught in a systemic cycle of oppression, poverty, and marginalization that has existed since the earliest colonial times. Without economic independence, Native Americans are not able to participate in mainstream party politics, and certainly not able to participate in capitalist enterprises.

Oneida (Wisconsin) Indian Rick Hill (chairman of the National Indian Gaming Association) concurs: "The tribes don't have any money unless we do gaming, because we don't have a tax base. We have lived in Third World poverty conditions, but gaming has proven to be mutually beneficial to state and tribal governments" (Lawrence 1999). Additionally, support is voiced by those who see some tribes using their casino profits to raise the standard of living in their respective communities. Tribes have earmarked funds to establish college scholarships, to construct clinics and hospitals, to build schools and day care centers, to open hotels, restaurants, gas stations, to fund retirement programs for their tribal Elders, and to make long-term business investments.

More important for some is the idea that casino profits can be used to develop cultural preservation programs. Cultural resource centers and museums are common on the reservations of gaming tribes, and money is often available for various preservation projects such as language reclamation and renewal initiatives, the building and maintaining of tribal archives, and cultural education programs. Profits are also often used to reacquire traditional land lost (usually stolen) during (and since) the colonial period, and to secure and protect culturally important or sacred places within a group's traditional landscape.[7]

On the other side of the gaming issue are those who see casinos and bingo halls as a blight upon the landscape. For example, Tim Giago, publisher and editor in chief of *Indian County Today*, says this about what he calls the "casino culture":

> Many years ago, when I worked as a 'keyman' at Harrah's Casino in Reno, NV, while attending school there, I never dreamed that huge, Reno-like casinos would eventually become a part of the landscape on Indian reservations. . . . It is almost scary to see this culture invading the quiet, peaceful lands of the Indian reservations. . . . The few real Indians [remaining] . . . have allowed [outside] casino managers to take control . . . to desecrate and insult the religious practices, traditions and culture of other Indian tribes. (quoted in Lawrence 1999)

Lora Abaurrea (1996) points out that many elderly tribal members "fear losing their traditional values to corruption and organized crime"; many see the "proliferation of gaming" as "a spiritual cancer eating away at what is left of the soul of Native American communities." There is also much concern about the dispersal of casino profits, with tribal members and outsiders alike asking: Who is accountable for how, why, and where profits are spent? Some, such as Jim Northrup of the Fond du Lac band of Lake Superior Chippewa, wants it to be known that, with few exceptions, "most tribal councils do not share the profits with the [tribal members]." He believes that gaming is creating a "class society" on many reservations "because not all members get to share in the profits." "Here at Fond du Lac," he wryly points out, "we get a ham" (quoted in Lawrence 1999).

The "paternalistic notion" mentioned above, that Indians are incapable of running sophisticated gaming operations without being swindled or taken advantage of by crooks and charlatans, is not entirely unfounded. Clay Akiwenzie (1996) states:

> The problems are practically uniform throughout Indian country. Disorganized, factionalized, and historically poor communities with limited infrastructure and little-to-no experience managing large sums of money are now being confronted with the daunting task of effectively managing a multi-million dollar corporation.

This statement (though perhaps a bit dated) reflects the fact that a number of gaming contracts signed with outside firms resulted in losses of millions of dollars to individual tribes. For example, the Interior Department reviewed thirty-seven contracts signed with outside gaming managers (before 1993) and "concluded that there were excessive fees amounting to $62.2 million in 18 of them" (Lawrence 1999). The government further concluded that "the management companies' risk and investment did not justify their fees—as high as 40% of net revenue." Additionally, the same probe reported the "startling revelation . . . that six tribes in Wisconsin and seven more in Michigan paid $40.3 million to lease gaming equipment that they could have bought for just $3.2 million" (Lawrence 1999).

Economic reality takes precedence for many (particularly "younger generation") Natives, who see gambling as an opportunity to advance their people and improve life in their community. For those reasons, Abaurrea (1996) suggests, "many are willing to face those stakes [corruption and organized crime] for economic salvation." And although it would be naïve to suggest that some gaming tribes are not being taken advantage of by "crooks and charlatans," it is equally naïve (not to mention ethnocentric) to suggest that "Indians are incapable of running sophisticated gaming operations without being swindled or taken advantage of." Indeed, many tribes (the Tigua included) have proven that they are more than equal to the task.

Another issue that has been discussed in Indian Country "but never resolved," and that strikes at the heart of the gaming debate, is the question of balance:

> How . . . [can Indian communities] best balance traditional cultural practices and moral belief systems with economic development. This idea of balance has been central to the debate over gaming on the Hopi Reservation in Arizona as well as on the Navajo Reservation which surrounds them. Both nations have chosen to reject gaming as a source of revenue because for them, the question takes on an either/or sensibility. . . . While this may seem rigid and anti-progressive to some people, it is a very real concern to many of the traditional people whose reality exists outside the world of profit margins and economic theory. (Akiwenzie 1996)

The question of balance, and the way in which the Tigua approached this issue, will be discussed below.

The Tigua Gaming Debate

In 1991 Texas passed its State Lottery Act and defined "lottery" as "procedures . . . through which prizes are awarded or distributed by chance among persons who have paid." In short, persons who "play" the lottery are gambling, risking a loss of money in hopes of a greater return. With the door now open to gaming in the state, and after seeing what some recognized tribes were able to achieve under the new gaming regulations, it was obvious that gaming was an issue that the tribe would have to consider as a way out of its weak economic situation.[8] The Tigua felt that in 1991 they were following, to the letter, the language of the 1987 recognition bill (Restoration Act), which clearly stated that tribal laws on gaming were to be identical to Texas law until amended. Unquestionably, the 1991 State Lottery Act passed by Texas represented an "amendment" to state gaming law.

Despite the openings provided by the passing of IGRA and, particularly, the blatant opening provided by the State Lottery Act, the tribe was unsure about embracing gaming as an economic option. The many issues and concerns swirling around Indian gaming were not unknown to the Tigua when they debated the question. Indeed, the decision to open a gaming operation was arrived at only after "long and sometimes bitter argument" (Cruz). The question of "balance" (as discussed above) was not lost on the Tigua as they searched for a way to resolve the many issues inherent in the debate. In the end (not unlike the debates that surrounded the tourism issue), the majority of the tribe determined that the argument boiled down to survival. The question was eventually solved pragmatically, but not without compromise. For example, to help avoid further controversy and to isolate the gaming activities, the decision was made to locate the casino as far as possible from the *tuhlah*, the site of most traditional activities. In discussing this process, Jesus states:

> As for the gaming . . . the gaming, yeah, you really have your problems, but were you going to trade jobs? I mean, the source is not there. Can you become self-sufficient and it is really a problem. . . . We, we're looking at what do we have as a resource to make money for the tribe? We looked at the center [*culture center*] as a resource to make money, tourism, but we don't have the resources to do that. So we started looking at it [*gaming*] and we said, "OK, first we have to see and think about how

to separate the gambling from the tradition, keep the tradition away from the gaming over there."

Friction between the so-called traditionalists and modernists led to some serious infighting, a commonly cited cause for intratribal conflict with regard not only to gaming issues, but various other issues related to "cultural progress." Traditionalists tend to be concerned about the harm (in this case) gaming can inflict on their group's cultural heritage, customs, and identities (see Akiwenzie 1996), whereas modernists tend to focus on the advantages of new technologies and the power and clout that can come along with a successful gaming operation. Of course, neither of these simplistic descriptions goes to the heart of the matter, as the gaming debate is nuanced and many-faceted.

My experience with the Tigua has led me to consider the importance of a third group, the "pragmatists." The Tigua community, as a whole, is very traditional and, as mentioned earlier, did not make the decision to go into gaming without contentious debate. The pragmatists won out, primarily because they were able to turn the purely traditionalist argument against itself. Not only did they argue that, realistically, they had no other economic options, not only did they simply point out that the influx of money would raise their collective living standard and educational attainment (which would allow them to play on a level field with their oppressors), but they argued that the casino money would actually allow them to better promote and secure their cultural heritage. This logic (which, largely, played itself out) centered on the notion that casino money could be used to promote cultural heritage through tribal-funded research, the expansion of the tribal archives, an updated museum, a funded traditional dance troupe, and the reacquisition of traditional land, among other possible uses. Although some argued that most of these initiatives could be funded through government grants, the sad truth is that government grant monies are extremely difficult to come by and that there was no guarantee that any of these needs, let alone all of them, would ever see a penny of funding from the government.

The real argument here revolved around the question of money and the role it would ultimately play in shaping Tigua culture. Although the Tigua clearly perceive their culture as traditional, the reality is that their tradition must be adjusted to the prevailing conditions (as discussed previously), and their community exists within the confines of an urban, capitalist, market system. Because for many in capitalist societies, money "stands for alienation, detachment, impersonal society, the outside" and because "its origins lie beyond our control," some traditional peoples fear that money takes on "a life of its own" and leads inextricably to cultural destruction (Carrier 2005).

Conversely, relations that are "marked by the absence of money" have become "the model of personal integration and free association, of what we take to be familiar, the inside" (Carrier 2005). These conflicting perceptions seem to imply that, by accepting a turn toward greater financial wealth, a community that follows the path of riches is simultaneously turning its back on traditional practice. This either/or notion, however, is not borne out by the evidence; cases abound that indicate that money is not incompatible with cultural perseverance. For example, Marshall Sahlins (1997: 52) suggests that "money can very well be the servant of custom not its master." He goes on to cite the Cree and several New Guinea Highland groups as examples of traditional communities who have used money to serve such a purpose (51–53). For the Tigua, however, the issue was not (as the pragmatists pointed out) to reach community-wide consensus about the morality of money as somehow inherently good or evil, but to reach community-wide consensus about how best to seize control over the influence money would have within the tribe.

This outcome is echoed in *A Handbook of Economic Anthropology* (Carrier 2005) in its critique of *Money and the Morality of Exchange* (Parry and Bloch 1989), when James Carrier states that the contributors to this collection "share the view that indigenous societies around the world take modern money in their stride, turning it to their own social purposes rather than being subject to its impersonal logic." This is possible because there are "two circuits of social life: one, the everyday, is short-term, individuated and materialistic; the other, the social, is long-term, collective and idealized, even spiritual," and because monetary relations are connected specifically to "the first category," societies are able "to subordinate" the influence of money "to the conditions of their own reproduction, which is the realm of the second category."

Being cognizant of the concerns surrounding the influence of sudden wealth on a community, though clearly important, does not necessarily mean that its every aspect can be controlled. For example, an additional concern among the Tigua traditionalists was that gaming would lead to an influx of tribal members who were only interested in cashing in on the casino bonanza. As Ralph Sturges, longtime chief of the casino-owning

Mohegan tribe in Connecticut, is quoted as saying: "Money is the greatest attraction in the world." However, because tribal membership rules were in place at the time of the casino opening, it would have been difficult (if not impossible) to exclude individuals who were obviously seeking monetary gain but who, nonetheless, met the existing membership requirements. Although, certainly, there were (and are) tribal members who only come around because of the money, this equation is a difficult one to quantify. Although some gaming tribes see a sudden surge in tribal enrollments, a pretty clear indication that the new members are likely interested in financial gain (see, for example, the Mashantucket Pequots, who saw their enrollment double), the Tigua did not experience a significant change in their enrollment numbers. There were other changes, however, that saddened a number of tribal members who believed some were only participating in tribal activities for reasons related to money. Maria, for example, states: "Now everything done here, now, everybody gets pay, and it's not about culture. It's about money. That's why there's jealousy around this Pueblo." While discussing the gathering of the food for the fiesta and how it used to be based on donations, Susana considers the impact of money on this traditional event: "You know, like I said, since we've come so much up in style now we had the money that, all this money, that we've made it a lot fancier for the fiesta. I heard a lot of bickering as far as getting paid; all this I have never heard . . . pay for following tradition?" Josephina expresses her unhappiness with the reaction of some of the Elders in volunteering to help at the various feasts: "There were quite a few Elders to take place [take part in] the fiesta feasts. You see very few Elders now. Before [the casino opened] we used to see a lot of Elders, not only men but women who used to take care of the fiesta. Back then we didn't have anything to depend on like we do now." In an admonition to the younger generation, Alonzo criticizes his perception of their attitude with the statement, "Don't just ask what are they going to give me [you] when they ask you to participate, no, I'm going to be like John Kennedy: ask not what the tribe can do for you but you go ahead and do for the tribe."

These concerns, although clearly important to the older generation, were seldom voiced by younger tribal members. This point is echoed by Jonathan Bloch and Maurice Parry (1989: 14) in a comment about research conducted by anthropologist Paul Bohannan with the Tiv of Nigeria (also see Carrier 2005):

It is not surprising, then, that when Bohannan writes about the Tiv's mistrust of money it always seems to be the elders who are deploring the situation. . . . Tiv elders talk about money in the way that we are apt to do—they make it into a condensed symbol of market relations, fetishise it by attributing to it an innate force independent of human will, and blame it for all the woes of their world.

Although the Tiv Elders' complaints were likely more related to their loss of authority over exchange marriage, and the Tigua Elders' concerns were over the role money plays in a perceived loss of cultural continuity, both groups appear to see money as the root cause of their problems. Perhaps for both, however, it is the perceived (and real) loss of authority and control over events that is most painful. My point is simply that the role of the casino and the influx of money as the root cause of the Elders' concerns might be somewhat overblown and may be better interpreted as simply the intergenerational complaints that are common in all societies. For example, Reyes describes the "respect, loss [of respect], a lot of respect has been lost." And Maria says: "When I was very young . . . everybody got together and there was unity between the people and the members." Additionally, comments made, primarily during the preparation phase of various ceremonies I attended, pointed to intergenerational rancor. For example, commonly heard comments include: "These kids think they know everything"; "You can't teach these kids anything; they think they know it all"; "This tribe is going to be in trouble when we die, nobody is going to know what to do"; and "They think they know tradition but they are doing it all wrong." In other words, at these events I heard the same complaints that are common at virtually any family function in almost any culture.

A rift of a much more serious nature did erupt shortly after the tribe started gaming operations, however, and (at least on the surface) appears directly related to traditionalists' concerns about the casino. In 1993–1994, the (then) war captain became embroiled in an argument that developed (reputedly) over the casino and its impact on traditional practices.[9] The dispute led to the development of a splinter faction within the tribe, with both sides claiming control over tribal offices. The side opposing the war captain eventually won out, but during the rift the sacred tribal drum, known as *Juan*, or *Juanchiro*, along with the two *abuelo* masks and several other sacred items, were hidden away. The drum, as discussed before, has played a powerful role in keeping the Tigua together throughout the years as it is perceived to be "like an old wise man," knowing everything about the Tigua. The Tigua believe it has a soul of its own, and the drum provides spiritual advice to the tribe. The drum's importance cannot be underestimated, and its return was of the utmost concern. After a 1995 criminal trial found the war captain not guilty of theft, the tribe upped its reward for the return of the drum from $500,000 to $1 million.[10] The drum was returned, but the hard feelings that had developed between tribal members linger to this day. Several tribal members continue to blame the casino for the development of this rift, as well as their current problems, stating: "The grandfathers are angry about the casino and this is our punishment."

Speaking Rock Casino Opens

After making the decision to pursue the gaming option, the tribe negotiated a compact with then Governor Ann Richards and reached an agreement on the issues and the percentage of money that would be earmarked for the state (purportedly 8 percent of total revenue) (see Schmidt 2004). Tigua attorney Tom Diamond left Austin after negotiating the compact, pleased that a fair deal had been arrived at. The following morning, however, he discovered that the state was backing out of the agreement. Perplexed by this development, the Tigua, nonetheless, responded by continuing to follow IGRA provisions. The next step (according to IGRA guidelines) was to sue Richards and the state in order to force them to negotiate a compact. The U.S. District Court ruled in the tribe's favor, and it appeared that the state would be forced to return to the bargaining table. Texas, however, appealed to the U.S. District Court on the grounds that its sovereign immunity was being impinged. The Fifth Circuit Court of Appeals upheld Texas's view on this issue and ruled that IGRA didn't apply to the Tigua, ignoring the idea that the most recent legislation (IGRA, which passed in 1988) should prevail over the earlier legislation (the Restoration Act, which passed in 1987). Further, the Fifth Circuit Court of Appeals ignored the principle of not adjudicating matters a previous court had settled.

Relations between Indian tribes, states, and the federal government are predicated on three centuries of law and treaties. However, it is often unclear where the dividing line between these three entities starts and ends (see Chapter Three). Although many observers (see, for example, Schmidt 2004; Gover 2002; Butterfield 2005; Skaibine 2002; Boylan 2002) were astounded by the findings against the tribe, the ruling, nonetheless, stood. The language of the Restoration Act stated that the tribe could do only what the state could do, and, clearly, Texas had legalized gambling.[11] The feeling around the Tigua reservation was that if the state was going to usurp the tribe's sovereignty and ignore them as a government entity, they would return the favor and ignore the state. The tribe and Diamond determined that they were within their legal rights to begin a gaming operation and simply started gambling, utilizing their own regulatory control.

> I mean, we did the whole thing [*decided to go into gaming without a state compact*], and then when we did that, we went out and put an ad that said we are interested in going into gambling. So, you know, send us your RSVP. But at the same time we put a clause saying if we decide to pick you [*as the gaming organization*] there is criteria that we got a right to investigate who are the players, who are the investors. We said, you know, we want to see your books. And, from there, we had, we had about ten [*applicants*]. There was one from Chicago, a contract that wanted to give us up front two million dollars. Someone wanted to give us one and one half million, some other company three million, and we said, "OK, do you comply with this?" [*our compliance guidelines*] and they say, "No." OK, that's when we got Seven Circles because they comply with everything. So, the plan's put together and that's what we did. (*Jesus*)

The Tigua contracted with Seven Circles Resorts to build and manage a high-stakes bingo parlor, which opened as Speaking Rock Casino in 1993. The bingo hall was immediately successful, and the tribe began to gradually add table games and slot machines.[12] After several years, the tribe bought out Seven Circles and began running the casino on its own. Most of the key casino management positions were held by tribal members, and many positions critical to day-to-day operations (e.g., security, food and beverage service, advertising and promotions, etc.) were likewise handled by the Tigua.

During the next decade, the tribe achieved a level of success that was, by any measure, astounding:

- Unemployment among tribal members dropped from over 50 percent to virtually zero.
- Casino employees (many non-Tigua) earned wages $2,500 above average along with full benefits.

- Speaking Rock (which earned roughly $60 million a year at its peak) had a payroll of $14 million.
- Local crime rates were reduced dramatically, making the casino's zip code the safest in the city.
- Eighty-seven percent of the tribal government's funds were generated through Speaking Rock; the tribe virtually stopped applying for federal grant funds.
- Polls showed 77 percent of city's residents backed the casino, and groups such as El Paso's City Council and Chamber of Commerce voiced their support.
- The tribe made charitable donations to the tune of $1.25 million (including $100,000 in flood relief to the city of Laredo and $100,000 to the victims of the World Trade Center assault).
- The tribe was able to build a recreation and wellness center that offered diabetes treatment, health classes, exercise rooms, and an Olympic-size pool for the whole community.
- Leaders put together a ten-year plan to build twenty-five houses a year and end homelessness (tribal members would buy their new homes on a sliding scale, not get them free).
- Leaders developed an educational program that monitored children closely during their school years (an investment that helped lead to a graduation rate of 98 percent [up from a dismal 10 percent] and the first generation of college graduates from the Tigua community) and built a library center with full Internet access (Schmidt 2004; also see Schulze 2001: 29).
- In order to further assist community members, the tribe designated a percentage of the casino profits to go to individual tribal members in the form of per capita payments. Rather than just hand the minor children a lump-sum payment, however, the tribe placed restrictions on who would be eligible:

So, with the help of the attorneys, we said, OK, were not going to just give money [*per capita distribution*] to everybody, like that, this is going to be the qualifications for the young kids. In other words, to get the money you need criteria. For the kids you must be eighteen and get your high school diploma or GED. Then you get your money. But, if you don't, you have to wait until you are twenty-two, but the money is still there for you. I think that then we said, OK, so much goes to the Elders for utilities, or meals or whatever, and for [*tribal*] programs. (*Cruz*)

It is important to point out here that IGRA requires all tribal gaming revenues to be used solely for governmental or charitable purposes. Much like state governments, who determine how lottery proceeds are to be spent, gaming tribes are forced to justify and account for where their profits go. As Darian-Smith (2004: 104) states:

> In direct contrast to the opulent expenditures of commercial casino operators such as Donald Trump, Indian tribes use gaming revenues to build houses, schools, roads, sewer and water systems; to fund the health care and education of their people; and to develop a strong, diverse future economic base.

Bush "Discovers" the Tigua

During its first five years of operation, Speaking Rock experienced minimal conflict with the state. Ann Richards was no longer in office, and the new Texas governor, George W. Bush, was apparently unaware a casino was operating in West Texas. He found out about it, however, after the Tigua donated (purportedly) $100,000 to Garry Mauro, Bush's Democratic challenger in the 1998 race for governor (Schmidt 2004). Mauro, who, unfortunately for the Tigua, lost to Bush, had advocated that Texas reach a revenue-sharing agreement with the tribe. After hearing about the donation, Bush suddenly (and clearly not coincidentally) began to attack the tribe and their casino. A prominent Bush spokeswoman, Karen Hughes, had the audacity to equate Tigua tribal gaming with illegal drug dealing. Texas, however, apparently only equates gaming with drug dealing when it is Indians who are profiting from it. The state, while fallaciously maintaining that casino gambling was illegal in Texas, conveniently forgot about its own role in the gaming industry (Schmidt 2004). As Kevin Gover (2002) points out:

> In Texas, the state conducts a state lottery. Licensed Texans can run raffles, bingo games, and "eight-liners," a form of slot machine. Texas allows "casino nights," scratch-off pull-tabs, and pari-mutuel racetrack betting on dogs and horses. In private places, Texans can play cards for money. Anyone familiar with Indian gaming laws knows that this array of legalized gambling in the State of Texas paves the way for Texas Indian tribes to offer a wide range of gaming activities on the reservations. According to the federal courts, though, the Tigua Indians of Ysleta del Sur Pueblo do not enjoy such rights. Even bingo. Even raffles. Even

eight-liners, lotteries, casino nights, racetracks and all those other things that are legal in the State of Texas.

Of course, Bush's view on Indian sovereignty was that they should not have any. His comment that "state law reigns supreme when it comes to the Indians, whether it be gambling or any other issue" (quoted in Schmidt, 2004) is astounding in its degree of arrogance and ignorance about Indian standing under the U.S. Constitution. A self-proclaimed strong advocate of state's rights (except when those state rights do not suit him, e.g., Florida in 2000), Bush made it clear that the state of Texas was not about to tolerate Indian self-determination. Immediately following his reelection as governor, Bush (purportedly) granted his attorney general, John Cornyn, $1.5 million to prosecute "illegal" gambling in the state. In fact, the money was used to set up a task force to pursue the Tigua. Although Bush claimed the pursuit was not politically motivated, it was obvious that his goal was retribution. Additionally, attacking Tigua gaming provided Bush the opportunity to placate his conservative political supporters (he was just beginning a run for the presidency at this time), as well as to protect the Texas lottery from competition (Schmidt 2004).[13]

In 1999 Cornyn filed suit against the Tigua, and once again the case went to the Fifth Circuit Court of Appeals. Predictably, this court once again ruled against the Indians.[14] The court claimed that the State Lottery Act had only legalized lotto, not all games of chance, despite its clear language that defined "lottery" winnings as "prizes [which] are awarded or distributed by chance among persons who have paid." Furthermore, it claimed that "the Restoration Act's ban on gaming was absolute, not conditional, and went on to state that the tribe had waived its sovereignty with respect to gaming, though nothing stated that explicitly" (Schmidt 2004). Cornyn, incredibly, had argued that the tribe was only an "association" under the Texas Penal Code, comparable to "a sorority or a fraternity." The Fifth Circuit, in a bizarre interpretation of Indian law, actually upheld this definition. An editorial written by the editors of *Indian Country Today* (2001) makes clear that Native Americans are paying close attention to the court rulings emanating from the state of Texas:

> The Fifth Circuit District Court of Appeals in New Orleans decided that the Tigua Indian Tribe of the Ysleta del Sur Pueblo . . . a federally recognized American Indian government, basically does not have the

rights of virtually every other federally recognized tribe in the country. . . . Cavalierly, the court decided to deny the status rights of the Tigua, agreeing with the state attorney general's position that "in Texas," Indian tribes are simple "associations" and have no more rights than "a sorority or a fraternity." . . . The Tigua are federally recognized and covered under the 1987 Pueblo Restoration Act. The act is but one of several legal bases that open the way for tribes to conduct economic enterprises, including gaming, in Texas and in any other state where federally recognized tribes reside. But, according to this troublesome ruling, Texas has the right to define the status of American Indians.

Because the impact of these rulings could eventually reverberate throughout the country, Indians and legal experts alike have been closely monitoring and dissecting the setting of this possible legal precedent. Carole Goldberg, professor of law at the University of California, Los Angeles, states: "The Fifth Circuit failed to apply the Supreme Court's Cabazon decision properly and failed to give proper weight to the Indian law canons of construction, which specify that ambiguous federal statutes should be interpreted so as to protect tribal sovereignty" (in Schmidt 2004; also see Gover 2002).

The question of ambiguity stems "from the last sentence of Section 107 (of the 1987 Pueblo Restoration Act) which mentions that the provisions of this subsection are enacted in accordance with the tribal resolution of March 12, 1986" (Gover 2002). Because this resolution "purports to endorse a complete ban on all gaming on the reservation," and the Senate Report continued (by accident) to contain language asserting that "the central purpose of the bill was still to ban gaming on the reservations," an ambiguity was created where the intent of Congress was to write a straightforward bill (Boylan 2002).[15] The fact that this bill contained language that gave the state and courts an opening to shut down Speaking Rock Casino was just the latest in a long line of mishaps visited upon the tribe through no fault of its own.

Conclusion

Speaking Rock Casino closed on February 12, 2002. Eight hundred people immediately lost their jobs, and tribal unemployment and welfare assistance soared. Nearly three thousand jobs were lost across the city, and an estimated $70 million in personal income was lost statewide. Tigua housing construction was forced to stop after 110 homes had been built. A plan to erect twenty-five gas station/convenience stores ended at six. Significantly, the tribe has been forced to make large cutbacks in programs such as elder care, health services, and education (Schmidt 2004). Additionally, paid vacations, retirement plans, medical insurance, and per capita payments have been canceled. Also stopped cold in its tracks was the Tigua program to quietly reacquire land lost during "the great land theft." For years, the Tigua had been purchasing their stolen land, content to pay fair market price for what was legally theirs. They preferred to get their land back in this manner, rather than to make waves going through a potentially very public and drawn out legal process. This attitude is consistent with a comment that was made by Tom Diamond back in the early 1960s. When someone asked him why the Tigua had never attempted to get their land returned sooner, he replied: "Because they didn't want to upset their neighbors." Indeed, the Tigua, who were long aware that their land had been stolen, had only brought up the possibility of filing a claim (when they did) as a way to provide leverage during recognition negotiations with the state and federal governments, not because they were interested in exploiting the land claim for its great financial potential.

Considering the turmoil and persecution the Tigua community has experienced throughout its tenure in El Paso, one would reasonably expect that this latest blow would cause widespread feeling of acrimony and resentment. It did not, however, come to me as a great surprise to find that many Tigua perceived the loss of the casino not as a personal or even Tigua-centered issue, but as a loss to the community of El Paso:

> It's not just something . . . for our people. It did help them a lot, there was work, there were job openings and if that job opening closed they put you in any position, but [the person] would still have a job. We were trying to get our people to help themselves, and it wasn't just our people; it was our community, our surroundings that we were working for too. We treat them the same as we would treat our tribal members; there is no favoritism on how we treated the people, just because you are an Indian didn't mean you had more rights to do this; it wasn't like that. If you worked for the tribe you were a part of the tribe. Hopefully they do consider themselves like that. (Cortez)

> It helped us out a lot . . . it was good, it has brought a lot of good to our people and even helped a lot of kids go to school and buy them a lot

of stuff like for school supplies. It wouldn't just help our people, it helped our [El Paso] fire department, our schools, we helped a lot of schools, not just our schools, we thought about El Paso and it wasn't just El Paso, there was an accident that happened in Del Rio, it was a tornado or something like that, our people sent some money down there and they delivered it down and they hand-delivered it, tried to help them out as much as we could. It brought a lot of good to the people in El Paso. (*Tito*)

This outlook would undoubtedly surprise many in capitalist, "free market," laissez-faire America, where the accumulation of wealth as an end in itself is often justification enough for seeking riches. Flying in the face of greed, self-promotion, and a business model that promotes the bottom line at any and all costs, community-minded Indian groups like the Tigua emerge as a threat to the status quo. Such an attitude is consistent with Puebloan cultural values in general and with the Tigua in particular. For example, I once asked a Tigua Elder about pharmaceutical corporations growing rich exploiting indigenous knowledge (intellectual property), and his response was direct: "I don't care," he said. "Now, let me ask you a question," he went on. "Do the medicines they make with Indian guidance help people?" I had to admit, "Yes, in fact they do." I was focused on being appalled that people were being taken advantage of for a profit, but as a Pueblo Indian his concern was for the common good. People were being helped, and that was more important to him than the loss of financial compensation. The value of sharing and helping others is engrained within the Puebloan worldview; however, it is decidedly not engrained within the worldview of most capitalists. The notion that many capitalists feel threatened by a business model that promotes generosity is compelling. Darian-Smith, for example, points out that

> many tribal governments involved in lucrative casino activities challenge the idea of economic profits as the overriding rationale for all activities. . . . In contrast to many other American businesses, tribes involved in gaming generally give substantial percentages of their profits on a voluntary basis to local non-Indian charities and community groups. . . . The point is that there are emerging alternative models, if only on the margins of mainstream capitalism, of how to conduct business and distribute business earnings. By promoting community service,

charitable contributions, and the value of sharing the wealth among those less fortunate so that society as a whole may benefit, Indian capitalism is also challenging the dominant logic in which economic gain is the only result that matters. (2004: 104)

The Tigua, who are continuing to fight for the return of their casino, are in many ways worse off financially now than they were when the casino opened. The overhead generated by their ownership of large buildings and landholdings, as well as the costs associated with maintaining the minimal staff necessary for the upkeep and maintenance of these holdings, is significant. Government funds, always difficult to come by, are temporarily stemming the flow, but soon the tribe will be broke. The few tribal members who still have jobs on the reservation have taken huge cuts in pay and benefits; some are in danger of losing their homes. A frequently cited concern involves the difficulty tribal children are now having affording their college education. Alonzo states:

> If the casino comes back it would be a good thing. There's a lot of kids that don't have the money to go to school and they want to go to school and that's one way of doing it. We are not getting the grants that we should get and I think we should help our young ones as much as we can to go to school. Pay their education, to do as much as we can for our people, because they are to be our leaders someday and we have to take care of them.

The casino closing seems to have hit the younger generations the hardest, not only because they can no longer afford to go to school, but because many have not lived through the extreme poverty of their Elders. Indeed, some Elders (especially those who opposed the casino) believe that it is the young who are being hardest hit. For example, Felipe points out that "this is very hard for the young generation because we create our own monster. Everyone, all the people, used to getting their money, and now they don't have it, they don't have anything. Yes, we create a monster." Others, such as pragmatic respondent Jesus, feel that the tribe should consider other ways of generating revenue and only reenter gaming with extreme caution. He points out:

> Even if we can get it back it's going to take three or four years to really get up [get the money coming in again] because if they do give us [gaming] they are going to put regulations, they are going to put, they are going to

tell us what to do with that money. The tribe's not hardly going to have any say at all, you know? It's going to be regulated by, it's just to them, it's just going to be an extension of the lottery that they already got and they're going to throw the Tigua a little bit. Even in hiring and firing it's going to be, they are going to be calling all the shots.

Interestingly, one of the rumors making the rounds in regard to the casino closing suggests that the state shut down the casino in order to pressure the Tigua into granting the state dictatorial power as a condition of allowing it to reopen. True or not, the point made by Jesus speaks to the predicament the state has forced the Tigua into. In fact, the similarities between the Tigua situation today, and the situation faced by Native peoples during the government implementation of the 1934 Indian Reorganization Act, are strong.

Concluding Remarks

Introduction

The United States of America was formed on the principle that "all men are created equal," and that all citizens have the rights of "Justice and Liberty." Unfortunately, as this research has clearly demonstrated, "equality," "justice," and "liberty" are not rights that have been extended to the Native occupants of this land. Indeed, Native individuals, communities, and organizations have been forced to react and respond to a system of domination that has firmly placed long-term indigenous viability in serious jeopardy. By inventing the "Indian," and, more importantly, by defining and legalizing "Indian identity," the United States has created a category that it can manipulate at will.

The invention and meaning of words, and the relationship among words, language, and law are issues that have been debated among scholars, politicians, and bureaucrats for hundreds of years (see Chapter Three). This endless debate is the product of a world that is made up of laws, nation-states, power relationships, and contested identities. The world that the Tigua (and countless other indigenous groups) occupy in the twenty-first century is harsh, unforgiving, and unfair. It is driven by profit and power and cares nothing for justice or the commonsense explanations of culture provided by scholars like M. Carrithers, David Maybury-Lewis, and others (see below under the section "Essentialized Culture"). Reality dictates that the Tigua and others prove their authenticity and cultural veracity, and it dictates, moreover, the rules, procedures, and guidelines that they must follow in order to gain recognition as a legitimate community of human beings. The real world does not allow free-flowing and free-forming culture from its indigenous peoples; it demands that change be documented and justified, measured and evaluated. Although this reality is, at least in the United States, unfair, capricious, and "fixed" by a power structure that is designed and determined to eliminate its Indian problem, the sad truth is that moral righteousness makes no difference.

Perhaps worse than this arbitrary system for proving authenticity is the paradox that surrounds the issue of contested identity, the fact that regardless of how Native American Indian peoples respond to the issue, they will be categorized as wrong-headed. The problem, as Arif Dirlik (1997: 73–74) suggests, is complicated by how the mechanisms of culture are understood:

> In academic circles engrossed with postmodernity/postcoloniality as conditions of the present, it is almost a matter of faith these days that nations are "imagined," traditions are "invented," subjectivities are slippery (if they exist at all), and cultural identities are myths. Claims to the contrary are labeled "essentialisms" and are dismissed as perpetuations of hegemonic constructions of the world.

In other words, if indigenous peoples argue along with the postmodernists that culture is subjective, imagined, and fluid, the dominant power structure rejects ethnic identity as invented and withdraws support from marginalized groups. By arguing that there are essential aspects to culture, however, cultural groups lock themselves into fixed categories that defy change. Either way, the long-term goal of Native cultural extinction will be realized by the dominant power (see Chapter Three under "Indian Identity"). Even a cursory examination of the elements that make up recognition legislation exposes a number of problematic issues that work against Native peoples. For example, when indigenous identity is reduced to an "essential" idea, the task of colonization has been greatly simplified from a legislative point of view. The fact that there are well over five hundred disparate Native communities makes no difference to the one-size-fits-all legislation. Furthermore, these legislatively drafted rules of identity allow the government to place repressive demands on group conformity by allowing rigid boundaries to be drawn around cultural identities, and reward the preservation of authentic culture over the real world need to survive through adaptation.

By embracing multiculturalism as a legal policy (rather than just as a political or moral philosophy), culture becomes reified, essentialized, and exclusionary. Indeed, it promotes the interests of some over the interests of the national collectivity and retards the notion that social homogeneity and equality are available for all. It goes against the fundamental belief that the United States is a melting pot. Ironically, however, it is clear that the ultimate outcome of the federal recognition policy (as it presently stands) will be the eventual extermination of the Indian as a unique entity (see Enrique Sam Colop 1983: 61, quoted in Warren 1998: 195–196). Equally ironic is that arguments against the development of identity politics are proffered by both the political left and right, though obviously for different reasons. The right argues that identity legislation grants privileges to certain groups at the expense of the mainstream, whereas many on the left argue that legalized identity policies, by delineating specific group identities, splinters the collectivity necessary for the overthrow of the capitalist system.[1]

Another aspect of the issue that works against Native peoples is that (as discussed in Chapter Three) groups typically do perceive their own culture as essentialized and, therefore, define themselves based on their perception of cultural boundaries as real and inviolable (see also Warren and Jackson 2002: 8–9). Because boundaries are a key component of ethnicity (symbolically expressed in modes of dress, livelihood, language, cuisine, music, ritual, religious belief, etc.), cultural groups conceptualize their boundaries as distinctive of their own identity. Moreover, by formulating boundaries, cultural identity can be perceived of as under threat and in need of protection. In protecting these perceived boundaries from "pollution" or "appropriation," groups simultaneously develop and utilize methods of cultural perseverance, a critical aspect of long-term cultural survival (see Harrison 1999). Maybury-Lewis (1997: 61) believes that the "mechanisms for maintaining the boundaries of the group are critically important, for it is they that enable the group to persist." Without boundaries, people would be unable to distinguish between who could (or could not) become a member of the group. Additionally, they "need to know how far an individual can deviate from the norms and behaviors of the group before s/he will be no longer considered a member of it. Above all, they need to know how much and what kinds of interactions members of the group may have with outsiders if the group is not to lose its identity" (61). It is particularly important for urban groups like the Tigua, who already share so much in common with their Mexican neighbors, because "ethnic groups are never isolates. They invariably have contact with others that are accessible and their members invariably interact with each other across the group boundaries, even where there is hostility between groups" (61–62).

By acknowledging the bounded nature of cultural identity, groups embark on the slippery slope that leads to cultural extinction through definition. If indigenous communities cease to perceive of culture as made up of essential attributes, however, their identity and uniqueness will be called into question, not only by the government but by the members of their own community. As Ward Churchill points out (see Chapter Three), "a more perfect shell game is difficult to imagine" (2004: 70).

Essentialized Culture

In a perfect world, much of what I have written could have been left unsaid. The Tigua of Ysleta del Sur Pueblo simply are who they are; they have become whom they have become. The specific mechanisms behind their transformation from precontact Tigua to twenty-first-century Tigua would be largely irrelevant. Their experience as displaced, dominated peoples, forced to adapt to a new physical environment as well as a new cultural environment (wrought by colonialism), would be interesting but certainly not contested. We could simply point out that all culture is dynamic and that it should not be surprising that particular historical events led the Tigua to adapt in culturally appropriate ways. We could dismiss the critics who argue that Tigua traditions are fraudulent or who suggest that Tigua cultural adaptations are uneven, incomplete, and invented or made up. We could point to the words of Carrithers (1992: 30), who has this to say about culture:

> The fact is this: human beings, in contrast to other social animals, do not just live in relationships, *they produce* [relationships] *in order to live.* In the course of their existence, they invent new ways of thinking and of acting—both upon each other and upon the nature which surrounds them. They therefore produce culture and create history. (emphasis in the original)

The notion that authentic indigenous culture is locked in some kind of time warp and that change signals cultural extinction has become deeply embedded within the psyche of Americans, including many elected and appointed government officials. This unrealistic and ethnocentric notion, however, only applies to indigenous culture; the culture of the nation-state is not only allowed to change but promotes that change as an aspect and outgrowth of modernity. This double standard is exposed by Maybury-Lewis (1997: 37–38), who points out that it is false to assume "that a culture or way of life cannot survive if the bearers of that culture have to change their ways of making a living." He goes on to suggest that it is also false to assume that traditional societies cannot change and that, if they did, they could not be said to have survived, for they would no longer be what they once were. But all societies in the world are in a constant process of change. Change of itself does not destroy a culture. In fact we expect modern societies to change—it is part of their modernity that they do so. Do their cultures therefore vanish? (37–38)

Present-day Tigua culture has, indeed, changed. In fact, it has changed largely in response to the many cultural changes that have taken place within the dominant culture that surrounds Tigua borders. Tigua culture has been constructed in reaction to their real world situation and can be understood as an outgrowth of their determination to survive socially. The fact that they (and the United States) have changed and will continue to change is not at issue. The force that regulates the terms and parameters within which change take place is, however, very much at issue.

The issue of cultural change or, more specifically, the state-sanctioned parameters within which indigenous cultural change is constrained, threatens the viability of groups around the globe. Worldwide, indigenous peoples are fearful that the nation-state (as an entity) is positioning itself to do away with the concept of indigeneity altogether.[2] Indeed, the issues brought forth by the Working Group on Indigenous Rights are instructive in what they reveal about the current relationship between oppressed and oppressor.[3] That the Working Group asks for the right of self-determination within existing states is not remarkable. That it goes on to ask for protection of indigenous peoples' own institutions of governance, protection of their own special relationship to the land, and protection of their traditional economic activities, speaks to the fear that indigenous peoples' cultural survival has been directly targeted. That the Working Group feels compelled to ask specifically for protection against genocide, however, is nearly incomprehensible. As Maybury-Lewis (1997: 56) states, "To ask not to be massacred (protection against genocide)" is a right all peoples should expect. It is very "significant that indigenous peoples should feel that they need specifically to ask for it and to have it guaranteed" (also see Wade 1997: 1). This sad commentary speaks powerfully to the unconscionable position indigenous peoples have been forced into as part of a worldwide program of cultural genocide.

How, specifically, are Native peoples expected to respond to the no-win situation into which they have been forced? If they collectively agree that Native culture is boundless, that change is arbitrary, group specific, and meaningless within the context of Western ideals, then any "New Age," "buck-skinner," "wannabe Indian" could legitimately petition for recognition. Indeed, this very threat compels some Native leaders to push for more and more stringent recognition criteria. By setting these strict bounds, however, the long-term viability of Native culture is placed in serious jeopardy, regardless of who is defining what those bounds are.

One possible response to this issue would be to devise a system that would accommodate the flow of culture, that would embrace the fluid aspects of "imagined boundaries," and that would remain open to an ongoing dialogue and deliberation between Indian groups and the government regarding the specific needs of the individual, the group, and the nation-state. This notion, termed "deliberative democracy" (see Benhabib 1996, 2002), though appealing in theory, fails to account for the imprecise manner in which deeply entrenched colonial relations of power operate (on its failure, see Hardt and Negri 2000; see also Coulthard 2004). It should, of course, be evident that any "deliberative democracy" would be couched in the discourse of hegemony, placing the dominator (once again) in the privileged position. For example, the current federal acknowledgment process has been largely built and modified over the years based on the input of Native peoples. However, the basic elements of the process mirror the entrenched values of the majority capitalist system by penalizing socialist models of inclusion. The current colonial system rewards self-service and the value of individualism by empowering the Indian "haves" over the Indian "have-nots," sanctioning the collectivity when new members are added, because increasing the number of members reduces the per capita funding available to each member. Indeed, one of the more important aspects of current Indian recognition policy (as discussed in Chapter Four) involves the acceptance of new members by the currently recognized groups. Petitioning groups rarely gain recognition without the express acquiescence and blessing of federally sanctioned communities, and because the federal Indian "entitlement pie" is ever-shrinking, there is nothing to be gained and much to lose by embracing new tribal acknowledgments. Wide support for stringent recognition criteria is voiced by many presently recognized tribes; indeed, the most common concerns tend toward criticisms not over the strictness of the guidelines but the perceived lack of strictness (see Miller 2004).

The gaming issue further feeds the fires of dissent as gaming tribes are loath to welcome new tribes who may cut into their annual share of gaming revenue, which for many of these tribes is already modest at best. In short, this particular form of "deliberative democracy" has resulted in "real" Indians gaining a voice over the "questionable" Indians, but by forcing the deliberation over recognition guidelines to unfold utilizing the terms, laws, language, and cultural values of the capitalist oppressor, the federal government has given up little power. Furthermore, it is notable that the self-serving and vindictive nature of the colonial power structure is reflected in the behavior of some of these "empowered" Indians. The Tigua provide an excellent example, as they very nearly lost their bid to gain recognition in 1968 based solely on the concerns of a handful of vindictive New Mexican Pueblo leaders. Their concerns had nothing to do with whether or not the Tigua were a legitimate Indian tribe (as clearly they were) but were based upon the petty belief that the Tigua were traitors to the Pueblo Revolt three hundred years ago and, for this reason alone, should not gain recognition (see Schulze 2001: 28; Miller 2004: 230). Then, in the mid-1990s, a self-serving Indian tribe from a neighboring state spent millions of dollars to help the state of Texas in its bid to close Speaking Rock Casino because it wanted to get rid of Texas-based competition (see "Speaking Rock Casino Today" in the Postscript). Clearly, capitalist values and conceptions of power are not confined to the colonial power structure, but their use by and against marginalized Native peoples must give hope to those who would like to see the Indian problem resolved through assimilation.

Another way to respond to the paradox that surrounds identity politics would be to develop a system of "strategic essentialism" whereby subaltern groups (in this case American Indians) could empower themselves by "*temporarily* essentializing" their culture. By putting aside their differences and focusing on the attainment of group goals, the collectivity could jointly force its views on the dominant structure (see Spivak 1987). Although also an attractive option, it is difficult to imagine how this process would play out under real world settings. To say, for example, that Native peoples share enough in common to enable them to speak with one voice seems particularly unrealistic, given the diverse backgrounds, needs, and histories of Native communities. Indeed, there are presently scores of existing national "pan-Indian" organizations, as well as many local and regional organizations, each of which has its own mission, goals, and agenda and has (at least so far) been unable to find a common voice.[4] In fact, it seems unlikely that these disparate organizations will ever be able to focus their energies in one direction because the clear impulse of colonialism is to splinter the community.

How are Native individuals and groups expected to respond to a system of domination that has concurrently defined them as one holistic entity while obfuscating solidarity with culturally disruptive policies? For example, the colonial government purposely initiated both intergroup and intragroup rancor by actively and obviously favoring "partial bloods" over "full bloods," and by openly rewarding "progressive" acquiescence over "traditional" cultural rigidity. Groups who went along with the systematic changes, for example, those who agreed to form U.S. government–initiated tribal councils, were rewarded with desperately needed funding. Groups and individuals who fought this usurpation of tribal sovereignty were punished, denied funds, and accused of standing in the way of "progress" by both the United States and "progressive" Indians alike. Further, the government significantly disrupted cultural continuity and group cohesion in the following ways: by stealing Native land and forcing communities to relocate to unfamiliar territories, by forcing changes to traditional economic systems, by forcing the enculturation of children at the various Indian schools, by persecuting Native religion, by creating poverty where once there was prosperity, by creating a body of Indian laws that were purposely designed to eliminate the Indian problem, by perpetuating a popular discourse that was filled with lies and myths and that encouraged (and encourages) discrimination, and by forcing traditional forms of governance to conform to a colonial model (see Chapter Three).

Moreover, as unique and diverse cultural entities were forced to identify under the single, colonially constructed classification "Indian," groups that had never even heard of one another were now treated as if they were a single body. Suddenly, indigenous peoples discovered that they were Indian and that as far as the colonists were concerned, there was only one Indian culture, one Indian worldview, one Indian religion, one form of Indian government, one Indian history, and one set of Indian traditions and behaviors. As a result, tribes that had traditionally fought one another as mortal enemies were now defined as a single group, tribes that were traditional and tribes that were progressive were now defined as a single group, tribes that were agricultural and tribes that were nomadic were now defined as a single group, tribes that were polytheistic and tribes that were monotheistic were now defined as a single group, tribes that were matrilineal and tribes that were patrilineal were now defined as a single group, tribes that were polygamous and tribes that were monogamous were now defined as a single group, tribes that were large and tribes that were small were now defined as a single group, and tribes that were politically conservative and tribes that were politically liberal were now defined as a single group.

Additionally, each Native community has been forced to tailor its response to colonialism and modernity based on particular community requirements. As previously noted in Chapter Three some (perhaps many) Native leaders are driven solely by a desire to effect change in their own specific community. Their efforts are focused on goals specific to their particular concerns, and they support political representatives (regardless of party affiliation) that can, have, or will address their specific needs, regardless of those representatives' views on national Indian policy. Poverty, the largest compounding problem faced by many Native communities, must be addressed on the community level with immediacy and a singular focus. Native peoples on many reservations are malnourished, sick, living in substandard housing, and dying at an alarming rate (see the demographic data in Chapter Three). Whether the diverse goals and political agendas of the various pan-Indian groups can be bridged in an effort to significantly move current Indian policy in a new direction is an issue that flies under the radar for many community-based Indian leaders.

The use of political strategies, such as "strategic essentialism" and "deliberative democracy," fail to work for American Indians at least partially because of the reasons listed above. The overarching impediment to solidarity, however, is not cultural heterogeneity but hegemonic legal parameters. Although the long-term issue of Indian solidarity is highly salient and continually debated by national Indian leaders, the direction this debate takes is largely constrained by the U.S. system of laws. Not only are Native leaders forced to negotiate policy within a deeply entrenched colonial system of power, but the limited sovereignty and self-determination the U.S. government affords Native peoples severally curtail the bounds and direction that solutions to present and future problems can entail. If provided true rights of sovereign nationhood, American Indians could approach this issue in a way that could promise true self-determination.[5] The likelihood of the United States agreeing to "grant" Native nations true nation-state status, however, is nonexistent. Meanwhile, Native peoples must continue to negotiate their future within the bounds of hegemony, the ultimate direction and outcome of which can only be determined by present and future Native leaders.

Tigua Resistance

For the Tigua, the question of how or why culture is defined or legalized has never been an issue. Indeed, it would be fair to say that few, if any, Native people conceive (or ever conceived) of their culture as a defined, legal entity. For most people, culture simply is, and terms like "authenticity," "real," and "proof" are far removed from any individuals' conception of who they are. It is governments and academics that now question the nature of culture, and it has only become an issue of debate because these institutions have sought to make it a debatable concept. The goals of hegemony require a level of control over subjugated peoples, and the creation of legal identities allows the dominant power to streamline the process by grouping people according to some simplistic classification such as race or ethnicity (see van de Burghe 1992; Wade 1997). Consequently, the issue of "real" culture has become less of a philosophical or moral question and more an issue of reality. Terms like "authenticity," "real," and "proof" have taken on a new and very serious connotation when used in reference to culture. The question for indigenous peoples (particularly unrecognized American Natives) is not relevant to the philosophical attributes of reified culture but to the reality of proving cultural continuity.

As a case study, the Tigua provide a glimpse of how one particular group went about "preserving" their culture and then went on to "prove" that they continued to be a "viable" group. That the Tigua could document their culture in a way that corresponded with government requirements might be thought of as a fortunate happenstance, but reality dictates that we seek to understand the specific mechanisms that allowed (and allows) Tigua culture to persevere as both real and legally recognized.

As alluded to in Chapter Two, C. N. Le (2006) points out that it is not the substance or content of ethnicity that should be the focus when exploring the issue of identity; rather, it is the social processes that produce, reproduce, and organize the boundaries of differentiation between ethnic groups that are important to understand. Indeed, as we have seen (in Chapters One through Three), historical occurrences, oral history, religious beliefs, ceremony, ritual, and senses of landscape, combined with the reality of diaspora, significantly affected and informed how Tigua senses of identity were maintained, modified, and perpetuated. Cultural practice served as a kind of repository of cultural memory for the Tigua, which when taken together provide a vivid picture of how the Tigua culture survived. To a lesser extent, the "Why?" of cultural continuity is also described in this book. Particularly during Chapter Four, I continually returned to the vital issue of cultural pride, to the Tigua refusal to give up on their own identity. In addition, I believe that the issue of power also played an important role in the ability of the Tigua to survive culturally throughout considerable persecution and turmoil. In short, I believe the Tigua were able to persevere culturally as an officially unrecognized tribe for so many years largely because they refused to acknowledge that they were being subjugated. In fact, they did not even seek recognition until forced to, and it had apparently never occurred to them that they were not real Indians. They simply went about their business, doing what they had always done, adjusting tradition and practice as needed, and generally ignoring the world that built up around them as much as they could.

The Tigua have resisted assimilation in myriad ways (as we have seen), but the best examples of Tigua resistance are found in the many shared stories of defiance, several of which have reached mythic proportions. The issue of resistance, and particularly "everyday forms of resistance," is an important notion to consider in understanding Tigua survival. It is important, here, to point out that the following discussion will focus on acts of Tigua resistance that appear to be directly concerned with "improving the terms" of their own oppression and not with acts that strive "to implant a new sociopolitical order" (Gledhill 1994: 93). Or, as Maurice Godelier puts it: "There must be resistance of some kind. . . . But to resist is not to propose or to think of an alternate model, a social alternative. Social resistance is not social revolution" (quoted in Eiss and Wolfe 1994). This distinction highlights the long history of the tribe as isolated and forced to react to oppression in specific, contextual, and personal ways. Indeed, most examples of Tigua resistance can be viewed as reactive (rather than proactive), and as John Gledhill (1994: 91–92) points out, "Reactive processes may be creative and dynamic, but they seem to be concerned primarily with contesting sovereignty and defending spaces of autonomy *within* oppressive social orders." In fact, the Tigua response to oppression appears to center around specific individual and community-wide (as opposed to pan-Indian or Pueblo Indian) issues. Generating senses of power internally and focusing that power on specific Tigua community needs allowed the tribe as a whole to feed on both individual and group success, as well as share the difficulty of setbacks. Using their shared history, experience, and political commitments, the tribe link themselves to both their past and each other (90).

Though their survival gave (and gives) hope to other "forgotten" tribes, it is clear that was never the direct intent of their resistive acts.

The issue of resistance is, of course, tied to the issue of power. I made reference in the Introduction to a belief held by many (for example, see Jorgensen 1972; Davis and Reid 1999; Ishiyama 2003) that Native peoples have been rendered powerless in the face of colonization. Although I agree that indigenous groups are engaged in a continuing power struggle with oppressive dominators, I do not agree that indigenous peoples are "powerless." Carrithers (1992: 26), for example, touches on this issue during a discussion about powerless people or (his term) "people without history." Disagreeing that Native peoples are simply passive, he states:

> Those without history, the primitive and isolated, could . . . have no moral purpose. Moreover, they could have had no effect upon their own lives and destiny, because in the long run the only active agent is the civilization which, developing independently, now bears down upon them. They were passive, inert, waiting to be discovered. Wolf stresses to the contrary that all people everywhere have a hand in their fate, that they are not just patients but agents as well. (26)

The Tigua provide a good example of the fallacious nature of the belief in powerlessness, as the following examples highlight. During an interview, Bill Wright (1993: 140) asked an Elder a question about past incidents of discrimination, wondering if the El Paso community was growing to accept the tribe. His response was enlightening: "They should understand that we are accepting them, not them accepting us." This response, I believe, epitomizes the Tigua worldview while succinctly explaining how policies of forced enculturation were deftly deflected by this small Pueblo community. They simply refused to acknowledge the white majority as more powerful. A similar example was provided by Jesus (see the section in Chapter Four, "Federal Acknowledgment") when he made the following statement in regard to the move from state to federal recognition: "The BIA says, 'OK, we recognize you but this is what you have to do.' I do not know but somebody else [in the tribe] said 'OK, we recognize the federal government but we will not do this' [agree to the government deal]." The use of this specific language, "We recognize the federal government," clearly indicates that the Tigua never viewed their relationship with the government as one-sided in terms of power. Indeed, even during their time under state control, they continually refused to be subjugated, and fought against the rules the state attempted to force on them. When they made concessions, such as their agreement to create tourist-themed attractions, it was on their terms, and there was seldom a case where they felt that they were being "ordered" to comply with state mandates.[6] Their response to religious persecution was likewise based on the notion that they were not going to give away the power to control their own system of belief. For example, the Tigua have incorporated aspects of Christianity into part of their traditional belief system, but did it "in our own way." They "tricked" the Spanish into believing that they had accepted Christianity while continuing to follow traditional religious practices. Not only did they mislead the Spanish, but they also selected elements from the colonizers' religion that appealed to their ethos and moved their religious beliefs in a direction that suited their needs (see Chapter Two).

These small acts of resistance, though mostly hidden (and themselves largely improvised), are still vital components within the overall resistance strategy. Gledhill (1994: 148) speaks to this in his description of resistance as an outgrowth of power relations, arguing that we should not necessarily give "politically organized resistance analytical priority over individual strategies which counter specific forms of domination, even in minute, everyday ways." K. T. Lomawaima (1993: 236–237) points to this issue when she outlines the failure of the federal government to alienate Indian people from the land. The government has been unsuccessful largely because of "Indian people's commitment to the idea of themselves. As individuals and as community members, Indian people clung stubbornly to making their own decisions, according to their own values." Moreover, as a part of this process, "they have created spaces of resistance within the often oppressive domains of education, evangelism, employment, and federal paternalism" (236–237). Donald Moore (1998: 350) expands on this when discussing the 1980s concept of "ethnographies of resistance" and its overlapping agrarian studies counterpart, "everyday forms of peasant resistance," which emphasized "the importance of daily cultural practices" that "infused the soul of popular histories. From this perspective, women and men made their own histories through cultural contestation." Additionally, Moore discusses the research of James C. Scott, whose work on rural politics in Malaysia is "arguably the most influential perspective on resistance in agrarian studies over the past decade" (350). Scott points to the "everyday forms of peasant resistance" which "emanated from the quotidian practices of subordinated actors":

The ordinary weapons of relatively powerless groups: foot dragging, dissimulation, desertion, false compliance, pilfering, feigned ignorance, slander, arson, sabotage, and so on. These . . . forms of class struggle . . . require little or no coordination or planning; they make use of implicit understandings and informal networks; they often represent a form of individual self-help; they typically avoid any direct, symbolic confrontation with authority. (350)

K. Sivaramakrishnan (2005: 351) largely agrees with this statement but adds: "Although it is right to stress that everyday resistance focuses on the point of enforcement to minimize domination, the precise strategy does depend on knowing where domination is coming from—that is, a reading of the intentions inherent in domination." The Tigua provide a number of examples that speak to this point. For instance, the Tigua have long continued to make collection forays into territory no longer under their control. By rule of law, the Tigua are "poaching" or "stealing" any resources they remove from particular areas. These collection excursions, though clearly dangerous, are carried out as a direct repudiation of a government policy designed to limit (if not prevent) cultural patrimony (see other examples below). Although some acts of resistance are symbolic and largely hidden from public view, I would add that the Tigua have shown a willingness to confront authority directly, both on the individual and group levels.

An important aspect of the issue of resistance relates to the "political implications or outcomes" associated with acts of resistance (Shaw 1999). For example, "some critical theorists (e.g., Foucault 1979) believe that where there is oppression or inequity, there will inevitably be resistance or challenges to oppression as well." Resistance can, therefore, be understood "as the 'flip side' of reproduction, where dominant beliefs, and ideologies that maintain structured inequities are challenged and weakened, rather than reinforced and strengthened." Indeed, the "image" and "message" embedded in practices of resistance are important because of their "potential to impact opinions and belief systems." The overarching intent of the practice of resistance, as well as the effect the act has on others, importantly influences community-wide reactions to oppression. Additionally, individual acts of resistance resonate within the individual as a "form of personal power," which may embolden tribal members on an individual level and lead to further acts.

Earlier in the book, I mentioned a Tigua Elder who threatened to cut down the telephone poles located on his property in response to a county inspector who told him he needed a building permit to add on to his home. The Elder reacted by rejecting the implementation of outsiders' rules.[7] This act sent a forceful message to the community that tribal members need not always succumb to the dictates of majority law. Perhaps the more important message was found in his determined reaction. Not only did he refuse to get the permit, which was an act of resistance in itself, but his threat to cut down the poles represented his determination to "push back." Numerous stories follow the pattern of Tigua members who, when confronted, not only fought against oppression but fought back.

Another Elder was summoned to the courthouse so the judge could order him to stop hunting on his land.[8] He refused to go when ordered to go, threatened to shoot the agent, threw the agent off his land, and after arriving in court the next day, he bluntly refused to follow the court order and subtly threatened to shoot any agent who attempted to enforce the decree.

A final example of an overt act (described in Chapter Two) was the willingness of tribal members to shoot at cars that got too close to their parade route. A more direct, blatant, unequivocal act of resistance is difficult to imagine.

Despite the best efforts of both the state and federal governments to subjugate the tribe, they have failed largely because the Tigua have steadfastly refused to relinquish the inherent power they hold over their own destiny. Power, as the Tigua understand, is a two-way street. The question of how an Indian tribe had existed, unknown to anyone but themselves, after spending over three hundred years in the El Paso region is also answered by their refusal to sacrifice control over their own destiny. Simply stated, the tribe never felt compelled to advertise their presence. Some people knew of their existence, many did not, and the Tigua simply did not care what outsiders thought, one way or another. They knew who they were, had strong pride in their identity, and held an unwavering faith in their own ability to survive. They were an "authentic" people then and now, not because they have proven it to outsiders, but because they have never given up the power to define who they are to outsiders.

Traditional Tigua

Another question posed as a part of this research related to the concept of tradition: "What is 'traditional' behavior, and how can it be tracked?" Although the word "tradition" is devoid of relevant meaning for many

"Westernized" people, it is a word that evokes significant and specific meaning when used by Native peoples. For the average American, engaging in the same act or behavior more than two or three times is sufficient reason to proclaim the "start of a new tradition." The number of new or made-up Western traditions, the vast majority of which have lost their meaning (if there ever was a meaning to begin with), is frankly astounding: Sweetest Day, Arbor Day, Groundhog Day, innumerable rites and rituals associated with weddings and funerals, sports-related traditions, individual family traditions, religious traditions; the list goes on ad nauseam. Although we like to think of ourselves as progressive, innovative, and technologically advanced, we also like to perceive of tradition as somehow sacrosanct and honor the notion that "tradition is 'supposed' to be conservative and 'old-fashioned'" (Ewins 1998). By viewing ourselves as both progressive and sensitive to the value of "tradition," what Simon J. Bronner (2000) refers to as "the biformity of tradition in American public usage," we gain the ability to embrace cultural change as inevitable, while concurrently rationalizing change as both measured and purposeful. This perception of tradition as contextually important is further exposed by Max Radin (1935: 67), when he points out that "in all its aspects it retains enough of its primary characteristics of vagueness, remoteness of source, and wide ramification to make it seem peculiarly strong to those who have recourse to it and peculiarly weak to those who mean to reject it."

In the United States, the underpinning philosophy of both major political parties is anchored to the conservative/progressive dichotomy; the notions that change should be either rejected or embraced. In reality, however, each side (following the curve of public opinion trends) tends to promote change either as a "necessary evil" (conservative), or as "forward-looking" (progressive). The luxury of allowing ourselves the right to both embrace tradition and accept change fulfills the real world needs of Western societies. This is not a luxury that is extended to non-Western peoples, however. Our very description of most non-Western cultures belies our true intentions regarding cultural change and our power to control how others change in ways we deem appropriate. We refer to these "fourth world" communities as "traditional," "preliterate," "small scale," "primitive," "tribal," and "prehistorical" (among the nicer terms), along with the more outdated standards "savage" and "barbarian." These labels evoke connotations that imply not only cultural stasis but cultural purity. Cultural tradition, according to this conception, is not supposed to change; it is fixed, frozen, and inalienable (Bronner 2000). Those who possess traditional culture provide citizens of Western nations a "living museum," they remind us of what it used to be like, and we gauge our sense of progress on the baseline they provide. Accordingly, change in traditional practice signifies that the tradition is "broken" and somehow no longer, or at least less, "authentic." The developments of new or comparatively recent traditions are not perceived of as adaptive but as fraudulent. The Western observer, as Rory Ewins (1998) suggests, "might be tempted to say, 'This chief says he's the traditional ruler of these people, but he's not really traditional at all. The whole basis of his authority is false' . . . which in turn is the subject of a whole debate about the 'invention of tradition.'"

The notion that most (if not all) traditions are "invented" was popularized in 1983 by the book *The Invention of Tradition* by Eric Hobsbawm and Terence Ranger. Anthropologists such as Jocelyn Linnekin (1983) and Roger M. Keesing (1989) helped to fuel the fire begun (perhaps unintentionally) by Hobsbawm, and now government authorities from Australia to Hawaii (see Trask 2003: 37–42) to Texas (see the section of Chapter Five titled "Contested Identity") have pounced on the idea of invented tradition as yet another way to weasel out of legal obligations by arguing that authentic or real culture does not exist (also see Warren 1998: 209). If the traditions that culture is based on are fraudulent or made up, it is no stretch to conclude that culture itself is a spurious notion. Therefore, anyone who claims an indigenous identity must be acting fraudulently; they must be attempting to receive benefits they are not rightfully entitled to. However, as I have been arguing throughout this book, to suggest that a changed culture is not a real culture is confounded by the reality of persisting cultural identities.

It is a simple matter to point to changes in particular customs (especially when accompanied by changes in indigenous language, dress, housing style, and subsistence strategy) and conclude that an indigenous culture has become acculturated. Part of the issue, at least, stems from the assumption by many that tradition and custom refer to the same concept. When one observes a change to custom, one assumes that as a result the tradition is broken. However, I agree with Hobsbawm (1983: 2), who points to differences between the two concepts. I perceive the differences between the two as analogous to the relationship that exists between the dependent and independent variables in statistical analysis. For example, Christmas (dependent variable) is a Christian 'tradition," whereas the "customs" (independent variables) associated with the celebration of

Christmas include trees, decorations, gifts, and eating certain kinds of food. Changes to the customary acts or behaviors associated with the tradition do not affect the overarching tradition itself. For an additional example, consider the "tradition" of the Tigua's June 13 Saint Anthony's Day Feast. This particular tradition is the product of numerous other traditions and customs. It represents the apex of the annual ceremonial cycle, but it is not a stand-alone event (the Christian tradition of Easter provides a basic corollary). Moreover, it is itself made up of numerous customs that may on occasion require adjustment based on particular needs. For instance, the tribe no longer needs to gather donations from their neighbors in more than a symbolic way, unlike the precasino times when those donations were critical to the event. Likewise, the numbers of tribal dancers, the gift basket presented to attending neighbors, and the location of the feast itself have changed over time. However, the tradition of the feast is "invariant," a trait that Hobsbawm (1983: 2) suggests applies to all acts of tradition. That some of the customs associated with the production of the tradition have changed does not necessarily imply that the "tradition" with which custom "is habitually intertwin[ed]" will also "inevitably" change, as Hobsbawm believes (1983: 3). In fact, the "tradition" of holding a feast day will always tie into the ceremonial practices and religious beliefs of the Tigua culture for as long as it persists.

Perhaps more important than the particular customs that comprise traditional acts is the way in which these acts relate to overall cultural cohesion. Whether the June 13 feast was "invented" or not (of course, every tradition must have some starting point) is meaningless in the face of the role it plays in the contemporary Tigua ethos. They can no more change that integral tradition any more than a Christian could change the traditional celebration of Christmas on December 25 (a tradition that is itself clearly made up and has undergone numerous changes in customary acts over time). That this particular invented tradition is followed by millions of Americans, and many others around the world, does not take away from the fact that it is both invented and fervently believed in and followed by so many. If Christmas, Easter, and countless other Christian and American traditions are perceived as authentic, indigenous traditions have at least as much right to the claim of authenticity. Indeed, more so if we consider the integral nature of many indigenous traditional practices. The United States, for example, could continue on quite well if Easter were declared fraudulent. That is not necessarily the case for indigenous peoples such as the Tigua, who perceive tradition differently and who experience tradition differently. The Tigua understand the crucial role tradition plays in their lives, including their pasts, present, and futures. For them, tradition has real salience as a vital component of their cultural and physical survival.

In fact, the Tigua are fully cognizant that their survival hinges on maintaining a proper balance between strict adherence to traditional practice and pragmatic acquiescence to the real word need to embrace both critical and incidental modifications to customary practice. They demonstrate a fundamental understanding of what tradition actually is as well as the role it plays in their daily lives. Raymond Williams (quoted in Bronner 2000) suggests that tradition serves as "the time-honored process of inheritance from an older generation [which] implies respect for elders and a certain duty to carry the process on." He goes on, however, to point out that "persistence through time is not necessarily a mark of honor if it is enforced irrationally." Tradition and custom, to the Tigua, signify the passing of knowledge; it is conceived of as a "gift," treated and passed on with respect.[9] It has meaning and fulfills a practical purpose whether the traditional act is expressed in dance, ceremony, song, perceptions of landscape, or cultural values such as sharing. Teyo exposes the core of Tigua perceptions of tradition when he equates the teaching of tradition, the passing of knowledge as a "gift," as a "part" of the giver and connected to a line of ancestors through time.

Tradition and custom are not separated from other aspects of culture, however, and although tradition is of vital importance to the community, and the role tradition plays in maintaining Tigua cultural perseverance has been well documented (see, for example, Greenberg 1998; Houser 1979; Minter 1976), there is also a wisdom and grounded sense of reality related to how the Tigua approach the notion of change. In a discussion about traditional dances with José, he makes it clear that small amounts of change invariably creep into the performances. "Are these dances identical to what they were twenty or fifty years ago? No, some little things get lost, new generations add things, its essence is the same, the meaning is the same, but it's impossible to keep change out altogether." In other words, the tradition persists, while the customs associated with it must occasionally be adjusted. In a discussion with Jorge about cultural change, he laughs, stating: "Yeah, you notice how it's OK for white culture to change, but us, no we're supposed to stay the same forever. New stuff, technology, laws, styles [of dress], food, music, you know, all that stuff is not supposed to make any difference to us." All human culture effects, and is affected by, change. Carrithers (1992: 9), for example, points out that when humans "do something that seems traditional, we do so in new conditions, and so are in fact re-creating tradition rather than simply copying it."

Change is a force that must be contended with if a community such as the Tigua is going to survive. Blindly, mindlessly following tradition and custom has never been an option for indigenous communities, whose survival is based on their ability to recognize change and adapt appropriately. During his fieldwork, Ewins (1998) questioned how the Fijians he encountered perceived of tradition, and came to the same conclusion:

> Traditions are a "link with the past," true, but they have changed a great deal already, as the history books amply show, and they remain open to change today. This wasn't a total acceptance of open-slather change in tradition on their part; there was usually some insistence that certain fundamentals should remain. . . . But there was also disagreement about what those fundamentals were.

Shelley S. Armitage (1998: 356), for example, argues that the loss of Tigua language skills, so often cited by linguists as "critical" to cultural transmission (see Berry 1980; Fishman 1972; Hernandez 1997; Mayher 1990; Padilla 1980), in reality assisted the Tigua in their ability to persevere. Her observation that "the Tiwa language was no longer functional as the language of commerce" and that their "bilingual skills" empowered them over other local Indian groups in their relationships with the Spanish, Mexican, and U.S. dominators speaks to their ability to respond rapidly to the fluidity of oppression. Moreover, the truly vital aspects of language, those relative to tradition and cultural memory, were preserved in the form of ritual, song, dance, and story (Armitage 1998: 358; see also Rappaport 1990: 13–14). Every generation inherits, in the words of Teyo, "a sacred trust," a responsibility to "protect and pass on tradition and custom." This responsibility was heightened, particularly in the past, because of dangerously low population numbers. Jesus often alludes to the extreme strictness displayed by the Elders when he was growing up, how determined they were to protect their cultural values, to ensure that the younger generation was capable of learning and passing on cultural knowledge. For example, he tells the story of kids being lashed with willow branches for going to the bathroom without permission during dance practices. Reyes makes this statement: "I remember when an Elder used to approach, that other person would bow his head and greet 'morning' or 'afternoon' until that Elder would greet likewise and then allow you to pass by saying 'pass by me.'" This extreme level of strictness was born of the necessity to fight against the debilitating effects of urban encroachment. As previously noted, however, the Tigua were able to turn this disadvantage into an advantage by using the threat of encroachment as a rallying point. As one tribal member states to Wright (1993: 139), "One of our big advantages over the other pueblos is that we have always been surrounded by white people. We learned to take the criticism of the white people and lived through all of that. We fight back and still keep our own customs." The strict adherence to traditional practice clearly assisted the tribe in their long-term ability to preserve, but it is equally clear that the need to be relentlessly protective has been lessened somewhat by the security (at least for now) of official recognition.

The ethnographic, ethnohistorical, and historical tracking of both change and perseverance within the Tigua community indicates that pragmatism and a clear understanding of reality have guided and shaped the perception and the practice of Tigua traditional and customary behavior. Tradition is not an empty word to the Tigua, but a meaningful component of life. Today, with around fifteen hundred tribal members, the need to be as strict as in the past has been somewhat lessened. Still (at least by "American standards") the Tigua continue to strictly monitor their young, and although exposure to the outside is not restricted, youngsters are carefully and firmly guided in their learning of Tigua values. In this community, where everyone, literally, knows everyone, problems (such as drug abuse) are identified and responded to quickly. The Tribal Council and Tribal Court work closely together to identify and address issues that affect the community's young.

Demonstrating kindness and politeness to outsiders is the Pueblo way, the Tigua way, and this value (tradition) is instilled in Tigua youth from a very young age. When I met Tigua children, I was always greeted, given a handshake, and asked about my well-being. Children who failed to follow this custom were gently but firmly reminded to properly greet "our guest." Relatives, particularly grandparents, are actively involved not only in the upbringing of related children but in the guiding and teaching of all the children in the community. This behavior is stressed as a traditional practice, and as Alonzo points out, "All these things should be important to our community, to preserve all our stories and legends, to preserve the Pueblo way and the Tigua way. It is important to the community but also to my grandchildren, all the grandchildren and other children on the reservation, to be knowledgeable about the past." Although the Tigua may stand on the brink of official "termination," it is patently clear that the Tigua, as individuals and as a community, will persist.

Overview

If the Ysleta del Sur Pueblo had been geographically located a mere 20 miles farther west, in present-day New Mexico, the Tigua could have averted many of the problems that they have suffered through during the past three hundred years. Their land would have been secured along with the other New Mexican Pueblos; their years of poverty would have been augmented through government "assistance" programs; their authenticity would never have been called into question; and their power as indigenous peoples would have been strengthened by the addition of the nineteen extant New Mexico Indian communities.[10] However (and perhaps ironically), the Tigua have survived to become the people they are today precisely because they have been forced to suffer through so much turmoil on their own. Their strength as a people and as a community correlates directly with their collective refusal to give up on their identity as American Indians.

The purpose of this book has been to explore the ability of the Tigua to survive against the onslaught of colonial rule and persecution, and I have sought to understand how this tribe was able to perpetuate their culture through many years of virtual obscurity. Additionally, my goal has been to explore and question the concepts of Indian identity and cultural extinction as they apply to the Tigua Indians of Ysleta del Sur Pueblo. The overarching goal has been to explore Tigua culture in an attempt to evaluate and understand the mechanisms utilized by the Tigua in perpetuating and preserving their Native identity for over three hundred years.

The 1680 diaspora played an important role in shaping the Tigua worldview as they rebuilt their lives and struggled to survive as an isolated Pueblo people. They attempted to maintain their previous lifestyle as much as possible, passing on traditional beliefs and practices and embracing their identity as Tigua Indians. Change was nothing new to this hundreds-year-old culture, however, and the bearers of that culture had faith that they would survive. The core of the Tigua ethos, the sense that their worldview was, and is, connected to their cultural history as Pueblo Indians, remains unchanged. A series of historical quirks, including domination under successive nation-states, arbitrary state borders, and residence in a state that was not legally bound to protect indigenous rights, led to a period of hardship and poverty that lasted for well over one hundred years. This hardship was greatly exacerbated by the theft of tribal lands. The government-sanctioned land theft forced the tribe to significantly alter its traditional subsistence strategy and greatly curtailed tribal members' access to their sacred landscape. By the early 1900s, high unemployment and poverty had forced many community members to relocate; racism and anti-Indian sentiments meant danger for those who openly embraced their Indian heritage; both the state and federal governments had forgotten the Tigua existed; and anthropologists and other researchers were describing Tigua culture as "moribund," if not already "extinct." In fact, traditional customs and practices were simply adjusted to account for the problems associated with urban encroachment.

Tigua oral tradition reveals much about tribal members' perceptions of identity and senses of community. Tigua narratives paint a vivid picture of a community that has spent many years in distress but is committed to survive by whatever means necessary. The cultural value of sharing precious resources is highlighted as vital to the physical survival of the tribe; however, it is the cultural survival of the community that is particularly stressed in Tigua oral history. The focus of virtually every community-wide story centers on group survival, on challenges met and overcome, on Tigua pride and perseverance, on outfighting and outsmarting all comers, and on defying to the death those who dare challenge the right of the community to practice its traditional behaviors. Pride in self-identifying as a Tigua Indian and pride in Tigua group survival resonate throughout historical documentation, including both written and oral sources. The Tigua hold a sense of Indian authenticity that is derived not through government legislation but through a heartfelt perception of self.

The Tigua community has a clear perception of its own identity and transmits that identity through multiple generations in specific ways. Cultural identity is strongly tied to sacred religious beliefs, and these beliefs are highly integrated within all aspects of traditional cultural behavior. Every aspect of life is ascribed with meaning and patterns of meaning, associated with not only practices but places (and senses of place) that are derived from the spiritual connection they ascribe to the interconnectedness between their ancestors (*abuelos*) and their traditional landscape. This sacred relationship is perceived as cyclical and never-ending. Indeed, the Tigua hold an unwavering belief that their very existence is tied inextricably to the sacred, that their sense of identity and community is rooted in their beliefs, traditions, landscape, ceremony, and spiritual life. Specific cultural mechanisms such as shared religious beliefs, a common history, and senses of community, combined with shared values, shared senses of family, and a commitment to tradition, have provided the Tigua a cultural continuity that lasts to this day.

Colonization and early U.S. expansionist policies (particularly the development of a corpus of Indian laws) played a deciding role in forcing the Tigua community into the status of "lost tribe," as the creation of new borders prevented the group from receiving the status and protection to which they were legally entitled. Although the tribe belatedly received federal status, its stolen land has never been returned, nor has it received monetary compensation or the legal right to use traditional property in culturally appropriate ways. Moreover, tribal sovereignty and Indian self-determination are largely a myth as they apply to the Tigua tribe. Based on the reality of desperate living conditions (a remnant of colonial rule), tribal leadership was bound to accept unconscionable concessions to their sovereign rights as part of their recognition criteria. This loss of rights led directly to the closing of the profitable Speaking Rock Casino, a successful gaming enterprise that operated from 1993 to 2002. The Tigua rights of sovereignty and self-determination were abrogated by the state of Texas utilizing dubious legal maneuvers, and this loss of rights presently threatens the Tigua's continued existence as a federally recognized tribe.

Postscript

Speaking Rock Casino Today

IN EARLY FEBRUARY 2002, the Tigua's decade-old casino was on the verge of closing. Unable to prevent the court order that would force the shutdown, tribal leadership moved to ensure that the closing would only be temporary. Following the advice of several prominent attorneys, including El Paso lawyer Norman Gordon and Santa Fe lawyer Bryant Rogers (who represented Indian tribes in New Mexico), the tribe entered into negotiations with Washington, D.C., lobbyist Jack Abramoff, a partner in the prestigious law firm Greenberg Traurig. Abramoff was well known in national Republican Party politics and had recently been profiled in the *Wall Street Journal* and *New York Times* as the country's "über lobbyist." Through the attorneys, the tribe set up a meeting with Abramoff for February 6, 2002, at which time he promised the tribe that he could help them reopen Speaking Rock Casino. If the Tigua would agree to pay $4.2 million, he stated, he could "influence" the necessary people in order to get a bill through Congress that would allow the tribe to resume gaming operations. However, Abramoff pointed out that he did not want other Indian tribes he represented to know about his deal with the Tigua, so he brought in his friend Michael Scanlon (a former press secretary for then House Majority Leader Tom DeLay) to head the operation. In fact, Greenberg Traurig (Abramoff's law firm) never registered as a lobbyist for the tribe (an illegal move). Instead, Abramoff told the Tribal Council he was willing to work for them pro bono, provided they hired his firm for consulting work (for $175,000 a month) once the casino reopened.

In order to impress the tribe with his powerful connections, Abramoff boasted about his many influential "friends." The list was impressive, including President George W. Bush, House Majority Leader Tom DeLay, Ohio Representative Bob Ney, and influential Bush adviser Grover Norquist. Abramoff, who always presented himself to tribal leaders as "close" to Bush, enjoyed telling people that he had "special influence" with "W," and told several tribal members that the president asked him for recommendations to fill key positions at the Bureau of Indian Affairs.[1] Indeed, a June 3, 2005, *Boston Globe* story, written by Michael Kranish, points to Abramoff's well-known political ties:

> Abramoff's calling card was his tie to Republican Party leaders. He boasted to the tribal leaders about his access to Bush, and noted that his law firm based in Miami, Greenberg Traurig, worked on the Florida case that helped put Bush in the White House. Scanlon, who sat by Abramoff's side as they met with the Tiguas, had previously boasted of Abramoff's ties to the president. "Jack has a relationship with the president," Scanlon told a Florida newspaper in 2001. "He doesn't have a bat phone or anything, but if he wanted an appointment, he would have one." Abramoff, in turn, boasted that Scanlon had access to his former boss, DeLay, the House majority leader.

The proposal outlined by Abramoff and Scanlon called for the crafting of a bill that would specifically allow the Tigua to reopen their gaming operation. Abramoff would use his connections to have the bill drafted and attached to an (as yet to be determined) important or popular bill that would be certain to pass. This is a common practice in Washington, and the tribe had no reason to suspect that (provided the right palms were greased) this proposal would not be successful. Scanlon, in a February memo to tribal leaders, however, appeared to begin laying the groundwork for the possibility that their plan might fail. He wrote: "Before going forward we would like to make it completely clear that this strategy is not foolproof. However, under no circumstances do we believe it could be classified as high risk either." This hedge was disconcerting, but the tribe decided to pay Abramoff and Scanlon, believing that, once again, they had little other choice. The notion that the casino closing had been planned as a way to shake down the tribe for money was not lost on Tigua leadership, but their feeling, according to one respondent, was that they would play along. "This is the way it works in this system, right? We pay, they let us open back up and we make the money back in a few months." As it turned out, the tribe was (as they suspected) involved in a scam, only it was not precisely the scam they had in mind. Indeed, they found themselves embroiled in what would become a national controversy that would lead to the fall of many of the above-named power brokers.

Abramoff and Scanlon, who went into great detail about what they could do for the tribe, failed to reveal what they had already done against the tribe. In fact, they had both been heavily involved in having the tribal casino closed, securing the assistance of Abramoff's close friend and former Christian Coalition director Ralph Reed. The *Washington Post* and other media reported that Abramoff and Scanlon worked behind the scenes in 2001 and 2002 to help support efforts by then Texas attorney general John Cornyn to close Speaking Rock Casino. The lobbyists were then representing Indian tribes in Mississippi and Louisiana who were trying to block competition in Texas. Apparently, Abramoff and Scanlon funneled $2 million from their tribal clients to Reed in order to assist him in building a church-based network to support Cornyn's court fight to close Speaking Rock. Additionally, the $4.2 million dollars the tribe paid upfront to Scanlon (ostensibly for public relations efforts) was shared equally with Abramoff, despite his promise to work for the Tigua pro bono. A collection of emails, confiscated as part of a congressional investigation into Abramoff and Scanlon (the Abramoff-Scanlon team stands accused of defrauding six Native American Indian tribes out of an estimated $86 million dollars), provides a clear picture of their true motives.

In an email dated February 5, 2002, Reed indicated to Abramoff that the final court order to close Speaking Rock might be only days away but complained that further appeals could slow the closing. Abramoff, who forwarded the email to his associate Scanlon, said of Reed: "Whining idiot. Close the fucking thing already!" Abramoff, however, did let Reed in on his honest feelings about the tribe in an email sent the same day, which referred to the tribe's previous support for Democrats, primarily Garry Mauro, Bush's Democratic challenger in the 1998 governors race: "I wish those moronic Tiguas were smarter in their political contributions. . . . I'd love us to get our mitts on that moolah!! Oh well, stupid folks get wiped out." Abramoff's urgency to get the casino closed soon became obvious when the following day he sent an email to Scanlon with the subject line, "I'm on the phone with Tigua!" The exchange:

ABRAMOFF: "Fire up the jet, baby, we're going to El Paso!!"
SCANLON: "I want all their MONEY!!!"
ABRAMOFF: "Yawzah!"

A couple of weeks later, on February 19, Tribal Council was set to vote on the Abramoff proposal, and Scanlon sent Abramoff an email that included an *El Paso Times* story that reported 450 casino employees would lose their jobs that day. "This is on the front page of today's paper while they will be voting on our plan," Scanlon wrote. Abramoff's response: "Is life great or what?"

In putting together their lobbying strategy, Abramoff and Scanlon told Tigua tribal leaders that they needed to contribute $300,000 to key lawmakers to get the legislation approved by Congress to reopen the gaming operation. Tribal leaders went along with the idea, sending checks to Abramoff to distribute to organizations such as the National Republican Senatorial Campaign Committee, the Superior California Leadership Fund, and the National Republican Congressional Campaign Committee. Abramoff, however, did not want to be publicly identified with the Tigua lobbying efforts and was angered when a tribal consultant included him in a group email. In response to this breach of secrecy, Abramoff emailed the tribal consultant: "Our presence in this deal must be secret as we discussed." Abramoff was more to the point in an email to Scanlon on the same subject later that day: "That fucking idiot put my name on an email list! What a fucking moron. He may have blown our cover!! Dammit. We are moving forward anyway and taking their fucking money." Meanwhile, Scanlon was changing his tune in regard to the prospects of their plan and its ultimate success. While in the process of selling the plan, Scanlon told tribal leadership that "under no circumstances do we believe [this plan] could be classified as high risk." However, two months after receiving the $4.2 million payment, he wrote the tribe the following memo: "With this political cover generated we feel pretty good about our prospects of tacking the legislation on and getting it through. . . . But please be advised—we are taking the most high-risk approach to this by using the election-reform bill as the vehicle." In fact, the attached Tigua bill had zero chance of passing, as both Abramoff and Scanlon knew when they were soliciting the funds.

Enlisting Representative Bob Ney (R-Ohio), Abramoff and Scanlon insisted to the tribe that Ney, chairman of the House Administration Committee, could reopen the Tigua's casino by attaching a provision to an election overhaul bill he had authored.[2] In order to entice Ney to go along with the plan, Abramoff asked the tribe to donate toward a Scotland golf trip for him and some staff members. Abramoff estimated the cost of the trip would be $100,000 or more and that they could funnel the money through Abramoff's (fraudulent) Capital Athletic Foundation. The tribe refused to cover the entire amount but did solicit donations from the Alabama-Coushatta tribe of Texas, whose Livingston casino was also shut down in 2002 and who stood to gain from the proposed bill. The Tigua, however, did purportedly donate $32,000 toward the cost of the trip, which bought them a meeting with Ney in his Washington office.[3] Ney, who thanked the tribe for the trip (not directly, but as one tribal member stated, "We could read between the lines"), reassured tribal leaders that everything was moving forward on their bill. What Ney failed to say was that he already knew the bill was dead in its tracks. Democratic Senator Chris Dodd (Connecticut) was sponsoring the election overhaul bill that the Tigua bill was to be attached to, but Dodd did not want an extraneous provision in it, a fact that was known to both Ney and Abramoff. Though Ney later claimed that he had been "duped" by Abramoff, Dodd stated in an interview that while their staffs had discussed the provision, "it was just rejected at the time." Although a Ney spokesman later claimed that when Ney learned about Dodd's opposition to the provision, "that was the end of it," the Tiguas said otherwise. Indeed, Ney held a conference call with them on October 8, 2002, after the election overhaul bill moved forward without the Tigua bill attached. During this call, Ney professed his disbelief that the Tigua bill had not been attached. In testimony before Senate lawmakers in November, a tribal spokesman stated: "Congressman Ney held a conference call with the Tribal Council . . . and told them about his disbelief that Senator Dodd had gone back on his word. He further reported that he would continue to work on the issue and believed that the tribe was entitled to their gaming operation." In fact, the efforts to assist the Tigua were halfhearted at best. After a failed attempt in 2002 to slip the Tigua gambling legislation into another bill, there are no records to indicate that any efforts were made by Ney or Abramoff and Scanlon to generate legislation for the tribe.[4] However, that did not stop Abramoff and Scanlon from attempting to get more money from the tribe. In March 2003, Abramoff proposed a plan to take out life insurance policies on all Tigua members who were at least seventy-five years old. The insurance payoff would have gone not to the Tigua, but to a Jewish boys' school that Abramoff founded and controlled.

Abramoff was able to build his reputation (which enticed the Tigua and others to hire him) at least partly on his claims of religious piety. Abramoff, who always appeared in public dressed in the proper religious garb, claimed to be a Hasidic Jew, painting a picture of himself as honest and aboveboard. As this narrative has made clear, his claim of pious religiosity is as fraudulent as his secular practices. Indeed, he allowed his true orthodoxy to rise to the surface when talking about Native peoples. On one occasion he sent an email stating: "I have to meet with the monkeys," referring to the Mississippi Choctaw tribe. On other occasions, he refers to tribal clients as morons, stupid idiots, troglodytes, and losers. The Tigua, who were taken in by this snake oil salesman, had no way to know that they were about to be robbed. As one Tribal Council member pointed out, "We were trying to play the game. . . . When you have one of the top lobbyists out there and he's telling you that you need to make contributions to that person, this person and that person—and we were desperate for time—you will do exactly what is asked of you."

This is not the system created by Native peoples but the system that Native peoples are, nonetheless, forced to engage as a contingency of survival. A larger struggle, however, lies on the horizon, a struggle that affects not just the Tigua but all American Indians. The long-term ability of all indigenous peoples in the United States to exercise their rights of sovereign nationhood and self-determination has been insidiously and deviously abrogated by a government bent on terminating, once and for all, the existence of the American Indian.

Notes

Introduction

1. "Tigua" is the Spanish spelling of Tiwa, and Ysleta del Sur (Isleta of the South) is used in order to prevent confusion with the Isleta New Mexico Pueblo. I use "Tigua" throughout the document to refer to the Ysleta del Sur Pueblo and "Tiwa" to refer to the Isleta del Norte Pueblo. "Tiguex" is used to refer to a former group of New Mexico communities that included many Tiwa Indians. I also use the word "Tigua" to refer to the Tiwa, Tiguex, and Tihua Indians that were forced to leave New Mexico as a result of the Pueblo Revolt. Corpus Christi de la Ysleta, San Antonio de Ysleta (a reference to the Tigua patron saint), and Corpus Christi de San Antonio de la Ysleta are classifications formerly used to designate Ysleta del Sur.

2. Texas, and therefore the Tigua, had seceded from the Union during the Civil War.

3. See Adam (2007, Postscript) for a detailed discussion of this issue.

4. This is one possible reason among several others. See Chapter Five.

5. See, for example, Fewkes (1902); Minter (1969); Houser (1979); Green (1974); Greenberg (1998).

6. I use the term "genocide" throughout this thesis, rather than the softer terms "ethnocide" and "culturecide," because I believe it is much more descriptive of what is actually taking place in the United States in regard to American Indians. Several definitions of the term have been offered, but I prefer the definition as initially coined by Raphael Lemkin in 1943: "The systematic and planned extermination of an entire national, racial, political, or ethnic group." I will argue that the laws and policies put into place in the United States are designed with the overarching, planned goal of eliminating its Native population. Moreover, if the culture of an entire people is rendered "extinct," whether through the process of direct violence or through legislative fiat, the ultimate outcome is the same.

7. See Chapter Five for an example relevant to the Tigua.

8. See Adam (2007) for a detailed discussion surrounding methodological issues.

9. Indeed, Keeshig-Tobias has commented that the "Indian" is nothing more than a figment of the white man's imagination (cited in Wright 1992: ix).

10. For example, see Means, "I am an American Indian, Not a Native American!" http://www.peaknet.net/~aardvark/means.html.

11. See Asch and Samson (2004); Barnard (2006); Kenrick and Lewis (2004); Omura (2003); Plaice (2003); Turner (2004); Saugestad (2004); Suzman (2003); Robins (2003).

12. Oddly, many of those who would deny indigenous peoples their privileges and rights as the descendents of aboriginal inhabitants have no problem accepting privileges (in the form of inherited wealth) from their own ancestors.

13. See Chapter Five (the section entitled "The 'Real' Tigua") and the Concluding Remarks ("Essentialized Culture") for further discussion.

Chapter 1

1. I use the term "oral tradition" to refer to shared cultural events, whereas I use the term "oral history" to refer to personal, firsthand experience.

2. See Adam (2002) for a detailed discussion relevant to the history of the New Mexican Pueblo peoples and the Tigua before 1680.

3. All the quotes presented in this book were taken verbatim from interviews conducted during my fieldwork, unless otherwise indicated. Several respondents asked to have their identity concealed and, for that reason, I have chosen to conceal all respondent identities through the use of pseudonyms. In some instances, information was masked in order to protect particular individuals' privacy. Throughout this book, long direct quotes from respondents will be indented.

4. See Map 1.

5. See Adam (2007, Appendix J) for the complete text and a comment.

6. It has been noted that the Tigua may not have been welcome in Isleta, and this idea cannot be discounted as a factor in their decision to remain. My argument is that their relationship with the land, which they had been building from at least 1680 (not to mention the investment of labor and resources in preparing a homestead) was firmly established, indeed culturally embedded, by the time of Isleta's reestablishment (in the early 1700s), and would have superseded any other consideration, political or otherwise.

7. It appears the retreating Spanish perceived that the internal and external conflict created by their existing policy (which, ultimately, led to the Pueblo Revolt) would need to be changed if they were to prosper in El Paso.

8. The rooster replaced the (increasingly) scarce eagle in the late 1800s as the Tigua symbol for "chief."

9. See Eickhoff (1996) for the history behind this appalling event.

10. Theodore Roosevelt did little to help the problem when he stated: "I don't go so far as to think that the only good Indians are the dead Indians, but I believe nine out of every ten are, and I shouldn't like to inquire too closely into the case of the tenth. The most vicious cowboy has more moral principle than the average Indian" (quoted in Hofstadter 1974: 274).

11. The decision, however, in the early 1990s to open the Speaking Rock Casino has brought with it change-related problems of a new kind, some good, some not so good (an issue to be taken up in Chapter Five).

12. See Chapter Four under "Federal Acknowledgment."

Chapter 2

1. The issue of identity legislation will be taken up in Chapter Three.

2. The Hopi reference relates to a specific dance that was performed in one village but has been discontinued due to the death of the last Elder who was knowledgeable about its traditional portrayal.

3. There is strong suspicion (among Tigua leaders, tribal attorneys, and tribal consultants) that TPWLD will not allow the Tigua to examine the pottery collection because they already know the shards connect the Tigua to Hueco, a fact that they have been fighting to downplay for many years, and an issue to be further discussed in Chapter Five.

4. Native tobacco wrapped in corn husks.

Chapter 3

1. See Adam (2007, Appendix E, Part A) for several examples.

2. For example, the infamous "one-drop rule" dictated that a person with *any* amount of "Negroid" blood was, by law, Negroid.

3. One need not wonder too much. For example, in the current *Cobell v. Norton* litigation, serious charges of mismanagement of Indian funds have been brought against the government. In brief, the government has "lost" billions of dollars of Indian trust funds, and it appears that in addition to the possibility that some of the funds were used to pay down the national debt (of all things), nobody from the Department of the Interior knows what happened to the money. Worse, they do not even care (see note 3, Chapter Four).

4. In fairness to Marshall, in the Cherokee ruling, as well as the *Worcester v. Georgia* case in 1832, the Supreme Court ruled that states could not pass laws conflicting with federal Indian treaties and that the federal government had an obligation to exclude white intruders from Indian lands. Angered by this ruling, President Andrew Jackson is said to have exclaimed: "John Marshall has made his decision; now let him enforce it."

5. Furthermore, the ruling stated that Indians "occupy a territory to which we assert a title independent of their will." They are in a "state of pupilage . . . and their relation to the United States resembles that of a ward to his guardian." The idea of a "trust relationship" comes from Chief Justice John Marshall's opinion. In *Worcester v. Georgia* (1832), Marshall expanded on the

idea of "trust" status by declaring that Indian tribes are "under the protection of the United States." Like any guardianship, the trust relationship implies rights and benefits, obligations and duties for both the trustee and the beneficiary. The unspoken message, of course, is, "Indians are not competent to handle their own affairs."

6. See Adam (2007, Appendix E, Part B) for more information on this ruling.

7. In regard to footnote 5 above: President Jackson, true to his word, and acting on what was known as the Georgia Compact, sent in the army to forcibly remove the Cherokee from their prosperous farms, moving them to the then wastelands of Oklahoma. Afterward, white land speculators freely moved onto thousands of acres of well-developed land near the East Coast.

8. The thirteen American colonies had already taken the step of negotiating agreements with militarily powerful Indian tribes, either to gain the tribes' alliance or, at least, to ensure the tribes' neutrality in the (then) imminent Revolutionary War.

9. The Bureau of Indian Affairs (BIA) was created in 1824 as the governmental body responsible for implementing and overseeing federal Indian policy and law and is the principal agency responsible for the administration of federal programs for Indian tribes. Tellingly, the BIA was initially incorporated as a part of the War Department but was transferred to the Department of the Interior in 1849.

Chapter 4

1. Legally, however, the Union never recognized the separation of the Confederate states (see Ostrowski 1997; McPherson 1991).

2. See Introduction.

3. See Friends Committee on National Legislation, "The Comments of Others on the Interior Trust Scandal," http://www.fcnl.org/issues/item.php ?item_id=1387&issue_id=112.

Chapter 5

1. Greenberg (personal and written correspondence) is the source for the following discussion of the Rio Grande Report.

2. I would add that in a discussion about this report with a prominent Tigua leader, I was informed that one of the authors contacted him about setting an interview time, which this busy individual was unable to do at the moment, but that he never received a follow-up call to set another meeting time. Indeed, I was told that not a single member of the tribe was interviewed as part of this report. Whether that is the fault of the Tigua or the researchers, this report should have made clear that information relevant to the Tigua was not ethnographic in nature.

3. "Plains Indian" cultural practices have traditionally dominated popular American discourse.

4. See Darian-Smith (2004: 57) for an interesting discussion about traditional Indian gambling.

5. See Adam (2007) for a summary of IGRA.

6. See Harvey (2000: 25) for a discussion about the creation of the IGRA.

7. The Tigua is an excellent example of a gaming tribe that did each of these things with its gaming revenue.

8. It should be pointed out that it was the 1991 Texas State Lottery Act that was primarily responsible for opening the door to Tigua tribal gaming, not a bill or lawsuit filed by the Tigua to get around the provisions of the Tigua recognition bill. In fact, because the IGRA superseded the Restoration Act's provisions, which prohibited gaming on the Tigua reservation under the state law provision, the tribe could have brought gaming to its reservation as early as 1988. However, the Tigua chose to abide by the recognition agreement (until 1991) despite this glaring loophole.

9. Apparently, this dispute was also related to the change in time of the January elections.

10. The "not guilty" verdict was largely the result of the "lifetime" status of the war captain and his responsibility to look after the sacred items. In legal terms, the war captain cannot "steal" these particular objects.

11. It is interesting to note that the Texas legislators opposed "gambling" before the 1991 State Lottery Act, but afterward legislators and other state officials reference only "casino" gambling as problematic.

12. I am greatly simplifying a very complex process here.

13. Bush declared in a widely circulated state report, "Casino gambling is not OK. It has ruined the lives of too many adults, and it can do the same thing to our children." He wooed religious conservatives by boasting in a presidential debate about his "strong antigambling record." But as president, Bush did not speak out against gambling. After promising not to take money from gambling interests, Bush's campaign fund accepted large contributions from gambling-related sources. His 2001 inaugural committee raised at least $300,000 from gambling interests, including gifts from MGM/Mirage, Sands, and a leading slot-machine maker. Bush later appeared at a Las Vegas casino for a fund-raiser for his reelection campaign (Kranish 2005).

14. See Adam (2007, Appendix H) for a discussion about this ruling.

15. See Adam (2007, Appendix H) for a detailed discussion regarding this ambiguity.

Concluding Remarks

1. See Kymlica (1997: 229–246) for an interesting discussion on "The Liberal Tradition."

2. Of course, eliminating this legal status concurrently eliminates the basis for extracting the rights that are owed to the descendents of indigenous populations.

3. Meeting under the auspices of the UN, the Working Group on Indigenous Rights issued a draft declaration concerning the rights that should be made available to all indigenous peoples (see Maybury-Lewis 1997: 56).

4. For example, the American Indian Movement, National Congress of American Indians, National Indian Youth Council, National Tribal Chairman's Association, and the Coalition of Eastern Native Americans.

5. Something similar to the model put together by the European Union, for example, could serve as a useful blueprint.

6. An exception would be the yearly trips they made to the state capital to "play Indian."

7. See Adam (2007, Appendix D, Story A).

8. See Adam (2007, Appendix D, Story B).

9. See Ewins (1998) for an interesting discussion linking tradition, knowledge, and biological evolution.

10. For example, when the New Mexican tribes ran into difficulty over their state gaming compact, they were able to use their collective numbers to force the state into a compromise (see Darian-Smith 2004; Mason 2000).

Postscript: Speaking Rock Casino Today

1. This was apparently news to Bush, whose spokeswoman said in response to a question about Abramoff that "they may have met on occasion . . . but the president does not know him." Abramoff, who is a Bush "Pioneer," having helped raise over $100,000 dollars for Bush's election campaigns, was apparently the more honest of the two when he told potential clients that he had personally met with Bush around a dozen times. Secret Service documents reveal at least seven meetings at the White House alone. And, according to a May 8, 2005, *USA Today* posting, his influence went beyond his meetings with Bush:

> WASHINGTON (AP)—In President Bush's first 10 months, GOP fundraiser Jack Abramoff and his lobbying team logged nearly 200 contacts with the new administration as they pressed for friendly hires at federal agencies and sought to keep the Northern Mariana Islands exempt from the minimum wage and other laws, records show. The meetings between Abramoff's lobbying team and the administration ranged from Attorney General John Ashcroft to policy advisers in Vice President Dick Cheney's office, according to his lobbying firm billing records."

Numerous media outlets have published reports that indicate Abramoff was, in fact, well known to Bush (see Adam 2007 for examples).

2. Ney, who had initially denied ever meeting with the Tigua (or having ever even heard of them), was forced to backtrack when the tribe released a photograph of tribal leaders meeting with him in a House hearing room on August 14, 2002.

3. In an email from Abramoff to the tribe dated August 10, 2002 (in preparation for Ney's meeting with the tribal leaders), he refers to the funding for the golf trip: "BN had a great time and is very grateful but is not going to mention the trip to Scotland for obvious reasons. He said he'll show his thanks in other ways."

4. See Schmidt (2005) and the *New York Times,* July 13, 2006, for details about the successful Tigua lawsuit against Greenberg Traurig.

References

Abaurrea, Lora. 1996. "Native Americans Are Cashing-In with Gambling Casinos on the Reservation." http://www2.sims.berkeley.edu/academics/courses/is190–1/s96/abaurrea/assign5.htm

Adam, S. K. 2007. *The Tigua of Ysleta del Sur Pueblo: A Case Study of Cultural Persistence Within an Urban Setting*. Ph.D. diss., Department of Anthropology, University of Bristol, UK.

Ager, Michael H. 1980. *The Professional Stranger: An Informal Introduction to Ethnography*. New York: Academic Press.

AILTP (American Indian Lawyer Training Program). 1993. *Indian Tribes as Sovereign Governments*. Oakland: AIRI Press.

Akiwenzie, Clay. 1996. *Modern* "'Small-Pox' for Native Culture." http://www.stanford.edu/group/Thinker/v2/v2n2/Akiwenzie.html.

Anschuetz, Kurt F. 2002. *Senses of Place and Constructions of Affiliation: Hueco Tanks State Historical Park*. Ethnographic Study no. 81293 [RGF 118], prepared for Cultural Resources Program, Texas Parks and Wildlife Department.

Armitage, Shelley S. 1998. "Tigua Pueblo: Materializing Language, Transmitting Memory." In *Multilingual America: Transnationalism, Ethnicity, and the Languages of American Literature*, ed. W. Sollors. New York: New York University Press.

Asad, Talal, ed. 1973. *Anthropology and the Colonial Encounter*. New York: Humanities Press.

Asch, Michael, and Colin Samson. 2004. "Discussion: On 'The Return of the Native.'" *Current Anthropology* 45, no. 2: 261–262.

Axtell, James. 1979. "Ethnohistory: An Historian's Viewpoint." *Ethnohistory* 26: 1–13.

Barker, Eugene C. 1946. "Annexation of Texas." *The Southwestern Historical Quarterly* 50, no. 1 (July).

Barker, Eugene C., and James W. Pohl. 2001. "Texas Revolution." In *Handbook of Texas Online*. http://www.tsha.utexas.edu/handbook/online/articles/TT/qdt1.html (accessed September 6, 2006).

Barnard, Alan. 2006. "Kalahari Revisionism, Vienna, and the 'Indigenous Peoples' Debate." *Social Anthropology* (European Association of Social Anthropologists) 14, no. 1: 155–159.

Basso, Keith H. 1996. *Wisdom Sits in Places: Landscape and Language Among the Western Apache*. Albuquerque: University of New Mexico Press.

Beard, Val. 2004. "Opinion." *Alpine Avalanche*. http://www.alpineavalanche .com/articles/2004/06/03/news/opinion/opinion01.txtiAlpine Avalanche.

Beckett, Patrick H., and Terry L. Corbett. 1990. *Tortugas*. Monograph no. 8. Las Cruces, NM: COAS Publishing and Research.

Bender, Barbara. 1993. "Introduction: Landscape—Meaning and Action." In *Landscape Politics and Perspectives,* ed. Barbara Bender. Providence: Berg.

Benhabib, Seyla. 1996. "Toward a Deliberative Model of Democratic Legitimacy." In *Democracy and Difference: Contesting the Boundaries of the Political,* ed. Seyla Benhabib. Princeton, NJ: Princeton University Press, pp. 67–94.

———. 2002. *The Claims of Culture: Equality and Diversity in the Global Era*. Princeton, NJ: Princeton University Press.

Berry, Christina. 2006. *What's in a Name? Indians and Political Correctness*. http://www.allthingscherokee.com/atc_sub_culture_feat_events_070101 .html.

Berry, John W. 1980. "Acculturation as Varieties of Adaptation." In *Acculturation: Theory, Models, and Some New Findings,* ed. Amado M. Padilla. Boulder, CO: Westview Press, pp. 9–25.

Bloch, Marc. 1954. *The Historian's Craft*. Manchester, UK: Manchester University Press.

Bloch, Maurice, and Jonathan Parry, eds. 1989. *Money and the Morality of Exchange*. New York: Cambridge University Press.

Block, W. T. 1976. *A History of Jefferson County, Texas, from Wilderness to Reconstruction*. Nederland, TX: Nederland Publishing. Originally written as M.A. thesis, Lamar University, 1974.

Bodley, John H. 1999. *Victims of Progress*. 4th ed. Mountain View, CA: Mayfield Publishing.

Bones of Contention: Native American Archaeology. 1998. BBC Worldwide.

Bonnichsen, Robson, and Alan L. Schneider. 2000. "Battle of the Bones." In *The Sciences*, a publication of the New York Academy of Sciences, July–August: 40–46.

Boylan, Virginia W. 2002. Testimony Before the Senate Committee on Indian Affairs on Implementation of the Texas Restoration Act, Public Law 100-89, Tuesday, June 18, 2002, 10 A.M., Room 485, Russell Senate Office Building.

Brah, Avtar. 1996. *Cartographies of Diaspora: Contesting Identities*. London: Routledge.

Bronner, Simon J. 2000. "American Concept of Tradition: Folklore in the Discourse of Traditional Values." *Western Folklore* 59, no. 2 (Spring): 143–170.

Brown, Roy B., Patricia Fournier, David V. Hill, John A. Peterson, and Mark Willis. 2004. "Settlement and Ceramics in Northern New Spain: A Case Study of Brown Ware Pottery and Historical Change." In *Surveying the Archaeology of Northwest Mexico*, ed. G. Newell and E. Gallago. Salt Lake City: University of Utah Press.

Brunner, Borgna. 2006. "American Indian Versus Native American: A Once-Heated Issue Has Sorted Itself Out. http://www.infoplease.com/spot/aihmterms.html.

Burke, Joseph C. 1996. "The Cherokee Cases: A Study in Law, Politics, and Morality." In *Native American Law and Colonialism, Before 1776 to 1903*, ed. John R. Wunder. New York: Garland Publishing, pp. 136–167.

Butterfield, Fox. 2005. "For a Tribe in Texas, an Era of Prosperity Undone by Politics." *New York Times*, June 13.

Callicott J. Baird, Miguel Acevedo, Pete Gunter, Paul Harcombey, C. Lindquist, and Michael Monticiono. 2006. "Biocomplexity in the Big Thicket." *Ethics, Place, and Environment* 9, no. 1: 21–45.

Canessa, Andrew, ed. 2005. *Natives Making Nation: Gender, Indigeneity, and the State in the Andes*. Tucson: University of Arizona Press.

Carrier, James G., ed. 2005. *A Handbook of Economic Anthropology*. Cheltenham, UK: Edward Elgar Publishing.

Carrithers, Michael. 1992. *Why Humans Have Culture: Explaining Anthropology and Social Diversity*. Oxford: Oxford University Press.

Castile, George Pierre. 1996. "The Commodification of Indian Identity." *American Anthropologist* 98, no. 4: 743–749.

Churchill, Ward. 1998. "A Breach of Trust: The Radioactive Colonization of Native North America." *American Indian Culture and Research Journal* 23, no. 4: 23–69.

———. 2003. *Perversions of Justice: Indigenous Peoples and Angloamerican Law*. San Francisco: City Lights Books.

———. 2004. "A Question of Identity." In *A Will to Survive: Indigenous Essays on the Politics of Culture, Language, and Identity*, ed. S. Greymorning. New York: McGraw-Hill.

Clifford, James. 1997. *Routes: Travel and Translation in the Late Twentieth Century*. Cambridge, MA: Harvard University Press.

Clifton, James A., ed. 1989. *Being and Becoming Indian: Biographical Studies of North American Frontiers*. Chicago: Dorsey Press.

Cohen, R. 1997. *Global Diasporas*. London: University College London.

Cohn, Bernard S., ed. 1987. *An Anthropologist Among Historians and Other Essays*. Oxford: Oxford University Press.

Comaroff, John, and Jean Comaroff. 1992. "Ethnography and the Historical Imagination." In *Ethnography and the Historical Imagination*. Boulder, CO: Westview Press.

Coulthard, Glen Sean. 2004. *Culture, Consent, and the State in the Struggles of Indigenous Peoples for Recognition and Self-Determination: Social Constructivism and the Politics of Critique*. http://www.law.uvic.ca/demcon/papers/Essentialism.doc.

Crapol, Edward P. 1997. "John Tyler and the Pursuit of National Destiny." *Journal of the Early American Republic* 17, no. 3: 467–491.

Craven, Jim. 2006. "September '00: Indian Affairs Head Makes 'Apology.'" Comments by Eugene Johnson (Selitz) and Jim Craven (Blackfoot), from AP report by Matt Kelly. http://www.chgs.umn.edu/Histories_Narratives _Documen/documents_on_Native_American_G/Revised_Apology.pdf.

Culin, Stewart. 1907. *Twenty-Fourth Annual Report of the Bureau of American Ethnology: Games of North American Indians.* Washington, DC: Government Printing Office. (Rev. ed. 1975) Dover Publications.

Darian-Smith, Eve. 2004. *New Capitalists: Law, Politics, and Identity Surrounding Casino Gaming on Native American Land.* Belmont, CA: Wadsworth/ Thomson Learning.

Davis, Sally M., and Raymond Reid. 1999. "Practicing Participatory Research in American Indian Communities." *American Journal of Clinical Nutrition* 69, no. 4: 755S–759S.

Deloria, Vine, Jr. 1969. *Custer Died for Your Sins: An Indian Manifesto.* London: Macmillan.

Deloria, Vine, Jr., and Clifford M. Lytle. 1983. *American Indians, American Justice.* Austin: University of Texas Press.

d'Errico, Peter. 1997. *American Indian Sovereignty: Now You See It, Now You Don't.* Text presented as the inaugural lecture of the American Indian Civics Project at Humboldt State University, Arcata, CA, October 24, 1997, sponsored by the HSU Center for Indian Community Development. http:// www.nativeweb.org/pages/legal/sovereignty.html.

———. 2005. "A Note on Names." http://www.umass.edu/legal/derrico/ name.html.

Dickerson, W. E. S. 2001. "Indian Reservations." In *Handbook of Texas Online.* http://www.tsha.utexas.edu/handbook/online/articles/II/bpi1.html.

Dirlik, Arif. 1996. "The Past as Legacy and Project: Postcolonial Criticism in the Perspective of Indigenous Historicism." *American Indian Culture and Research Journal* 20, no. 2: 2, 26n2.

Donakowski, Darrell W., and Victoria M Esses. 1996. "Native Canadians, First Nations, or Aboriginals: The Effect of Labels on Attitudes Toward Native Peoples." *Canadian Journal of Behavioural Science* 28, no. 2: 86–91.

Dozier, Edward P. 1970. *The Pueblo Indians of North America.* New York: Holt, Rinehart, and Winston.

DuMars, Charles T., Marilyn O'Leary, and Albert E. Utton. 1984. *Pueblo Indian Water Rights.* Tucson: University of Arizona Press.

Dutton, Bertha. 1983. *American Indians of the Southwest.* Albuquerque: University of New Mexico Press.

Eickhoff, Randy. 1996. *Exiled: The Tigua Indians of Ysleta del Sur.* Plano: Republic of Texas Press.

Eiss, Paul, and Thomas C. Wolfe. 1994. *Deconstruct to Reconstruct: An Interview with Maurice Godelier.* http://www.umich.edu/~iinet/journal/ vol1no2/deconstruct.html.

Ellis, Florence Howley. 1979. "Isleta Pueblo." In *Handbook of North American Indians*, ed. Alfonso Ortiz. Washington, DC: Smithsonian, vol. 9, pp. 351–365.

Ewins, Rory. 1998. *Changing Their Minds: Tradition and Politics in Contemporary Fiji and Tonga*. Christchurch, New Zealand: University of Canterbury, Macmillan Brown Centre for Pacific Studies.

Feld, Steven, and Keith H. Basso. 1996. *Senses of Place*. Seattle: University of Washington Press.

Fenton, William N. 1952. "The Training of Historical Ethnologists in America." *American Anthropologist* 54, no. 3 (July–September): 328–339.

Fewkes, J. Walter. 1902. "The Pueblo Settlement Near El Paso, Texas." *American Anthropologist* 4, no. 1: 57–72.

Fishman, Joshua A., ed. 1972. *Readings in the Sociology of Language*. New York: Mouton Publishers.

Forbes, Jack D. 1960. *Apache, Navajo, and Spaniard*. Norman: University of Oklahoma Press.

Forrest, Earle R. 1929. *Missions and Pueblos of the Old Southwest: Their Myths, Legends, Fiestas, and Ceremonies, with Some Accounts of the Indian Tribes and Their Dances; and of the Penitentes*. Cleveland, OH: Arthur H. Clark.

Fuller, John D. P. 1935. "Slavery Propaganda During the Mexican War." *The Southwestern Historical Quarterly* 38, no. 4 (April).

Gabriel, Kathryn. 1996. *Indian Gaming in Mythology, History, and Archaeology in North America*. Boulder, CO: Johnson Books.

Garcia, Maria Elena. 2005. *Making Indigenous Citizens: Identities, Education and Multicultural Development in Peru*. Palo Alto, CA: Stanford University Press.

Gavaki, Efrosini. 1993. *Maintenance and Transmission of Ethnic Identity: The Case of the Greeks in Canada*. National Europe Centre, Australian National University. http://dspace.anu.edu.au/bitstream/1885/41781/2/gavaki1.pdf.

Geis, Michael. 1987. *The Language of Politics*. New York: Springer.

Gerald, Rex E. 1974. "Aboriginal Use and Occupation by Tigua, Manso and Suma Indians." In *Apache Indians III*, ed. Kenneth F. Neighbours, Myra Ellen Jenkins, and Rex E. Gerald. New York: Garland Publishing.

Gledhill, John. 1994. *Power and Its Disguises: Anthropological Perspectives on Politics*. London: Pluto Press.

Godelier, Maurice. 1999. *The Enigma of the Gift*, trans. Nora Scott. Cambridge: Polity Press.

Gover, Kevin. 2002. "For Want of a Comma, a Casino Is Lost." *Indian Country Today*, March 20. http://www.indiancountry.com/content.cfm?id=1016546067.

Gray, Shannon. 1994. "Tigua Ethnobotany." M.A. thesis, Miami University, Oxford, Ohio.

Green, A., and K. Troup. 1999. *The Houses of History: A Critical Reader in Twentieth-Century History and Theory*. Manchester, UK: Manchester University Press.

Green, Thomas. 1973. *Yo Soy Indio: An Analysis of a Contemporary Nativistic Movement.* Ph.D. diss., Department of Anthropology, University of Texas at Austin.

Greenberg, Adolph M. 1998. *Tigua Land Tenure and Land Use Practices: An Ethnographic Assessment.* Research report prepared and submitted to the Tigua tribe and tribal attorney Tom Diamond.

————. 2000. *Ysleta del Sur Pueblo and the Rio Grande.* Research report prepared and submitted to the Tigua tribe and tribal attorney Tom Diamond.

Griffin, Roger A. 2001. "Compromise of 1850." In *Handbook of Texas Online.* http://www.tsha.utexas.edu/handbook/online/articles/CC/nbc2.html (accessed November 4, 2008).

Guenther, Mathias. 2006. "Discussion: The Concept of Indigeneity." *Social Anthropology* 14, no. 1: 17–32.

Guibernau, Montserrat, and John Rex, eds. 1997. *The Ethnicity Reader: Nationalism, Multiculturalism, and Migration.* Cambridge: Polity Press.

Guitar, Lynne. 1998. "The Requirement." In *Historical Encyclopedia of World Slavery,* ed. Junius P. Rodríguez. Santa Barbara, CA: ABC-Clio.

Hackett, Charles Wilson. 1913. "The Retreat of the Spaniard from New Mexico in 1680, and the Beginnings of El Paso II." *Southwestern Historical Quarterly* 16, no. 3 (January).

————. 1937. *Historical Documents Relating to New Mexico Nueva Vizcaya, and Approaches Thereto, to 1773.* Vol. 3. Washington, DC: Carnegie Institution of Washington.

Hale, Kenneth, and David Harris. 1979. "Historical Linguistics and Archeology." In *Handbook of North American Indians,* ed. Alfonso Ortiz. Washington, DC: Smithsonian, vol. 9, pp. 170–177.

Hammond, G. P., and A. R. Rey. 1940. *Narratives of the Coronado Expedition.* Albuquerque: University of New Mexico Press.

Hardt, Michael, and Antonio Negri. 2000. *Empire.* Cambridge, MA: Harvard University Press.

Harrison, Simon. 1999. "Cultural Boundaries." *Anthropology Today* 15, no. 5: 10–13.

Harvey, Sioux. 2000. "Winning the Sovereignty Jackpot: The Indian Gaming Regulatory Act and the Struggle for Sovereignty." In *Indian Gaming: Who Wins?* ed. A. Mullis and D. Kamper. Contemporary American Indian Issue Series no. 9. Los Angeles: UCLA American Indian Studies Center.

Hernandez, H. 1997. *Teaching in Multilingual Classrooms: A Teacher's Guide to Context, Process, and Content.* Upper Saddle River, NJ: Prentice Hall.

Hickerson, Nancy Parrott. 1994. *The Jumanos: Hunters and Traders of the South Plains.* Austin: University of Texas Press.

Hobsbawm, Eric, and Terence Ranger, eds. 1983. *The Invention of Tradition.* Cambridge: Cambridge University Press.

Hofstadter, Richard. 1974. *The American Political Tradition, and the Men Who Made It.* New York: Vintage Books.

Houser, Nicholas P. 1979. "Tigua Pueblo." In *Handbook of North American Indians,* ed. Alfonso Ortiz. Washington, DC: Smithsonian, vol. 9, pp. 336–342.

———. 2003a. "Selected Oral History Interviews Made in Ysleta and the El Paso Region in 1966." *Ysleta del Sur Pueblo Archives,* vol. 5, 183–312.

———. 2003b. "Tigua Indian Scouts in Defense of the Pass of the North: Three Centuries of Service." *Ysleta del Sur Pueblo Archives,* vol. 5, 175–182.

Hurd, Greg. 2004. "Kansas-Nebraska Act Turned Indian Lands into Slavery Battleground." *Lawrence Journal-World,* September 5. http://www2.1jworld.com/news/2004/sep/05/kansasnebraska_act_turned/.

Indian Country Today. 2001. "There Isn't No Indians in Texas: A Red Alert." http://www.indiancountry.com/content.cfm?id=2736.

Irwin-Williams, Cynthia. 1979. "Post-Pleistocene Archeology." In *Handbook of North American Indians,* ed. A. Ortiz. Washington, DC: Smithsonian, vol. 9, pp. 31–42.

Ishiyama, Noriko. 2003. "Environmental Justice and American Indian Tribal Sovereignty: Case Study of a Land-Use Conflict in Skull Valley, Utah." *Antipode* 35, no. 1: 119–139.

Jahoda, Gustav. 1999. *Images of Savages: Ancient Roots of Modern Prejudice, in Western Culture.* New York: Routledge.

Jorgensen, Joseph G. 1972. "The Sun Dance Religion: Power for the Powerless." Chicago: University of Chicago Press.

Keesing, Roger M. 2003. "Do Native Peoples Today Invent Their Tradition?" In *Taking Sides: Clashing Views on Contemporary Issues in Cultural Anthropology,* ed. Robert L. Weisch and Kirk M. Endicott. Guilford, CT: McGraw-Hill/Dushkin.

Kenrick, Justin. 2006. "Discussion: The Concept of Indigeneity." *Social Anthropology* (European Association of Social Anthropologists) 14, no. 1: 17–32.

Kenrick, Justin, and Jerome Lewis. 2004. "Indigenous Peoples' Rights and the Politics of the Term 'Indigenous.'" *Anthropology Today* 20, no. 2.

Kranish, Michael. 2005. "Gambling, GOP Politics Intertwine: Casino Payments Seen as Influential." *Boston Globe,* June 3.

Kriesberg, Louis. 2003. "Identity Issues." Beyond Intractability Knowledge Base Project, eds. Guy Burgess and Heidi Burgess. Conflict Information Consortium, University of Colorado, Boulder. http://www.beyondintractability.org/essay/identity_issues/.

Kroeber, Alfred L. 1966. *An Anthropologist Looks at History.* Berkeley: University of California Press.

Kunal, Parker. 2004. "Thinking Inside the Box: A Historian Among the Anthropologists." *Law and Society Review* 38, no. 4 (December): 851–860.

Kuper, Adam. 2003. "The Return of the Native." *Current Anthropology* 44, no. 3: 389–402.

Kyle, Richard. 1995. *The New Age Movement in American Culture.* New York: University Press of America.

Kymlica, William. 1997. *Multicultural Citizenship.* Oxford: Clarendon Press.

Lamberth, Royce C. (District Court Judge). 2005. "Indian Trust Fund Scandal." Friends Committee on National Legislation. http://www.fcnl.org/issues/item.php?item_id=1387andissue_id=112.

Lange, Charles H. 1979. "Relations of the Southwest with the Plains and Great Basin." In *Handbook of North American Indians,* ed. Alfonso Ortiz. Washington, DC: Smithsonian, vol. 9, pp. 201–205.

Lawrence, Bonita. 2004. "'Real' Indians and Others: Mixed-Blood Urban Native Peoples and Indigenous Nationhood." Lincoln: University of Nebraska Press.

Lawrence, Neal. 1999. "Midwest Today: Gambling on a New Life." http://www.midtod.com/highlights/gambling.phtml.

Le, C. N. 2006. "Assimilation and Ethnic Identity." Asian-Nation: The Landscape of Asian America, June 16. http://www.asian-nation.org/assimilation.shtml.

Lee, Roger A. 2005. "The U.S.-Mexican War (1846–1848)." http://www.historyguy.com/Mexican-American_War.html.

Lemkin, Raphael. 1943. *Axis Rule in Occupied Europe: Laws of Occupation, Analysis of Government, Proposals for Redress.* Washington, DC: Carnegie Endowment For International Peace.

Limerick, Patricia Nelson. 1987. *Legacy of Conquest: The Unbroken Past of the American West.* New York: Norton.

Lindauer, Owen. 1998. "Archaeology of the Phoenix Indian School." *Archeology* (March).

Linnekin, Jocelyn. 1983. "Defining Tradition: Variations on the Hawaiian Identity." *American Ethnologist* 11: 241–252.

Linton, Ralph. 1942. "Nativistic Movements." *American Anthropologist* 45 (April): 230–240.

Logsdon, Paul. 1983. "Salinas National Monument: Mighty Missions of Long Ago." *New Mexico Magazine,* March, pp. 20–23.

Lomawaima, K. T. 1993. "Domesticity in the Federal Indian Schools: The Power of Authority over Body and Mind. *American Ethnologist* 20: 227–240.

Loren, Diana, and Emily Stovel. 1997. "Approaching a Reconciliation for Ethnic Construction in Archaeology and Identity Politics." Paper presented at "All for One and One for All: (Re)Constructing Identity in the Ancient World," Graduate Student Symposium, Department of Classical and Near

Eastern Archaeology, Bryn Mawr College, October 17–18. http://www.brynmawr.edu/archaeology/guesswho/loren.html.

Mason, W. Dale. 2000. "Indian Gaming: Tribal Sovereignty and American Politics." Norman: University of Oklahoma Press.

Maybury-Lewis, David. 1997. "Indigenous Peoples, Ethnic Groups, and the State." Needham Heights, MA: Allyn and Bacon.

Mayher, John S. 1990. *Uncommon Sense: Theoretical Practice in Language Education*. Portsmouth, NH: Boynton/Cook.

McIntosh, Peggy. 2003 [1989]. "White Privilege: Unpacking the Invisible Knapsack." In *Applying Anthropology: An Introductory Reader*, ed. A. Podolefsky and P. Brown, 7th ed. Boston: McGraw-Hill.

McKeehan, Wallace L. 2001. *Adams-Onís Treaty of 1819*. http://www.tamu.edu/ccbn/dewitt/adamonis.htm.

McPherson, James M. 1991. "The Hedgehog and the Foxes." *Journal of the Abraham Lincoln Association* (University of Illinois Press) 12.

McPherson, Robert S. 1992. *Sacred Land, Sacred View*. Salt Lake City, UT: Brigham Young University Press.

Miller, Mark. 2004. *Forgotten Tribes: Unrecognized Indians and the Federal Acknowledgment Process*. Lincoln: University of Nabraska Press.

Minter, Alan H. 1976. "Tigua Indians of Pueblo de Ysleta del Sur: Their Present Status and Condition." *El Campanario* 7, no. 3 (September).

Mintor, Alan. 1969. "The Tigua Indians of the Pueblo de Ysleta del Sur, El Paso County, Texas." *West Texas Historical Association Year Book* 45: 30–44.

Monette, Richard A. 1996. "Treaties." In *Encyclopedia of North American Indians*, ed. F. Hoxie. Boston: Houghton Mifflin.

Moore, Donald. 1998. "Subaltern Struggles and the Politics of Place: Remapping Resistance in Zimbabwe's Eastern Highlands." *Cultural Anthropology* 13, no. 3: 344–381.

Moyer, Judith. 1999. "Step by Step Guide to Oral History." http://dohistory.org/on_your_own/toolkit/oralHistory.html.

Murphy, Dan. 1993. *Salinas Pueblo Missions National Monument, New Mexico: Abo, Quarai and Gran Quivira*. Tucson, AZ: Southwest Parks and Monuments Association.

Noble, David G. 1982. "Salinas: Archaeology, History, Prehistory." *Exploration: Annual Bulletin of the School of American Research*. Santa Fe, New Mexico.

O'Brien, Sharon. 1989. *American Indian Tribal Governments*. Norman: University of Oklahoma Press.

Olsson, Karen. 1998. "Being Some Brief Observations Concerning the Indians of El Paso, the Texians of Austin, and the Sundry Devotees of Breakfast Bingo." The Bush Files, from the pages of the *Texas Observer*, June 19. http://www.bushfiles.com/bushfiles/KingBushandtheTigua.html.

Omura, Keiichi. 2003. "Comment: 'The Return of the Native.'" *Current Anthropology* 44, no. 3: 395–396.

O'Neal, John William. 1969. *Texas, 1791–1835: A Study in Manifest Destiny.* M.A. thesis, Department of History, East Texas State University.

Ortiz, Alfonso. 1972. *New Perspectives on the Pueblos.* Albuquerque: University of New Mexico Press.

———. 1979. "The Pueblo Revolt." In *Handbook of North American Indians,* ed. Alfonso Ortiz. Washington, DC: Smithsonian, vol. 9, pp. 194–197.

———. 1994. *The Pueblo Indians of North America.* Frank W. Porter, gen. ed. New York: Chelsea House Publishers.

Ostrowski, James. 1997. *Was the Union Army's Invasion of the Confederate States a Lawful Act? An Analysis of President Lincoln's Legal Arguments Against Secession.* Delivered at the Mises Institute's conference on the political economy of secession. http://www.lewrockwell.com/ostrowski/ostrowski31.html.

Oussatcheva, Marina. 2006. "Institutions in Diaspora: The Case of Armenian Community in Russia." WPTC-01–09. http://www.transcomm.ox.ac.uk/working%20papers/WPTC-01–09%20Marina.doc.pdf.

Padilla, Amado M. 1980. "The Role of Cultural Awareness and Ethnic Loyalty in Acculturation." In *Acculturation: Theory, Models and Some New Findings,* ed. Amado M. Padilla. Boulder, CO: Westview Press, pp. 47–84.

Parry, Jonathan, and Maurice Bloch. 1989. *Money and the Morality of Exchange.* Cambridge: Cambridge University Press.

Parsons, E. C. 1939. *Pueblo Indian Religion.* Chicago: University of Chicago Press.

Pevar, Stephen L. 2002. *Rights of Indians and Tribes: The Authoritative Guide to Indian and Tribal Rights.* 3rd ed. Carbondale: Southern Illinois University Press.

Pierre, Pat. 2004. Quoted in *Blind Your Ponies: On-Line Curriculum Development for Native Students.* http://www.madlat.ca/presentations/Making%20IT%20Click/Lambert_Session11.ppt.

Plaice, Evie. 2003. "Comment: 'The Return of the Native.'" *Current Anthropology* 44, no. 3: 396–397.

Pletcher, David M. 2001. "Treaty of Guadalupe Hidalgo." In *Handbook of Texas Online.* http://www.tsha.utexas.edu/handbook/online/articles/TT/nbt1.html.

Plog, Fred. 1979. "Western Anasazi." In *Handbook of North American Indians,* ed. Alfonso Ortiz. Washington, DC: Smithsonian, vol. 9, pp. 108–130.

Powell, John Wesley. 1891. *Indian Linguistic Families of America North of Mexico.* Bureau of American Ethnology Annual Report 7. Washington, DC: Government Printing Office.

Prince, L. Bradford. 1915. *Spanish Mission Churches in New Mexico.* Cedar Rapids, IA: Torch Press.

Radin, Max. 1935. "Tradition." In *Encyclopedia of Social Sciences*. New York: Macmillan, vol. 15, pp. 62–67.

Ramos, Alcida Rita. 1998. *Indigenism: Ethnic Politics in Brazil*. Madison: University of Wisconsin Press.

Rappaport, Joanne. 1990. *The Politics of Memory: Native Historical Interpretation in the Colombian Andes*. New York: Cambridge University Press.

Robins, Steven. 2003. "Comment: 'The Return of the Native.'" *Current Anthropology* 44, no. 3: 397–398.

Sahlins, Marshall. 1997. "On the Anthropology of Modernity, or, Some Triumphs of Culture over Despondency Theory." In *Culture and Sustainable Development in the Pacific*, ed. Antony Hooper. Canberra: Asia Pacific Press.

Sando, Joe S. 1976. *The Pueblo Indians*. San Francisco: Indian Historical Press.

———. 1992. *Pueblo Nations: Eight Centuries of Pueblo Indian History*. Santa Fe, NM: Clear Light Publishers.

———. 1998. *Pueblo Profiles: Cultural Identity Through Centuries of Change*. Santa Fe, NM: Clear Light Publishers.

Saugestad, Sidsel. 2004. "Discussion: On 'The Return of the Native.'" *Current Anthropology* 45, no. 2: 263–264.

Schmidt, Rob. 2004. "Tough Times for Tiguas: How a State and a Court Shut Down a Successful Casino." *Indian Gaming Business*.

Schmidt, Susan. 2005. "Abramoff Ex-Firm Settles with Tribe: Former Lobbyist Was Paid Millions on Both Sides of Casino Issue." *Washington Post*, February 12, p. A2.

Schroeder, Albert H. 1979. "Pueblos Abandoned in Historical Times." In *Handbook of North American Indians*, ed. Alfonso Ortiz. Washington, DC: Smithsonian, vol. 9, pp. 236–254.

Schulze, Jeffrey M. 2001. "The Rediscovery of the Tigua: Federal Recognition and Indianness in the Twentieth Century." *Southwestern Historical Quarterly* 105, no. 1.

Secakuku, Ferrell. 2005. "Supawlavi Village, Hopi Nation." http://www.indigenousgeography.si.edu/themes.asp?commID=1andthemeID=8andlang=engandfullCopy-1.

Seed, Patricia. 1995. "Ceremonies of Possession: Europe's Conquest of the New World, 1492–1640." Cambridge: Cambridge University Press.

Senjkovic, Reana. 2002. "Folklore (Epilogue)." Institute of Ethnology and Folklore Research. http://www.ief.hr/page.php?id=154andlang=en.

Shanley, Kathryn. 2000. "Lady Luck or Mother Earth? Gaming as a Trope in Plains Indian Cultural Traditions." *Wicazo Sa Review* (Fall).

Shaw, Susan M. 1999. "Conceptualizing Resistance: Towards a Framework for Understanding Leisure as Political Practice." Paper presented at the Ninth Canadian Congress on Leisure Research, May 12–15, Acadia University,

Wolfville, Nova Scotia. http://www.lin.ca/resource/html/cclr9/CCLR9
_64.pdf.

Simmons, Marc. 1979. "History of the Pueblos Since 1821." In *Handbook of North American Indians*, ed. Alfonso Ortiz. Washington, DC: Smithsonian, vol. 9, pp. 178–193.

Simmons, William S. 1988. "Culture Theory in Contemporary Ethnohistory." *Ethnohistory* 35: 1–14.

Sivaramakrishnan, K. 2005. "Some Intellectual Genealogies for the Concept of Everyday Resistance." *American Anthropologist* 107, no. 3: 346–355.

Skaibine, Alex. 2002. Testimony Before the Senate Committee on Indian Affairs on Implementation of the *Texas Restoration Act*, Public Law 100-89, Tuesday, June 18, 2002, 10 A.M., Room 485, Russell Senate Office Building.

Smith, Linda T. 1998. *Decolonizing Methodologies: Research and Indigenous Peoples*. Dunedin, New Zealand: University of Otago Press.

Snipp, C. Matthew. 1988–1989. "On the Costs of Being American Indian: Ethnic Identity and Economic Opportunity." *Institute for Social Science Research* 4, no. 25.

Spivak, Gayatri Chakravorty. 1987. "Can the Subaltern Speak?" In *Marxism and the Interpretation of Culture,* ed. Cary Nelson and Lawrence Grossberg. Chicago: University of Illinois Press.

Spradley, James P. 1980. *Participant Observation*. New York: Holt, Rinehart, and Winston.

Stegmaier, Mark Joseph. 1996. *Texas, New Mexico, and the Compromise of 1850: Boundary Disputes and Sectional Crisis*. Kent, OH: Kent State University Press.

Stockes, Brian. 2001. "Tigua Enrollment Is Stalled in Senate." *Indian Country Today*, January 3. http://indiancountry.com/content.cfm?id=484.

Sutherland, Anne. 1999. "*Journal of Political Ecology:* Case Studies." *History and Society* 6.

Suzman, James. 2003. "Comment: 'The Return of the Native.'" *Current Anthropology* 44, no. 3: 389–402.

Theodossopoulos, Dimitrios. 2003. "Ethnic Stereotypes and Their Ethnographic Alternatives in Southeast Europe." *Journal of Mediterranean Studies* 13, no. 2 (special issue).

Theodossopoulos, Dimitrios, and Keith Brown, eds. 2004. "Stereotypes and Otherness in Southeast Europe." *History and Anthropology* 15, no. 1 (special issue).

Thick, Edward. 2005. "Tigua Indians: Food for Thought." *Borderlands*, an El Paso College Community College History Project. http://www.epcc.edu/nwlibrary/borderlands/09_tigua.htm.

Thomas, Linda, and Shân Wareing, eds. 1999. *Language, Society, and Power*. London: Routledge.

Thuen, Trond. 2006. "Discussion: The Concept of Indigeneity." *Social Anthropology* (European Association of Social Anthropologists) 14, no. 1: 17–32.

Timmons, W. H., Lucy F. West, and Mary A. Sarbers, eds. 1988. *Census of 1841 for Ysleta, Socorro, and San Elizario*. El Paso, TX: El Paso Historical Commission.

Tonkin, Elizabeth. 1992. *Narrating Our Pasts: The Social Construction of Oral History*. Cambridge: Cambridge University Press.

Trask, Haunani-Kay. 1991. "Natives and Anthropologists: The Colonial Struggle." In (2003) *Taking Sides: Clashing Views on Contemporary Issues in Cultural Anthropology*. Guilford, CT: McGraw-Hill/Dushkin.

Truesdell, Barbara. 2006. *Oral History Techniques: How to Organize and Conduct Oral History Interviews*. Bloomington, IN: Center for the Study of History and Memory, Indiana University.

Tuan, Yi-Fu. 1977. *Space and Place: The Perspective of Experience*. Minneapolis: University of Minnesota Press.

Turner, Terry. 2004. "Discussion: On 'The Return of the Native.'" *Current Anthropology* 45, no. 2: 264–265.

van de Burghe, P. 1992. "Tourism and the Ethnic Division of Labour." *Annals of Tourism Research* 19, no. 2: 234–249.

Van Hear, N. 1998. *New Diasporas: The Mass Exodus, Dispersal, and Regrouping of Migrant Communities*. London: University College London Press.

Vicenti, Carey N. 1995. "The Reemergence of Tribal Society and Traditional Justice Systems." *Judicature* 79, no. 3 (November–December).

Wade, Peter. 1997. *Race and Ethnicity in Latin America*. London: Pluto Press.

Wallace, Anthony F. C. 1956. "Revitalization Movements." *American Anthropologist* 58: 264–281.

Warren, Kay B. 1998. *Indigenous Movements and Their Critics: Pan-Maya Activism in Guatemala*. Princeton, NJ: Princeton University Press.

Warren, Kay B., and Jean F. Jackson, eds. 2002. *Indigenous Movements, Self-Representation, and the State in Latin America*. Austin: University of Texas Press.

Washburn, Wilcomb E. 2006. "Indians and the American Revolution," http://www.americanrevolution.org/ind1.html.

Whiteley, Peter M. 1987. "The Interpretation of Politics: A Hopi Conundrum." *Man* 22, no. 4.

Woodbury, Richard. 1979. "Prehistory." In *Handbook of North American Indians*, ed. Alfonso Ortiz. Washington, DC: Smithsonian, vol. 9, pp. 22–30.

Woodbury, Richard B., and Ezra Zubrow. 1979. "Agricultural Beginnings." In *Handbook of North American Indians*, ed. Alfonso Ortiz. Washington, DC: Smithsonian, vol. 9, pp. 43–60.

Wright, Bill. 1993. *The Tiguas: Pueblo Indians of Texas*. El Paso: Texas Western Press.

Wright, Ronald. 1992. *Stolen Continents: The Americas Through Indian Eyes Since 1492*. Boston: Houghton Mifflin.

Yellow Bird, Michael. 1999. "Indian, American Indian, and Native Americas: Counterfeit Identities." *Winds of Change: A Magazine for American Indian Education and Opportunity* 14, 1.

Index

About the Author

S. K. Adam is a cultural anthropologist with a focused interest in visual and applied anthropology. Additionally, he is interested in methodological issues and ethics in research. He has researched extensively in the American Southwest and conducted small-scale research projects in Egypt, South Africa, and Kenya.